THE ENLARGED EUROPEAN UNION

BOOKS OF RELATED INTEREST

The Swiss Labyrinth: Institutions, Outcomes and Redesign
edited by Jan-Erik Lane

Europeanised Politics? European Integration and National Political Systems
edited by Klaus H. Goetz and Simon Hix

Recasting European Welfare States
edited by Maurizio Ferrera and Martin Rhodes

The Changing French Political System
edited by Robert Elgie

Compounded Representation in West European Federations
edited by Joanne B. Brzinski, Thomas D. Lancaster and Christian Tuschhoff

Politics and Policy in Democratic Spain: No Longer Different?
edited by Paul Heywood

Britain in the Nineties: The Politics of Paradox
edited by Hugh Berrington

Crisis and Transition in Italian Politics
edited by Martin Bull and Martin Rhodes

Southern European Welfare States: Between Crisis and Reform
edited by Martin Rhodes

The Euro-Mediterranean Partnership: Political and Economic Perspectives
edited by Richard Gillespie

The State in Western Europe: Retreat or Redefinition?
edited by Wolfgang C. Müller and Vincent Wright

The Regions and the European Community
edited by Robert Leonardi

The Regional Dimension of the European Union
edited by Charlie Jeffery

National Parliaments and the European Union
edited by Philip Norton (new in paperback)

The Crisis of Representation in Europe
edited by Jack Hayward

The Politics of Immigration in Western Europe
edited by Martin Baldwin-Edwards and Martin A. Schain

THE ENLARGED EUROPEAN UNION

Diversity and Adaptation

Editors

PETER MAIR
JAN ZIELONKA

FRANK CASS
LONDON • PORTLAND, OR

First Published in 2002 in Great Britain by
FRANK CASS PUBLISHERS
Crown House, 47 Chase Side, Southgate
London N14 5BP, England

and in the United States of America by
FRANK CASS PUBLISHERS
c/o ISBS, 5824 N.E. Hassalo Street
Portland, Oregon, 97213-3644

Website: www.frankcass.com

British Library Cataloguing in Publication Data

The enlarged European Union : diversity and adaptation
1. European Union 2. Nationalism – European Union countries
3. European Union countries – Economic integration
4. European Union countries – Social policy
I. Mair, Peter II. Zielonka, Jan, 1955–
337.1′42

ISBN 0 7146 5287 3 (cloth)
ISBN 0 7146 8255 1 (paper)

Library of Congress Cataloging-in-Publication Data

The enlarged European Union : diversity and adaptation / [edited by]
Peter Mair, Jan Zielonka.
p. cm.
Includes bibliographical references and index.
ISBN 0-7146-5287-3 (cloth) – ISBN 0-7146-8255-1 (paper)
1. European Union countries – Emigration and immigration. 2. European Union – Ethnic relations 3. European Union countries – Economic integration. 4. Europe – Politics and government – 1989– 5. Group identity – Europe. 6. European Union countries – Social policy. 7. National characteristics, European. I. Mair, Peter. II. Zielonka, Jan. 1955–
JV7590 .E47 2002
940.56–dc21 2001008502

This group of studies first appeared in a Special Issue of *West European Politics* (ISSN 0140-2382) Vol.25, No.2 (April 2002), [The Enlarged European Union: Diversity and Adaptation].

Printed in Great Britain by MPG Books Ltd., Bodmin, Cornwall

Contents

Acknowledgements

This volume includes papers from two research projects conducted jointly by the Robert Schuman Centre of the European University Institute and the Group of Advisors at the European Commission. We are grateful to Giuliano Amato, Jacques Delors and Jean Luc Dehaene for chairing successive parts of the projects. Official reports of these projects can be obtained via the RSC website at http://www.iue.it/RSC/PublicationsRSC-PP.htm. Needless to say, neither of these institutions share responsibility for the individual arguments presented in this volume.

Introduction: Diversity and Adaptation in the Enlarged European Union

JAN ZIELONKA and PETER MAIR

It is now taken as given that the European Union will be a much more diversified entity following its planned eastward enlargement. The applicant states from Eastern Europe are much poorer than the current West European member states. Their democracy and in some cases even their statehood is newly established and presumably more fragile. Their economic, legal and administrative structures are less developed. They also have their own distinct histories, societies and cultures. And although they all share the aspiration to join the Union, their visions, interests and priorities do not necessarily converge with one another nor with those of current EU members. In fact, in view of the numerous structural differences between the current and prospective EU member states, it is difficult to expect there to be a major and durable alignment of their respective political preferences and behaviour after enlargement.

The European Union is trying hard to reduce many of these structural differences before the accession date. But how much can possibly be accomplished in the relatively short time before the first round of enlargement? Since pressure is mounting to speed up accession and at the same time to make it inclusive, it is highly unlikely that the Union will take in only the most unambiguously EU-compatible countries from the region. Hence by opening the doors and ushering in such a large degree of diversity, it is inevitable that some of the admission criteria are going to be compromised. But does this mean that the process of European integration will be slowed or even halted? Will it have the effect of paralysing the EU institutions, leading to an escalation of the sort of disputes that may prevent any collective endeavours?

This collection intends to examine the various forms of diversity that are likely to persist after the admission to the Union of several post-communist countries and seeks to assess both the real level of diversity as well as its implications. Will diversity lead to actual divergence in structure and policy?[1] Need we fear a possible paralysis of European institutions after the enlargement? In order to answer these questions, differences and similarities in the fields of macro-economics, welfare systems, democracy, institutional infrastructure, civic orientations and popular culture are scrutinised, as well as the processes of adaptation to Europe that are already under way among the candidate members. The presentation of this range of empirical evidence is intended to challenge many of the theoretical assumptions about the scope, form and meaning of diversity in the process of European integration, and especially in the context of the forthcoming eastward enlargement. In fact, the map of unity and diversity in the enlarged EU proves to be extremely complex, and does not simply correspond to the old East–West divide. Moreover, the division lines themselves are constantly changing, with the enlargement process constituting an important factor forcing adaptation and serving to push individual states into a single regulatory framework, if not necessarily in a common political direction. The European effect works unevenly in different functional areas as well as in different territories, and there are other 'unifying' factors at play, with globalisation (or perhaps simply Americanisation) in particular producing different models and loyalties than Europeanisation as such.[2] In addition, there are also centrifugal forces within the candidate countries that continue to generate diversity rather than unity across Europe.

A certain degree of diversity is, of course, unavoidable, but it needs to be emphasised that this applies not only to the future enlarged European Union, but also, and already, to the current Union of 15 quite diversified member states. Moreover, it is clear that not all types of diversity need prove detrimental to the process of European integration. Diversity can have either positive or negative connotations, depending on context and objectives, and much of its effect clearly depends on what is being sought, in which field, and under what particular set of circumstances. Let us therefore begin with an effort to conceptualise the impact of diversity on the process of European integration and to ask whether the increased level of diversity is a bane or blessing for the enlarged Union.

DIVERSITY AND EUROPEAN INTEGRATION

In the theory of European integration the concepts of fusion, convergence, cohesion and integration are often used as synonyms,[3] and this inevitably leads to a tendency to demonise any sort of diversity. For many students and practitioners, the progress of European integration is simply measured by the degree to which the Union is able to achieve greater cohesion. The failure of European integration, on the other hand, is illustrated by examples of persisting and irreconcilable differences among individual member states. But why is diversity seen as problematic?

The reasons for criticising diversity are many. One is a misguided perception of the ultimate aim of integration. If European unity is the aim of integration, differences in structure and behaviour are seen as something to be overcome or even as something fundamentally undesirable. But unity as such was never the ultimate aim of integration.[4] In the extreme, of course, such an aim could lead to the creation of an Orwellian-like state that is not only totalitarian, but also inefficient,[5] a scenario that is of particular relevance in the context of eastward enlargement. Moreover, homogenising tendencies in the process of European integration have also made it necessary for the Union to develop and 'legalise' the concepts of subsidiarity and flexibility,[6] although, interestingly enough, such subsidiarity discourse has scarcely been applied to the issue of eastward enlargement, with the new applicant states being denied the opportunity for the various opt-outs that have already been negotiated by some current member states in the areas of foreign, monetary, social or border-related policy (for example, the Schengen *acquis*). In fact, an insistence on total alignment with EU norms and regulations remains the prevailing discourse in the process of enlargement, not only for tactical but also for strategic considerations.

This uneven treatment of current and prospective EU members suggests a resistance to accepting the unknown 'other' as a partner in a well-established project – and this is yet another reason for demonising diversity. This is a quite natural psychological reaction to change and has been experienced in previous cases of enlargement. When Spain, Greece and Portugal attempted to join the then European Communities, for instance, fears of migratory flows and the import of lax legal Mediterranean culture were quite widespread.[7] Identity formation involves a distinction being made between the 'self' and the 'other', and despite their persisting European quest, the countries that lay behind the Iron Curtain have long been stigmatised as a different 'other'. As Giuliano Amato and Judy Batt have observed:

> The division of Europe has left its mark on perceptions in the West, reinforcing long-standing prejudices about the East as "backward" and less "civilized" than the West, not fully "part of Europe". The prospect of enlargement to the East has brought these prejudices to the fore, further contributing to the tendency to portray the increasing diversity that it entails as a new and uniquely threatening challenge for the EU.[8]

For the applicant states, enlargement represents what Wagener in this volume refers to as their 'return to Europe' after many years of Soviet domination;[9] for many of the current member states, on the other hand, enlargement looks more like a missionary crusade, in which the applicant countries are sometimes treated as an equivalent of medieval barbarians that need to be taught the superior Western ways of doing business and politics.[10] In other words, the view is that they should resemble EU prototypes or otherwise be kept at bay with the use of export quotas and Schengen. At the same time, however, it is evident that no single EU prototype actually exists.[11] Current EU members are themselves very diversified and one can argue that the *acquis communautaire* contains rules that are technical rather than normative, and which, as such, can hardly represent a serious factor in identity formation. In fact, EU identity is closely linked to a pan-European culture and history of which the candidate states are an incontestable part. To put it another way, it is evident that European identity can hardly remain the exclusive commodity of an organised group of the powerful and the rich.

Another reason for attacking diversity emerges from the positivist predilection for social and institutional engineering that is widespread among both social democratic and Christian democratic political parties. The Union is seen as a means of controlling the very complex and diversified European environment through the use of communitarian solutions. While the liberal approach tolerates and even praises diversity of structure and action, the positivist approach is about disciplined crafting aimed at curbing various forms of diversity, especially those that might lead to a durable divergence. This requires a careful selection of targets (agenda setting), elaboration of conditions, safeguards and time-tables, active guidance and regular screening.[12] Failure to meet certain targets or deviation from the envisaged route is evaluated in a very negative sense. The EU policy of enlargement in this sense is concerned with engineering and crafting. The applicant states are confronted with the requirement to implement a set of conditions that are aimed at making them EU-compatible. Their progress in meeting these conditions is subject to regular screening. Accession is meant to take place only once the applicants meet the envisaged targets.

But can crafting and engineering ever succeed in a complex European environment? So many of the existing European arrangements have developed in such an ambiguous and often disguised manner that, despite all the pretentious rhetoric, it is difficult to believe that any were the result of careful engineering. There is little reason to assume that the eastward enlargement will not follow a similar path. In fact, the EU has never spelled out the main objectives of its enlargement policy (although various and at times contradictory statements have been made by successive presidencies, the Commission, as well as individual MEPs). Its accession conditions are often imprecise, impractical and in conflict. The screening process is superficial and subject to discretionary interpretations. And the successive decisions taken within the process of enlargement result from hard and largely unpredictable political bargaining that does not resemble any carefully crafted blue-print. Moreover, the Western European experience shows that engineering does not eliminate diversity, but only modifies it. As a recent comprehensive study of the impact of EU policies and legislation on the member states suggested:

> The process patterns and policy outcomes of Europeanization have not been uniform across the member states, and do not reflect either the well defined will of a "unified supranational actor" or a pervasive problem-solving rationality which imposes itself "automatically" as to increase the overall efficiency of European policy decisions in the context of a transnational interdependence of policy problems. Instead, the political reality of European policy-making is 'messy' insofar as it is uneven across policy areas and member states, institutionally cumbersome, and subject to the dynamics of domestic politics each with its own particular logic. As a consequence, the outcomes of European policy-making tend to be much more diverse than one would expect and preclude any simplistic explanation of Europe-induced changes.[13]

In other words, despite crafting and engineering, diversity already appears as a normal state of affairs within the European Union, and in this regard eastward enlargement will change little.

DIVERSITY AND EUROPEAN INSTITUTIONS

Fears of destroying the existing delicate balance of power in the Union also prompt criticism of diversity, with the side-effect that the process of enlargement is both used and abused by individual member states in order to enhance their own partisan positions. The often less than dignified inter-state bargaining during the Nice summit offers a case in point. More generally, those in favour of looser forms of European co-operation may advocate a speedy and wide-reaching enlargement as a means of undermining the federalist ambitions of other member states, and this in turn leads to fears that the latter will be tempted to pursue more advanced forms of integration within a smaller and more convergent European core.[14] Of course, the creation such a core might have serious negative implications for the entire process of European integration. Most crucially, it would imply abandoning the so-called community model in which all member states are treated on an equal basis, undertaking the same mutual obligations and following the same rules. The *acquis communautaire* represents the essence of this model and it is for this reason that the applicant states are denied any opt-outs from its components.[15]

In the short run the import of additional diversity from Eastern Europe may indeed result in a more inter-governmental rather than a federative mode of European co-operation. This need not be the case in the long run, however. Although each previous wave of enlargement implied a certain increase of diversity, communitarian solutions nevertheless gradually became the norm in many new fields. It might also be argued that it is precisely the creation of a European core that could lead to more diversity, and perhaps even real divergence. The core would add an extra layer of institutional co-operation without abandoning existing layers within the EU itself, and its creation could even lead to serious conflicts. Some of the current member states would be worried about being excluded from the core, while others would fear, rightly or wrongly, that the core opens the door to Franco-German domination. Hence, while the idea of a core Europe has been raised many times in the history of European integration, it has nevertheless not been implemented. Instead the Union has developed more modest forms of diversification in the form of temporary or permanent opt-outs, subsidiarity and flexibility.

Increased diversity is also believed to carry the risk of paralysis and immobility in the decision-making system. It is already difficult to get 15 states in line, and adding extra states to the list may well prevent the emergence of any meaningful consensus in the future. The addition of new states will also create the need for additional special arrangements and transition periods that would further complicate the decision-making system. Moreover, a more complex decision-making system is seen as likely to be less efficient and less transparent, thus leading to negative implications for the Union's legitimacy.[16] Again, however, this does not need to be the case. Decision-making deadlock might have already been anticipated in a Union of 15 diverse member states, and yet it is often avoided through the escape routes devised by the actors involved.[17] Indeed, according to Adrienne Héritier, who has extensively studied the Union's ways of accommodating diversity, it is precisely this 'logic of diversity' which initiates a spontaneous acceleration of policy making by political regulatory competition and mutual learning.[18] The emergence of various escape routes has become 'second nature to European policy-making in all its inter-linked arenas' producing policy innovation and contributing to democratic legitimisation. According to Héritier, it is arguably simpler to accommodate more rather than less diverse member-state interests within one polity: in the heterogeneous polity, accommodation and compromise seeking becomes the cardinal feature of decision making.[19] Similar conclusions have been reached by Lisa Martin, who argues that a diversity (or as she puts it, a heterogeneity) of interests creates opportunities for trade-offs among actors and so increases the likelihood of agreement rather than stalemate.[20] True, diversity combined with the consensus-based decision-making system can sometimes lead to paralysis. But this is more likely to be the fault of the consensus-based decision-making system than of the diversity as such.[21] Nor is diversity necessarily inimical to the democratic system. On the contrary, diversity, albeit cited as pluralism, is more commonly seen as indispensable to democracy.

Finally, the import of additional diversity from Eastern Europe is seen to increase the sheer costs of European integration. Since the applicant states are poorer than the current member states, and since most also have larger agricultural sectors, their potential accession inevitably raises questions concerning the sustainability of existing EU programmes. Should vast agricultural subsidies be extended to new members such as Poland or Romania that still maintain a fifth of their labour force in the agricultural sector? Should the greatest beneficiaries of EU cohesion policy, including Greece, Portugal or Spain, agree that most of the cohesion funds now shift to new members from Eastern Europe? Can the existing redistributive system survive the eastward enlargement without a drastic increase in individual states' contributions?

The European Commission provided a partial answer to these questions in its *Agenda 2000* document,[22] which envisaged modest reforms of the Common Agricultural Policy and the Cohesion Funds combined with certain caps on the subsidies extended to new members. Thus, for example, subsidies were not to exceed a certain percentage of the national GDP and should be matched by domestic funds. In this way, the contributions by the individual member states to the EU budget would not have to be increased and the EU budget itself would remain balanced.

But although the Commission analyses and proposals may be valid, they have failed to convince many politicians in the most affected countries or those various pressure groups such as farmers or trade unions that represent non-competitive sectors of industry.[23] In this case, however, it is necessary to consider the interests of the Union as a whole as well as those of particular and sometimes parochial forces within it. Thus, for example, the net economic gains of enlargement to the Union are estimated to be greater than the potential costs.[24] Moreover, the EU cohesion funds are envisaged not as a gift or a kind of social policy, but as a means by which weaker economies may be compensated for opening their markets.[25] And even if one cannot fully endorse the economic argument that integration is likely to benefit the rich rather than poor and peripheral countries (see the contribution by Daniel Gros to this volume), it is undeniable that the applicant states from Eastern Europe are already shouldering heavy costs in the form of the structural adjustments that are necessary to conform to the existing *acquis communautaire*. Thus, for example, it is estimated that the additional investment cost simply for the environmental *acquis* is likely to be around two per cent of GDP over a period of 15 years.[26] In addition, and even more crucially, it is evident that the calculation of costs and benefits cannot be confined to the economic sector alone, and that the security and political gains from enlargement are likely to be much higher than the strictly economic gains. In fact, one may argue that integrating more divergent countries such as Romania will bring about greater political and security rewards than integrating more 'EU-compatible' countries such as the Czech Republic, Hungary or Slovenia.

For all of these reasons, it can be argued that there is little reason to fear the various kinds of diversity in the Union that enlargement will bring. While diversity can at times jeopardise certain forms of co-operation, it can also facilitate co-operation and hence foster further integration. Diversity teaches adaptation, bargaining and accommodation. It is a source of competition, self-improvement and innovation. As such, it may also prove not only an important prerequisite of democracy, but also of efficiency, in that it may be argued that it is only highly diversified and pluralistic societies acting in a complex web of institutional arrangements that are able to succeed in conditions of modern competition.

IDENTIFYING THE 'FAULT LINES' IN THE ENLARGED UNION

Democracy, Culture and Politics

But where precisely are the 'fault lines' likely to lie in the newly diversified and enlarged European Union? For a first answer to this question, Dieter Fuchs and Hans-Dieter Klingemann have examined the extent to which the citizens across the wider Europe share political values and behaviour. They also try to establish the extent to which there are systematic differences between Western, Central and Eastern Europe, and to locate the possible cultural cleavages. In fact, their data reveal few differences across Europe in the political values and behaviour that are essential to democracy. In other words, no sharp threshold can be identified between West and East; instead, there is a continuous decline in the extent of a democratic community. The potential for Europeans in Western, Central and Eastern Europe to consider each other as democrats, and to integrate this understanding in their collective identity is thus considerable. At the same time, however, Albania and the Slav successor states to the Soviet Union (Russia, Ukraine, Belarus and Moldova) represent an important exception, in that in all elements of the Fuchs and Klingemann analysis, these particular countries reveal a sharp contrast not only with the Western European states, but also with those in Central and Eastern Europe. From the point of view of political culture, this analysis suggests that the eastern border of the EU would have to be drawn to the west of these countries. This does not imply that there exists a wholly homogenous political culture further to the west, however. Levels of self-responsibility differ markedly between Sweden and Spain, for example, and a number of Central and Eastern Europeans already approximate to the Spanish pattern. In addition, while per capita GDP in Slovenia may well be close to Western levels, its citizens nevertheless reveal a much lower level of civic engagement and social trust.

David D. Laitin also analyses the political cultures of applicant states, but this time with a focus on language configuration, religious beliefs and popular culture. His findings are in line with those of Fuchs and Klingemann: there is no clear-cut cleavage between the current EU member states and the applicant states from Central and Eastern Europe. Laitin also shows evidence of a pan-European culture that is rapidly infusing the applicant countries of the East. This transcendent European culture exists in conjunction with national cultures, which remain vibrant in both the West and the East. More to the point, the differences among national cultures within the current EU member states are considerable, and the national cultures of the applicant states fall well within the extremes set by these existing member states. In fact, Laitin argues that the cultural practices of the applicant states are more proximate to the cultural practices of the original six EC members than are the cultural practices of the later entrants. Applicant peripheral states often have more motivation to assimilate into the norms of the centre than is the case for the populations closer to the centre.

The argument of Vladimir Tismaneanu is much more sombre, even though here too there is confirmation that the key divides are not necessarily those between the current EU, on the one side, and a collectivity of all Eastern applicant states, on the other. Post-communist transitions have led to the emergence of three different groups of polities – Central European successes such as the Visiegrad three, protracted middle-of-the-road transition states such as Bulgaria and Romania, and quasi-democracies such as Russia, the Ukraine and Moldova – which vary in terms of the extent to which a genuine democratic culture and practice can be seen to have become inculcated. What we see here, therefore, is not just a diversity created by the meeting of East and West, but a diversity within each of the two broadly defined communities themselves. We have, in other words, a heterogeneous set of political cultures. But Tismaneanu is also concerned to draw attention to the sheer vulnerability of the post-communist systems, plagued by a Leninist legacy, on the one hand, and an all too brief period of democratic experimentation, on the other, and the core of his argument is devoted to teasing out nine threats to the fledgling democracies which, in turn, could well impact on the overall legitimacy and effectiveness of the European project. But though sombre, Tismaneanu's analysis also reinforces the argument raised above, which is that the gains from enlargement should not simply be seen in terms of economics alone. As he rightly reminds us, and as has also been consistently pointed out by students of southern Europe, the attraction of membership in the European Union – the 'magnetism' of a united Europe – can serve to strengthen the hand of democratic forces in regimes which have had a long history of non-democratic government.[27] In this sense, enlargement also involves an important political imperative. Moreover, integration within Europe may serve a more practical purpose by helping to build the institutions which can protect democracy from its enemies. As Tismaneanu points out, it is not so much that each and every post-communist political culture is more vulnerable to non-democratic forces than each and every political culture in the West – the fault lines simply do not operate like that – but rather that Western institutions have now developed to an extent that they afford substantial protection against such forces, whereas such protection is often absent in the East. It is all very well to build on the gains of liberalism in the post-communist polities, he concludes, but it is also necessary to take account of the sheer fragility and vulnerability of those gains.

The question of the fragility of the democratic order in the post-communist democracies is also addressed in Darina Malova and Tim Haughton's overview of the new institutional structures that have developed during the 1990s. And here also the beneficial effect of the pull exerted by the EU is highlighted. But Malova and Haughton also point to a paradox which appears to develop here, in that the need to adapt to the demands of the EU, and particularly the 'fast-track' procedures which have been adopted in order to satisfy the requirements of the *acquis,* may yet hinder consolidation in those polities where neither the actors nor the institutions have fully settled into place. In other words, while EU magnetism encourages the consolidation of democracy, the practice of integration often poses severe institutional and legitimacy problems. Far from easing democratic fragility in post-communist Europe, enlargement may well accentuate it, at least in the shorter term. Nor are the possible solutions to these problems always necessarily favourable for democracy. Thus in drawing attention to processes of adaptation to the enlarged EU, Malova and Haughton suggest that one of the ways in which the applicant states can better prepare themselves for entry is by strengthening their executive arms of government, a move which would reflect a recognition of where effective power now lies within the EU system. At the same time, however, they also recognise that this might well undermine the new commitment to pluralism that has tended to accompany democratisation, particularly in East-Central Europe. In this case, then, a solution which implies convergence on an apparent existing EU pattern, and hence one which seems to demand a negation of the existing diversity of constitutional and institutional forms, might well prove counter productive.

Market Institutions, Economics and Welfare

As Laszlo Bruszt points out, it is at the level of market institutions that the greatest diversity can be seen. Yet again, however, there is no simple East–West contrast involved here. In fact, Bruszt points to three sources of divergence in the enlarged Europe. The first is the growing divergence within the East itself, and between the different countries, with the dominance of a nationalist agenda and/or the 'capture of the state' by powerful economic interests in particular countries driving a gap between the more and less reform-minded polities. Nor, as he argues here, is this simply a problem that can be solved by various anti-corruption measures – it goes much deeper than that. The second source of divergence involves the building of institutions of economic development, and here the border between clusters of countries does almost inevitably follow the traditional East–West divide, with even the reform-minded polities of East-Central Europe still lagging behind the current EU member states. This gap, however, is likely to prove bridgeable with time. The third source of divergence is to be found within the post-communist countries themselves, across regions, sectors and social groups – dividing the more 'internationalised' or 'Europeanised' parts from the rest of the economy. But while Bruszt associates this problem only with the non-EU members, it is nevertheless clear that a similar divide can be identified within the more established democracies, albeit perhaps at a less acute level. Indeed, it is precisely the consequences of such a divide that have sometimes been associated with the recent rise of right-wing populist parties in Western Europe, many of which appear to win support among those seen to be losing out in the shift to adapt to the needs of an increasingly gloablised economy.[28]

The contribution by Daniel Gros demystifies one of the most popular stereotypical assertions about eastward enlargement, that is, the assertion that embracing poor economies from Eastern Europe will lead to various economic problems that may well hamper European integration. Gros does not deny that there is indeed a serious economic gap between the current member states and the applicants from Eastern Europe. The total GDP at market prices and current exchange rates of the ten associated countries from Eastern Europe amounts to only four per cent of the GDP of the current European Union, or about one-ninth of the GDP *per capita*.[29] The applicant countries are more dynamic than the current EU members, however, and, as Gros suggests, this is likely to prove more crucial for the future of European economic integration. When one looks at the experience of previous waves of enlargement, problems were usually caused by richer member states such as Belgium rather than by poorer, but more dynamic, states such as Portugal or Ireland. In other words, as Gros argues, it is the differences in economic 'health' rather than wealth that is the more important criterion in the evaluation of economic developments in the enlarged Union, and in this respect the applicant countries are doing pretty well compared to the current member states. Growth rates are generally expected to remain higher in the applicant states than in the current EU member states.

Economic data also show that divergence is cutting across the traditional East–West divide. For instance, Austria's GDP per capita is more than double that of Portugal: $25,666 compared to $10,167 (figures for 1997). Slovenia's GDP per capita ($9,039) is nearly as high as that of Portugal. In terms of broad indicators of economic structures it is also difficult to find strong systematic differences between the candidates and the current EU members. Thus Gros shows that even the share of agriculture in the GDP of most of the candidates is quite similar to that of the poorer member states, while the candidates' share of industry in GDP is also not notably different from some current member states. In fact, it is very difficult to make any firm judgement about systemic differences in economic structure because there are such large differences even among the present EU members. There are also significant discrepancies between individual applicant states, or even within individual states where quite prosperous areas have developed around capitals or in regions bordering on the more affluent West. All this, according to Gros, does not need to hamper the economic growth in the Union. On the contrary, enlargement is likely to stimulate the overall economic growth within the enlarged EU with related benefits for European integration.

Economic gaps between Eastern and Western Europe are also of course followed by social gaps, the subject of the analyses by Hans Jürgen Wagener and János Mátyás Kovács in this collection, and it is these social gaps that are even more feared by the EU public and experts. There is some concern that poverty and unemployment will prompt huge migratory flows from new to the old EU member states, and hence put the entire Western European welfare system under strain. Some applicant countries have been slow to introduce any serious reforms of their over-centralised, rent-seeking, paternalist and often corrupt welfare systems, while those in the region who have embarked on the road to social reforms seem to prefer the American rather than European social model – the former relying largely on neo-liberal solutions, with the latter attempting to combine economic growth with social protection.

Kovács focuses especially on this latter question in his assessment of the directions of the social reforms, if any, that are being undertaken by the applicant states. And here again, the key question is whether this will imply more divergence or more convergence within the enlarged European Union. Kovács does not question the statistical evidence that indicates some striking social gaps between the two parts of Europe, especially in real wages and living standards.[30] However, he also points out that most of these statistics fail to take account of the sizeable unregistered 'shadow' economy in the region, in that citizens in many of the applicant states have long been accustomed to coping with social shortfalls through household production, the farming of small private plots, or through work in the 'second' informal economy. Moreover, some statistics paint too negative, if not misleading, a picture of the development of the applicant countries' social problems. For instance, although unemployment has risen sharply in all applicant states since the beginning of the post-communist transition, the current high levels are actually comparable to those prevailing within parts of the existing Union. Kovács also warns against the risk of elevating manifestations of social differences between East and West to an almost mythical level, cautioning against a presentation of Eastern Europe simply as a region of abandoned children, street beggars and tuberculosis patients that may spread its social diseases westward in the aftermath of EU enlargement.

This is not to deny that Eastern Europe does indeed have serious social problems inherited from decades of communist domination and from the unprecedented economic recession of the 1990s, and the path-dependent character of the problems is amply highlighted by Wagener's analysis of the adaptation within social security systems. However, Wagener also shows how countries in the region have already initiated reforms of their social security systems, and how in at least some cases these reforms have already brought about some impressive improvements. Moreover, accession to the Union is likely to produce further improvements in social standards in the region, largely through economic impulses accelerated by enlargement than through the EU redistributive system as such. Finally, and from a strictly formal point of view, Wagener also points out that social problems should not represent a serious obstacle to accession, in that the social *acquis* comprises a mere 70 directives. What Wagener refers to as the 'return to Europe' in this area therefore offers more degrees of freedom. He also adds that when compared to the established democracies in Western Europe, the new democracies of Eastern Europe, much as those in Latin America, tend to encounter less resistance from entrenched interests when seeking to implement radical reforms.

At the same time, as Kovács admits, social transformation in Eastern Europe has as yet often been quite modest, sometimes inconsistent, and not truly comprehensive. Most notably, in some cases the reform of health and education has been lagging behind the reform of social welfare. However, he insists that Eastern European reforms echo Western European efforts at welfare reform, with the neo-liberal arguments being used by local politicians serving to make a virtue out of the necessity of introducing austerity measures in the economy. Convergence of social systems is thus possible, but it is necessary to adopt a dynamic rather than static view of such convergence, and to accept that it is globalisation rather than Europeanisation as such that constitutes the prime motivator. In this sense, there may not be any stable Western model to be emulated, for by the time any new rules of play are agreed, the position of the goalposts might have shifted.[31] It is also necessary to recognise that, as in the West, individual applicant countries also have their own social particularities, such as the corporatist role of the Solidarity trade union in Poland's social policy, the strength of social-democratic tradition in the Czech Republic, or the substantial weight of informal welfare in Hungary. In fact, all of these diverse social models in both parts of the continent are being forced to introduce similar reforms under the pressure of global economic competition and interdependence, and, in some respects, as Wagener suggests, it is evident that some of the applicant states from Eastern Europe have managed to cope with this global pressure more quickly and more effectively than is the case among some of the current EU member states. Here again, then, the idea of a clear border between East and West proves too simple and misleading, with path dependency and reform, both being constrained by global pressures, producing increased heterogeneity in the West and in the East.

CONCLUSION

The forthcoming Eastern enlargement is often cited as threatening to water down the entire integration project. Indeed, for some Eurosceptics, this is part of the appeal of enlargement. Among those committed to the Union, however, there are many voices expressing a fear that increasing diversity and differentiation will preclude more advanced forms of European integration.

In many respects, as this collection shows, these fears are ill-founded. Diversity exists both among the existing EU member states as among the applicants, and the line between unity and diversity does not follow the post-war East–West border. Moreover, it has been the end of the cold war rather than the prospect of enlargement as such that has forced the EU to rethink and readjust the integration project. Enlargement is a response to the new post-cold war developments. It is not in itself the source of the difficulties. The fact that the long-standing ideological and military East–West divide no longer exists cannot but affect the shape and ambition of European integration, and those who seek to proceed with integration as if nothing had happened in Europe a decade ago risk acting like home-owners who insist on running an air conditioning system in a house that no longer has any walls.[32] In short, it is the European integration project that needs to be adjusted to enlargement, and not the other way around.

All this does not mean that we need to endorse all kinds of diversity. But it does suggest that Europe needs to learn to cope with diversity in a more creative, pragmatic and relaxed manner. This would hardly be possible without more information about what precisely the evolving patterns of diversity in the new Europe involve, and this collection of papers is intended to help us accomplish that aim.

But there is another side to this argument, and this time one which applies particularly to the newly established democracies of post-communist Europe and how precisely they are adapting. It is now little more than a decade since the democratic forces in Eastern Europe seized control from the communist regimes. This was one of the high points in a the world-wide 'third wave' of democracy, and involved the creation of more or less pluralist political regimes which, after half a century of communist rule, were finally restored to democratic control and accountability. It was, by any standards, a remarkable transformation, and that so many of these states have managed to build and maintain more or less full democratic legitimacy in the succeeding decade is no mean achievement. Now, however, many of these countries are on the verge of joining the European Union system, a system which itself is often depicted as one lacking proper mechanisms of popular accountability and control, and as one which suffers from a much decried democratic deficit. True, the European Union insists that the applicant states meet formal democratic criteria, and this is an important condition. But it is also evident that the practice of EU democracy often works against transparency, accountability and active popular participation.[33] What it appears to offer instead, as Scharpf has suggested, is a government for the people rather than a government of the people, and one based on what he calls output-oriented legitimacy rather than input-oriented legitimacy.[34]

In other words, having secured democracy after decades of non-democratic rule, the post-communist polities are now seeking entry to a system in which democratic values do not necessarily seem to be prioritised. Democracy was an object of struggle in Eastern Europe. In many respects, however, it seems increasingly a matter of indifference within the more comfortable West. Here also, then, may be a source of diversity. But in this case it may be a decidedly welcome one. For it is perhaps in the enlarged Europe that the practice of democracy will finally acquire a much-needed impulse.

NOTES

This introduction greatly benefited from thoughtful comments by Helen Wallace and Ania Krok-Paszkowska.

1. While diversity involves difference, divergence usually implies moving further apart. See also Christina Schäffner, Andreas Musolff and Michael Towson, 'Diversity and Unity in European Debates', in Andreas Musolff, Christina Schaffner and Michael Townson (eds.), *Conceiving of Europe: Diversity in Unity* (Aldershot: Dartmouth 1996), pp.1–14.
2. See Tanja A. Börzel and Thomas Risse, *When Europe Hits Home: Europeanization and Domestic Change* (Florence: RSC/EUI Working Papers, no. 56, 2000).
3. See, for example, Wolfgang Wessels, 'An Ever Closer Fusion? A Dynamic Macropolitical View on Integration Process', *Journal of Common Market Studies* 35 (1997), pp.267–99, or

Robert Leonardi, *Convergence, Cohesion and Integration in the European Union* (London: Macmillan 1995), pp.33–59.

4. This is regardless of the preamble to the Treaty on European Union that talks about 'creating an ever closer union'. See, for example, the 1989 address by Jacques Delors in Bruges, reprinted in Brent F. Nelsen and Alexander C.-G. Stubb (eds.), *The European Union. Readings on the Theory and Practice of European Integration* (London: Lynne Rienner 1994), pp.51–64.
5. Those who insist that their aim is a qualified rather than a total unity therefore need to make it clear what mixture of diversity and unity they want to achieve. However, this is usually not the case even in otherwise very competent analyses. See, for example, Eric Philippart and Monika Sie Dhian Ho, 'From Uniformity to Flexibility: Management of Diversity and its Impact on the EU System of Governance', in Gráinne de Búrca and Joanne Scott (eds.), *Constitutional Change in the EU. From Uniformity to Flexibility?* (Oxford: Hart Publishing 2000), pp.299–336.
6. See T. Koopmans, 'The Quest for Subsidiarity', in Deirdre Curtin and Ton Heukels (eds.), *Institutional Dynamics of European Integration. Essays in Honor of Henry G. Schermers* (Dordrecht: Martinus Nijhoff Publishers 1994), and Alexander C.-G. Stubb, 'Negotiating Flexible Integration in the Amsterdam Treaty', in Karlheinz Neunreither and Antje Wiener (eds.), *European Integration After Amsterdam. Institutional Dynamics and Prospects for Democracy* (Oxford: Oxford University Press 2000).
7. See Loukas Tsoukalis, *The European Community and its Mediterranean Enlargement* (London: Allen and Unwin 1981).
8. Giuliano Amato and Judy Batt, *Final Report of the Reflection Group on The Long-term Implications of EU Enlargement: The Nature of the New Border* (Florence: Robert Schuman Centre and Forward Studies Unit, EC 1999), p.11.
9. Vaclav Havel, 'Overcoming the Division of Europe', Speech to the European Parliament, Strasbourg, 16 Feb. 2000 (http://www.hrad.cz).
10. Heather Grabbe, *A Partnership for Accession? The Implications of EU Conditionality for the Central and East European Applicants* (Florence: RSC/EUI Working Papers, no. 12, 1999). See also Alina Mungiu-Pippidi, 'Facing the Desert of Tartars: the Eastern Border of Europe', in *Europe Unbound* (London: Routledge 2002).
11. See, for example, Helen Wallace, 'Whose Europe is it Anyway?', *European Journal of Political Research* 35/3 (1999), pp.287–306, and Helen Wallace, 'The Domestication of Europe: Contrasting experiences of EU Membership and Non-membership', Daalder Lecture, Leiden University, 1999.
12. Graham Avery and Fraser Cameron, *The Enlargement of the European Union* (Sheffield: Sheffield Academic Press 1998).
13. Adrienne Héritier, 'Differential Europe: The European Union Impact on National Policymaking', in Adrienne Héritier *et al.*, *Differential Europe. The European Union Impact on National Policymaking* (Boston: Rowman & Littlefield 2001), p.2.
14. See Helen Wallace and William Wallace, *Flying Together in a Larger and More Diverse European Union* (The Hague: Working Documents of the Netherlands Scientific Council for Government Policy, no. 87, 1995); and Jonathan Story, 'The Idea of the Core: The Dialectics of History and Space', in Geoffrey Edwards and Alfred Pijpers (eds.), *The Politics of European Treaty Reform* (London: Pinter 1997), pp.15–43.
15. This does not mean that the interpretation and application of the *acquis* is always rigid and inflexible. See Claus-Dieter Ehlermann, 'How Flexible is Community Law? An Unusual Approach to the Concept of Two Speeds', *Michigan Law Review*, 82/5–6 (1984), pp.1274–93.
16. See, for example, Fritz W. Scharpf, *Governing in Europe: Effective and Democratic?* (Oxford: Oxford University Press 1999).
17. See William Wallace, 'Government without Statehood: The Unstable Equilibrium', in Helen Wallace and William Wallace (eds.), *Policy-Making in the European Union* (Oxford: Oxford University Press, 3rd edn. 1996).
18. See Adrienne Héritier, *Policy-Making and Diversity in Europe. Escaping Deadlock* (Cambridge: Cambridge University Press 1999), p.2.

19. Héritier, *Policy-Making and Diversity in Europe*, p.8.
20 Lisa L. Martin, 'Heterogeneity, Linkage and Common Problems', in Robert O. Keohane and Elinor Ostrom (eds.), *Local Commons and Global Interdependence* (London: Sage 1995), pp.79–91.
21. Note Nicholas Rescher's argument: 'Consensus is not a criterion of truth, is not a standard of value, is not an index of moral or ethical appropriateness, is not a requisite for co-operation, is not a communal imperative for a just social order, is not, in itself, an appropriate ideal ... Consensus is no more than one positive factor that has to be weighed on the scale along many others.' See Nicholas Rescher, *Pluralism: Against the Demand for Consensus* (Oxford: Clarendon Press 1993), p.199.
22. European Commission (1997), *Agenda 2000* (http://europa.eu.int/comm/agenda2000/rapid 9716fr.htm).
23. It should be stressed, however, that according to successive Euro-barometer polls, public opinion in Spain, Portugal and Greece is more in favour of enlargement than that in countries such as Germany or Austria. It would also clearly be wrong to interpret the result of the Irish negative vote on the Treaty of Nice as a sign of opposition towards the Eastern enlargement. Moreover, as Urlich Sedelmeier pointed out, an analysis of the negotiations leading to the so-called Association Agreements between the EU and Central and Eastern European states reveals that the main opposition to a more far-reaching accommodation was not primarily the result of national differences among member states, but came predominantly from sectoral policy, both within the Commission and within the member state governments. See Ulrich Sedelmeier, 'East of Amsterdam: The Implications of the Amsterdam Treaty for Eastern Enlargement', in Neunreither and Wiener, *European Integration After Amsterdam*, p.232. See also Jose Torreblanca, 'Overlapping Games and Cross-Cutting Coalitions in the European Union', *West European Politics* 21/2 (1998), pp.134–53.
24. See R.E. Baldwin *et al.*, 'The Costs and Benefits of Eastern Enlargement: The Impact on the EU and Central Europe', *Economic Policy* 24 (April 1997), pp.125–76.
25. See Robert Leonardi, *Convergence, Cohesion and Integration in the European Union* (London: Macmillan 1995), p.4; and Liesbet Hooghe (ed.), *Cohesion Policy and European Integration* (Oxford: Oxford University Press 1996), pp.5–6.
26. Alan Mayhew, *Recreating Europe: The European Union's Policy towards Central and Eastern Europe* (Cambridge: Cambridge University Press 1998).
27. See Jan Zielonka and Alex Pravda (eds.), *Democratic Consolidation in Eastern Europe, Vol. 2: International and Transnational Factors* (Oxford: Oxford University Press 2001). See also Leonardo Morlino, *Democracy Between Consolidation and Crisis: Parties, groups and citizens in southern Europe* (Oxford: Oxford University Press 1998).
28. See, for example, Hans-Georg Betz, *Radical Right-Wing Populism in Western Europe* (New York: St. Martin's Press 1994).
29. It is important to keep in mind, however, that most statistics do not take into account the sizeable unregistered 'second' or 'shadow' economy in this region. See also below. For some basic economic data comparing the eastern and the western part of the continent see e.g. http://www.evd.nl/main.asp or http://www.worldbank.org/eca/eu-enlargement/index.html.
30. For instance, in the mid-1990s more than one-third of Poles and Hungarians were found to be living in poverty with falling life expectancy. The data for Bulgaria and Romania are even more dramatic. See, for example, Daniel Vaughan-Whitehead, 'Economic and Social Gaps, New Hidden Borders in the Enlarged Europe?' *EUI Working Papers* (RSC, No. 29 Florence, 2000), esp. pp.19–20.
31. For a recent assessment of the changing face of the West European welfare regimes, see Maurizio Ferrera and Martin Rhodes (eds.), *Recasting European Welfare States* (London: Cass 2000).
32. Timothy Garton Ash, 'Europe's Endangered Liberal Order', *Foreign Affairs* 77/2 (1998), p.61.
33. As Ralf Dahrendorf recently noted: 'The Union has now laid down very serious tests of democratic virtue for so-called accession countries. If, however, it applied these tests to itself, the Union, the result would be dismal.' See Ralf Dahrendorf, 'Can European Democracy Survive Globalisation?', *Policy-Network Analysis*, 15 Oct. 2001.
34. See Scharpf, *Governing in Europe*, esp. chapter 1.

Eastward Enlargement of the European Union and the Identity of Europe

DIETER FUCHS and
HANS-DIETER KLINGEMANN

Until the Maastricht Treaties (1991), the European Community was primarily an economic community legitimated by economic efficiency criteria.[1] Maastricht, however, initiated the transformation of the Community into a European Union (EU), which continued with the Treaty of Amsterdam (1997). These treaties vest greater powers in EU institutions. The EU is thus increasingly a supranational regime, substantially restricting member states' scope for action, and whose decisions directly affect citizens' lives. These decisions also affect politically sensitive areas that had hitherto been dealt with at the nation-state level (including social and moral issues). These developments have been politicising the EU and, consequently, engendering legitimation problems. The discussion on the democratic deficiencies of the EU, which has arisen only since this transformation of the European Community, is an expression of the legitimation issue. Many feel the EU can attain democratic legitimacy only if a European demos with a collective identity takes shape.[2] This can be maintained even if the democratic deficiencies of the EU were to be eliminated institutionally by substantially expanding the rights of the European Parliament. A viable European democracy requires a European demos that conceives of itself as a collectivity, considers itself represented by the Parliament, and makes the latter the addressee of relevant demands. However, in view of the cultural plurality and heterogeneity of European nation states, it is doubtful whether the constitution of a European demos with a tenable collective identity is possible at all.[3]

A further transformation of the EU must increase these doubts. At the 1992 Copenhagen summit, the then EU heads of government decided that the countries of Central and Eastern Europe could become members of the EU if they so desired and if they meet certain criteria for accession. There are now a number of candidates for accession, and negotiations are being conducted with a first group of countries. For a number of reasons, eastward enlargement is likely to make it even more difficult to develop a European identity. First, because the territorial limits of Europe are vague: where does it end in the east, or where should it end? A clearly defined territory is at least a useful, indeed necessary, precondition for the cognitive constitution of an 'us' that distinguishes itself from 'others' and which is the vehicle of a collective identity.[4] Second, including additional nation states increases the cultural plurality of the EU still more. And, third, it cannot be excluded that, over and above this pluralisation, there is a cultural gap between Western Europe and Central and Eastern Europe. Such a gap can be caused by different traditions and historical events in the distant past but also by socialisation and experience in the opposing societal systems in which people in Eastern and Western Europe lived from the end of the Second World War until the collapse of the communist states.

A collective identity can develop only on the basis of commonality among the members of a definable community. It is an open question how comprehensive this commonality must and can be in the case of a European demos. We assume that homogenising the plurality of national cultures to form a European nation is a project that is neither practicable nor useful. For a European demos before which the EU regime can be legitimated and which participates in the democratic processes in Europe, common political values and behaviours are presumably quite sufficient. With this premise in mind, our empirical goal is to establish the extent to which such commonality exists in individual countries or whether there are serious and systematic differences.

This analysis is structured by two theoretical considerations. First, we assume that political value orientations and behaviours can be organised in meaningful patterns. In determining these patterns we draw on the concepts of the democratic community and various types of democratic community. The most important criterion is support for democratic rule and rejection of autocratic rule. The greatest possible agreement on these preferences is a necessary condition for a European demos. However, fundamental support for democracy reveals nothing about the ideas on how democracy should be specifically implemented and structured. To settle this question, further values and behaviours must be taken into account. They form specific patterns, and, with reference to the democratic theory debate, we distinguish different types of democratic community.

Second, our analysis of differences in political values and behaviours considers not only individual countries but groups or families of countries. The country groups are distinguished on the basis of criteria proposed by Huntington, Lipset and Reisinger.[5]

The planned analysis can contribute only to discovering the *potential* for the formation of a European demos with a collective identity. Empirically established, objective commonality can have an identity-forming effect only if it is perceived as such and finds its place in the self-description of the collectivity. However, this transformation of objective commonality into the subjective self-understanding of a collectivity presupposes a great deal. In the case of a European demos, one of the prerequisites is certainly a European public[6] that can make latent commonality visible and allow it to become part of people's self-conception. However, this is not the subject of our study. We limit ourselves to the priority investigation of whether there is such commonality at all.

The study proceeds in three steps. First, the concepts of democratic community and types of democratic community are presented. The empirical analysis follows. It begins by explicating the classification of countries and by stating a number of theoretical expectations. In the empirical analysis itself, we first establish the extent to which the societal community in individual countries and groups of countries can be considered democratic at all. We then determine what type of democratic community predominates in these countries and groups of countries. In a third and final step, we summarise the empirical findings and draw a number of conclusions on the formation of a European demos with a collective identity.

THE CONCEPT OF THE DEMOCRATIC COMMUNITY

The demos of a democracy is a certain form of societal community. And like every societal community it is constituted through two mechanisms.[7] First, by *drawing a boundary* that defines who is included and who is excluded. In modern societies, citizenship provides a formal boundary. But it can have a constitutive effect only if it is subjectively assimilated by members of the community. This requires cognitively identifiable criteria, and one important such criterion is a clear territorial boundary. Second, a societal community takes shape through the *ties* between members on the basis of things actually or presumed to be shared. Only through these two mechanisms does a mere aggregate of individuals become a community that presents and can describe itself as such, and with which members can also identify.

The form of societal community that interests us is the demos, which, as the subject of a democratic form of government, should be a democratic community.[8] If it is to be accepted as such, it has to exhibit certain minimal characteristics. The institutional order of a democracy (kratos) can function only if there is a corresponding community (demos). In determining the properties of a democratic community we draw on an analytical model that divides democracy into three hierarchically structured levels.[9] The topmost level is that of *political culture*, whose constitutive elements are the fundamental values of a democracy. The next level is that of *political structure*, which consists of the democratic system of government of a country, generally laid down by the constitution. This structure can be understood as a selective implementation of the cultural values of a community for the action context of politics, and this system of government is also legitimated by recourse to these values. The lowest level in the hierarchy is that of the *political process*. The political process is concerned with the realisation of the collective goals of a community by the actors. Their action is controlled by the political structure, and this means, among other things, that normative expectations about the behaviour of political actors are associated with the constituted system of government in a given country. The three levels thus form a control hierarchy that begins with culture and ends with the process or actual activity on the part of actors. What attributes must a community have at these three levels if it is to be deemed democratic?

At the *cultural level*, a democratic community is characterised above all by support for the fundamental values of democracy. They include the idea of self-government or sovereignty of the people. And this includes mutual recognition of citizens as free and politically equal. Since the birth of democracy in ancient Athens, the two values of freedom and political equality have been essentially bound up with that of democracy.[10]

A democratic community cannot be as clearly identified at the *structural level* as at the cultural level. On the one hand, it must be expected that the regime in the citizens' own country is supported in so far as it is a democracy and not an autocracy. Otherwise approval of the idea of democracy would be completely non-committal. On the other hand, the idea of a democracy can be institutionally embodied in different ways. For this reason, many people may basically want a democracy but not in the form that exists in their country. People may therefore support or criticise the democracy implemented in their country for a variety of reasons.[11] They may support it because it is a democracy and as such has institutionalised the idea of democracy. They may criticise it because they feel that the reality of democracy in their country fails to meet their own normative ideas of democracy, and because they also assume there are alternative forms of implementation that produce a better democratic reality. Such people can be described as 'critical democrats'.[12] Both possibilities are compatible with the prerequisites for a democratic community.

The *process level* is concerned with the realisation of political objectives by producing collectively binding decisions. In pluralistic societies, such goals are always controversial, and conflicts about them are the very essence of democratic processes. A democratic community is thus not characterised by consensus, however understood, about the political goals to be attained but only by actual compliance with the procedural norms for taking action as laid down by the constitution, and which are intended to regulate everyday political conflicts.

Figure 1 shows these attributes of a democratic community in the form of 'the more – the more' statements. They constitute operational definitions that provide a point of reference for later empirical analysis. As we have argued, a democratic community is characterised at the process level by compliance with the democratically established legal norms. The prohibition of violence or force as a political instrument has pre-eminent status among these legal norms, because it affects the essence of successful integration into a community. The figure therefore contains an independent operational definition of force as a means of politics.

Having established the characteristics of a democratic community, we proceed to differentiate different types. For the purpose of our study we combine a theoretical with a pragmatic approach. Theoretically, we follow the contemporary discussion in political philosophy,[13] and pragmatically we are guided by indicators available in the 1995–99 *World Values Survey*. We

FIGURE 1
OPERATIONAL DEFINITIONS OF A DEMOCRATIC COMMUNITY

System level	Basic elements	Operational definitions
Culture	Values	The stronger support is for a democracy and the more strongly autocracy is rejected, the more closely the societal community will correspond to a democratic community. The more strongly other citizens are recognised as free and equal, the more closely the societal community will correspond to a democratic community.
Structure	Rules and institutions	The stronger support for or critique of democracy in one's own country is based on democratic norms, the more closely the societal community will correspond to a democratic community.
Process	Actions	The less citizens use force as a political means, the more closely the societal community will correspond to a democratic community. The more closely citizens conform to the democratically determined norms of action, the more closely the societal community will correspond to a democratic community.

begin with a simplified description of the types, bringing in a dimension at the cultural level that has hitherto been neglected by empirical democracy research, namely the ethos of a community. It has two points of reference, first, the ethical values by which a person orders his life and, second, the ethical values governing relations with other members of the societal community.

This ethos of the community is the subject of one of the most important democracy theory debates to have been conducted in recent decades. It is not dealt with in detail at this point but the aspects that are important for the analysis – the differentiation of the democratic community – are reiterated. The debate has been provoked by the tension between the freedom of individuals and the demands of the community. Differing normative positions are apparent primarily in the priority given to the one or the other. This general continuum, with the poles individualism and community, can be divided into two dimensions, which have already been mentioned in discussing the ethos of the community. The one dimension addresses the fundamental question of who bears the principal responsibility for shaping and determining a person's life: the individual himself or the state, which represents a specific form of community institutionalisation. The other dimension is concerned with the just as fundamental question of how relations between individuals should be. The one alternative is performance-driven competition between individuals in the various marketplaces and the other is co-operation and solidarity in dealing with one another.[14] Crossing these two dichotomous dimensions produces a typology with four normative models of democracy and the corresponding types of democratic community: libertarian, liberal, socialist and republican (see Figure 2).

The contrasting and, as it were, pure models are the libertarian and socialist communities. On both dimensions they give clearest priority to one or other alternative. The liberal model differs from the libertarian primarily through equality of opportunity in competition between individuals in the economic and political markets as a criterion of justice. And justice is the most important standard by which to evaluate societal institutions. The most prominent advocate of this model is Rawls.[15] Given differences in ability and temperament, equality of opportunity can be ensured only through legal regulation and redistribution by government. Government thus plays an extremely important role in shaping the life of the individual. The liberal model differs from the socialist model in three ways. First, redistribution by government is concerned only with the most equal possible distribution of the primary goods that are absolutely necessary for the individual to organise his life autonomously. Second, the principles of competition and

FIGURE 2
TYPES OF A DEMOCRATIC COMMUNITY

		Responsibility for one's own fate	
		Self	*State*
Relationship with others	*Competition*	Libertarian	Liberal
	Co-operation (Solidarity)	Republican	Socialist

performance are constitutive for the relationship between individuals in everyday interaction in the marketplace, in politics, and in other areas of society. And, third, in the event of conflict, individual freedom always has unrestricted priority over the equal distribution of the other primary goods.

Among other things, this means that, in contrast to the socialist model, basic social rights ought not to be included in the constitution. Ensuring equality of opportunity can be only a political task, which, in practical terms, results in the establishment of a more or less comprehensive welfare state. Overall, the role of government in the liberal model is thus relatively less restricted than in the socialist model. This difference is not visible in the dichotomised typology. From an institutional point of view, the ethical values of the libertarian community mean as little government as possible and as comprehensive a market as possible; and those of the socialist community mean a comprehensive welfare state and a limited market. The liberal community occupies an intermediate position.

The republican community differs most strongly from the others. Moreover, it can be considered the normatively most demanding. In contrast to the liberal community, common values are of crucial importance, and, in case of doubt, are given priority over the unrestricted freedom of the individual. The lifestyle of a republican community is 'essentially co-operative and solidaristic'.[16] It differs from the liberal and especially from the socialist community by a fundamentally anti-etatist and anti-paternalism attitude. In this regard it resembles the libertarian community. According to republican ideas, community values should be implemented not by government, and thus on behalf of the citizens, but by the community of citizens themselves.[17] For this reason the self-organisation of the citizenry in local units is an essential republican postulate. The republican community is thus a participatory and solidary community. The solidarity concept differs considerably from that upheld in the socialist community. It presents

FIGURE 3
TYPES OF A DEMOCRATIC COMMUNITY (SCHEMATIC DESCRIPTION)

	Libertarian	Liberal	Socialist	Republican
Cultural level				
Responsibility for one's own life	Self	Self + State	State	Self
Relationship with others	Competition	Competition + Equal opportunities	Solidarity (abstract)	Solidarity (specific) Trust
Ethic idea of the good		Tolerance		Tolerance
Structural level				
Ownership of means of production	Private ownership	Private ownership	Private ownership + State property	
Management of enterprises	Entrepreneur		Entrepreneur + Employee	
Process level				
Political motivation				High
Civic engagement (voluntary associations)				High

itself as voluntary support for people in need through no fault of their own, or as voluntary charitableness. Solidarity in a socialist community, by contrast, is exercised through collectively binding decisions by the state and, moreover, is characterised by a strong concept of equality.

The ideas about a republican community that were developed in the context of normative democracy theory have been taken up in an empirical research context especially by Putnam.[18] Putnam himself uses the concept of *civic community*. The dimensions and attributes of the civic community are compatible with our analytical distinctions. Putnam assumes from the outset that the civic community is democratic, and accordingly exhibits corresponding attitudes towards the democratic system of government. He therefore concentrates on the ethos of the community and the behaviour of its members that it engenders. At the level of political culture, Putnam sees several values as characteristic of the community. In the first place he emphasises political equality, while stressing – fully in keeping with the republican tradition – that this includes equal rights *and* duties for all. This value is particularly important for the relationship between individual members of the community and its institutions. The other values are concerned with interactions among members of the community. They should be guided by solidarity, tolerance and trust. The citizens of a civic community are thus explicitly not egoistic-rational people, as is assumed, for example, in the libertarian model of democracy. A decisive characteristic of a civic community is, according to Putnam, a strong commitment among citizens to political participation. Putnam makes two specifications in this regard. First, an orientation towards the public good: 'Participation in a civic community is more public-spirited, more oriented to shared benefits.'[19] On the other hand, the decisive form of participation is in voluntary associations. According to Putnam, active membership in voluntary associations contributes to the generation of the values mentioned and the associated ability and willingness for co-operative behaviour in realising the public good.

Figure 3 shows the four types of democratic community schematically in terms of the attributes described above. The two dimensions underlying the typology in Figure 2 have naturally been taken into account. A characteristic is used in describing a type of democratic community only if this is clearly justified on the basis of the democracy theory discussion.

EMPIRICAL ANALYSIS

Classification of Countries and Theoretical Expectations

As the predecessor of the European Union, the European Community came into being during the period of the East–West conflict. It therefore included only Western European states, with France and Germany as the core countries. They provided relative economic and cultural homogeneity, and the border question did not arise. To the west, north and south, the border was defined by the coastline, and to the east by the Iron Curtain. After the collapse of communism, the eastward border dissolved, and the question where the eastern bounds of Europe ought to be set and who should be considered potential members of the EU came onto the agenda.[20]

Depending on what criteria are applied, this question finds a variety of answers. The criterion of our study is the similarity of political communities in the countries of Central and Eastern Europe to those of the Western European countries that have hitherto constituted the European Union. The basic assumption is that the potential for the formation of the European demos with a collective identity is proportionate to the similarity of political values and behaviours. Before we tackle the empirical analysis, we classify the countries under study and attempt on this basis to formulate what we expect of the analysis.

Political values and behaviours are influenced by various factors; most importantly, perhaps, by durable cultural traditions.[21] A useful starting point for classifying countries is thus the distinction between civilisations drawn by Huntington. He postulates a historical cultural borderline within Europe that divides the Western-Christian peoples from the Muslim and Orthodox peoples. This dividing line ultimately goes back to the division of the Roman Empire in the fourth century, consolidated in the sixteenth century. If one were to take account of this cultural border only, the frontier of Europe would be clearly definable. It would run where Western Christianity ends and Islam begins.[22] This definition is based above all on religion, and this is dichotomised: Protestant and Catholic vs. Orthodox and Muslim. For the purposes of our analysis, this is too great a simplification. We therefore draw on two further criteria to produce a more differentiated classification of countries, basing our procedure on democracy theory approaches and findings.[23]

These two additional criteria are the different empires in which the peoples concerned lived for centuries, namely the British, Habsburg, Russian and Ottoman empires. The links between these empires and specific religions (Protestant, Catholic, Orthodox and Muslim) are obvious, but it can be assumed that the respective system of government has an independent impact on fundamental values. They are, for example, to be associated with the extent of autocratic rule in the different empires or with the different degree of separation between state and church.

The Soviet Empire can be regarded as a specific variant. Russia formed the centre of this empire, and its sphere of influence included first the other Soviet republics, and second the countries of Central and Eastern Europe within the Iron Curtain. Unlike the other empires, the Soviet Union and its satellite states had definitely no religious basis. The impact on the political attitudes and behaviours of the citizenry is affected by the autocratic system of government and the egalitarian ideology.[24] Reisinger suggests that this impact varies depending on the length of time during which a country had a Leninist regime.[25]

In addition to religion, empire and Leninist regime, we draw on a fourth characteristic, the level of socio-economic modernity. It is operationalised by per capita GDP. The modernity and wealth of a country are among the most important preconditions for the formation and stability of a democracy and for the development of democratic and liberal values. This has been repeatedly established by Lipset,[26] and can be considered one of the best confirmed findings of empirical democracy research.

Tables 1 and 2 classify countries in terms of the dimensions explained. Description in terms of 'empire' and 'modernity' (Table 1) is relatively unproblematic. It is a little more complicated with 'religion', since most countries are mixed in this respect. Table 2 shows the shares of individual

TABLE 1
CULTURAL HERITAGE. A CLASSIFICATION OF COUNTRIES BY EMPIRES, DURATION OF LENINIST REGIMES AND MODERNITY

Countries	Empires (crude classification)	Modernity (GDP ppp in US $)
Anglo-American countries		
USA	British (-)	29.080
Australia	British (-)	19.510
New Zealand	British (-)	15.780
Western European countries		
Norway	None (Sweden) (-)	24.260
Sweden	None (-)	19.010
Finland	Russian (-)	19.660
West Germany	None (Prussia) (-)	24.345
Spain	None (Spain) (-)	15.690
Central European countries		
East Germany	None (Prussia)/Le 41	17.995
Czech Republic	Habsburg/Le 41	10.380
Slovakia	Habsburg/ Le 41	7.860
Hungary	Habsburg/ Le 43	6.970
Slovenia	Habsburg/ Le 18	11.880
Croatia	Habsburg/ Le 18	4.930
Baltic countries		
Estonia	Russia/ Le 50	5.090
Latvia	Russia/ Le 50	3.970
Lithuania	Russia/ Le 50	4.140
South-Eastern European countries (mainly Orthodox)		
Yugoslavia	Ottoman/ Le 18	3.500
Romania	Ottoman/ Le 43	4.270
Bulgaria	Ottoman/ Le 43	3.870
South-Eastern European countries (mixed-Muslim)		
Macedonia	Ottoman/ Le 18	3.180
Bosnia-Herzegovina	Ottoman/ Le 18	2.358
Albania	Ottoman/ Le 45	2.170
Eastern European countries		
Russia	Russia/ Le 74	4.280
Ukraine	Russia/ Le 74	2.170
Belarus	Russia/ Le 74	4.820
Moldova	Ottoman/ Le 50	1.450

Notes: Le = years of Leninist rule (Reisinger 1999 and own calculations for Albania, East Germany; and the former Yugoslav states); Modernity: GDP purchasing parity power in US dollars 1997.

TABLE 2
CULTURAL HERITAGE. A CLASSIFICATION OF COUNTRIES BY DENOMINATION

Countries	P %	C %	PC %	O %	M %	OM %	S %	T %	CL
Anglo-American countries									
USA	***36***	25	**61**	0	0	1	18	80	**P**
Australia	***48***	26	**74**	1	1	2	3	79	**P**
New Zealand	***60***	14	**74**	0	0	0	4	78	**P**
Western European countries									
Norway	***82***	1	**83**	1	1	2	4	89	**P**
Sweden	***81***	5	**86**	1	4	5	1	92	**P**
Finland	***80***	3	**83**	2	0	2	1	86	**P**
West Germany	***39***	33	**72**	0	1	1	1	74	**P**
Spain	1	***82***	**83**	0	0	0	1	84	**C**
Central European countries									
East Germany	***18***	5	**23**	0	0	0	1	**24**	**T**
Czech Republic	2	***39***	**40**	0	0	0	3	43	**C**
Slovakia	10	***73***	**83**	0	0	0	3	86	**C**
Hungary	17	***55***	**72**	2	0	2	1	75	**C**
Slovenia	2	***69***	**71**	2	1	3	1	75	**C**
Croatia	0	***82***	**82**	1	1	1	1	85	**C**
Baltic countries									
Estonia	10	0	10	***16***	0	**16**	2	**28**	**T**
Latvia	***19***	18	**37**	18	0	18	5	60	**P**
Lithuania	2	***77***	**79**	4	0	4	2	85	**C**
South-Eastern European countries (mainly Orthodox)									
Yugoslavia	1	6	7	***64***	8	**72**	2	81	**O**
Romania	2	5	6	***87***	0	**87**	3	96	**O**
Bulgaria	1	1	2	***52***	12	**64**	1	67	**O**
South-Eastern European countries (mixed-Muslim)									
Macedonia	0	1	1	***45***	24	**69**	0	70	**O**
Bosnia-Herzegovina	2	14	16	26	***27***	**53**	1	70	**M**
Albania	0	6	6	20	***67***	**87**	0	93	**M**
Eastern European countries									
Russia	0	0	0	***48***	5	**53**	1	54	**O**
Ukraine	0	6	6	***56***	0	**56**	1	63	**O**
Belarus	0	8	8	***54***	0	**54**	0	62	**O**
Moldova	0	0	0	***83***	0	**83**	1	84	**O**

Notes: P = Protestant; C = Catholic; PC = sum of Protestant + Catholic; O = Orthodox; M = Muslim; OM = sum of Orthodox + Muslim; S = Sects; T = proportion of respondents mentioning a denominational affiliation; CL = generalised denominational classification. Cell entries are data generated by the World Values Survey 1995–99.

religions in each country as a percentage. In the last column (CL) the country is classified in terms of modal denomination. The columns PC (Protestant and Catholic) and OM (Orthodox and Muslim) demonstrate the dominant dividing line postulated by Huntington.

Countries have been assigned to one of seven groups on the basis of the four dimensions (see Tables 1 and 2). Although our study is concerned with European countries, the United States, Australia and New Zealand have also been taken into account. According to Huntington, these countries form an independent culture complex within Western-Christian civilisation that differs systemically from Europe. This difference has recently been empirically established also at the level of political attitudes and behaviour.[27] Including this group of countries provides a contrasting backdrop to the particularity of European nations. Moreover, they most clearly represent one of the types of democratic community that we have identified (libertarian community).

We have chosen to label the groups of countries by geographical region. Such regions are relatively neutral concepts, while being, in a certain sense, effective factors in generating common characteristics. Spatial proximity between countries and peoples facilitates communication and increases the probability of similar historical experience. All four dimensions relate to the formation and stability of democracies on the one hand, and to the development of democratic and liberal attitudes and behaviour on the other.[28] Since we cannot make any precise assumptions about the relative weight of individual dimensions and relations between the various scale points, only limited a priori assumptions are possible on the basis of this classification. We begin with the 'democratic community', which is characterised by acceptance of the fundamental values of every democracy. In this regard, the situational factor of the collapse of the communist systems is likely to have an effect. We therefore expect a democracy to be supported by a majority in every country. The factors we have used in classifying countries would therefore have to take effect in *relative differences* between countries and groups of countries. If the major historical dividing lines postulated by Huntington, separating the Western-Christian peoples from the Muslim and Orthodox peoples, is indeed the decisive borderline, the Anglo-American, Western European, Central European and Baltic countries would be more democratic than the South-Eastern and Eastern European lands.

If all four dimensions – not only 'religion' but also 'empire', 'Leninist regime' and 'modernity' – are taken into account, expectations are somewhat more differentiated. On the basis of these dimensions, we can posit the following ordinal sequence in the extent to which a democratic community exists: (1) the Anglo-American and Western European countries (perhaps Spain and Finland might be somewhat marginal); (2) the Central European countries; (3) the Baltic countries; (4) the South-Eastern European countries (with the exception of Albania); (5) the Eastern European countries (including Albania). In all the following tables of empirical results, the groups of countries are listed in this presumed order. If one wishes to provide an empirically testable simplification, the extent to which a democratic community exists in individual countries can be assumed to vary along a geographical northwest–southeast axis.

Two central criteria were applied in differentiating between types of democratic community (see Figure 2 above). First, whom the citizens feel should bear primary responsibility for a person's fate (the individual himself or the state), and, second, how relations between fellow citizens ought to be (competitive or solidary). The two criteria can also be understood as a specification of the more general individualism-collectivism dimension. In formulating our expectations we drew on a study by Lipset.[29] He postulates a substantial difference between American and European cultures, an 'American exceptionalism'. In this context he is concerned only with Western Europe. The distinction Lipset makes resembles that proposed by Huntington[30] between North American and Western European cultures. However, Lipset focuses on different aspects. In his view, the exceptionality of American culture has been primarily determined by the ethos of the Protestant sects that immigrated from Britain. Central to the American ethos is a marked individualism with a strong ethic of self-responsibility and an anti-etatist attitude. This has produced a society with a weak central government and a strong market. Another two features that characterise the American ethos also trace back to the traditions of the Protestant sects.[31] On the one hand, this is a pronounced work ethic that derives ultimately from the idea of 'predestination'. On the other hand, it is an ethic moralism with respect to questions of good life and true action.

Lipset contrasts the American ethos with the etatist and solidarity attitudes among Europeans, which have led to the formation of welfare states. Of the factors given in Tables 1 and 2 that shape the political attitudes and behaviours of the citizenry, Lipset thus cites British origins and the tradition of the British Empire, and the religion of the Protestant sects. However, since the ethic of the Protestant sects and the structure of the political and economic systems grounded on it are considered the most important causes for the extraordinarily successful modernisation process in the United States, the modernity factor also comes into play. On the basis of

Lipset's study we can formulate a number of expectations about the type of democratic community in the countries under study.

Lipset takes no account of Central and Eastern European countries. If we assume that autocratic regimes – like those of the Ottoman and Russian Empires and the Soviet imperium – foster etatist orientations and weaken individualist attitudes, we can on this basis formulate expectations about the type of democratic community to include the countries of Central and Eastern Europe. We restrict ourselves to the two criteria underlying the typology in Figure 2, on the assumption that, at a more general level, both are based on the individualism-collectivism (or etatism) dimension. On this dimension at least three types of democratic community can be placed. The libertarian community is closest to the individualist pole, the socialist community to the collectivism pole, with the liberal community between the two. If we apply these criteria, the Anglo-American countries can be assumed to exhibit a tendency towards the libertarian community, Western European countries towards the liberal community, and the countries of Central and Eastern Europe towards the socialist community. The latter is likely to apply most strongly for the Slavic successor countries to the Soviet Union.

Democratic Community

Two questions are to be settled in the first step of the empirical analysis. First, the extent to which the societal communities in the countries under study are democratic, and, second, how marked the similarities or differences between these countries are. The analysis is guided by the expectations formulated in the previous section.

The criteria for a democratic community have been laid down as operational definitions (see Figure 1). With the exception of 'mutual recognition as free and politically equal citizens', indicators of all the attributes of a democratic community are contained in the World Values Survey 1995–99. The distributions of attitudes and behavioural dispositions measured by these indicators are shown in Table 3.

The empirical findings displayed in Table 3 are not interpreted in any detail.[32] They serve primarily as background information for the following systematic comparison, to which we can refer as needed. Before we tackle this comparison, a few remarks on methods are appropriate.

The countries under study are described and localised by aggregating individual characteristics of citizens. The advantages and disadvantages of this strategy are well known, and they have been comprehensively discussed. Our approach differs from most in that we make a priori assumptions that are theoretically justified. On the one hand we define the democratic community

TABLE 3
EMPIRICAL EVIDENCE OF CITIZEN SUPPORT OF A SET OF CRITERIA FOR A DEMOCRATIC COMMUNITY

Countries	Culture		Structure		Process	
	DEM[a] %	AUT[a] %	PSC %	CGI %	VIO %	LAW %
Anglo-American countries						
USA	88	5	35	27	83	98
Australia	83	6	30	23	85	97
New Zealand	88	3	14	11	87	95
Western European countries						
Norway	93	3	67	60	91	97
Sweden	93	5	27	39	88	93
Finland	75	10	34	23	91	94
West Germany	93	1	40	20	85	88
Spain	92	8	31	25	76	97
Central European countries						
East Germany	91	2	38	12	85	90
Czech Republic	88	4	33	18	80	86
Slovakia	88	4	36	30	73	82
Hungary	83	5	32	30	80	89
Slovenia	82	6	28	24	70	85
Croatia	95	13	45	38	87	74
Baltic countries						
Estonia	85	6	30	36	83	91
Latvia	79	8	24	19	83	83
Lithuania	87	15	29	23	76	90
South-Eastern European countries (mainly Orthodox)						
Yugoslavia	88	10	24	29	74	92
Romania	89	22	11	16	77	94
Bulgaria	80	19	36	43	79	96
South-Eastern European countries (mixed-Muslim)						
Macedonia	73	15	21	16	79	89
Bosnia-Herzegovina	87	26	32	57	72	97
Albania	98	65	43	35	93	92
Eastern European countries						
Russia	51	20	7	16	82	85
Ukraine	75	17	13	29	78	81
Belarus	75	17	12	26	83	80
Moldova	71	16	14	33	66	82

Notes: DEM: Support of democratic rule; AUT: Support of autocratic rule; PSC: Support of political system of one's own country; CGI: Confidence in governmental institutions; VIO: Illegitimacy of violence; LAW: Law abidingness. Cell entries are percent positive support.

a) The addition of both percentages can exceed 100. There are respondents who equally support democratic and autocratic rules.

in general and the types of democratic community on the basis of a number of specific characteristics. On the other hand, we determine which countries best represent the democratic community and its types. These are the benchmark countries of our analysis. We assume that all respondents can be described and related to the benchmark countries through a combination of the properties constitutive to the respective community. By using discriminant analysis as a statistical technique we are able to answer two questions. First, how important the specific characteristics (indicators) are in predicting the membership of a respondent in the predefined group on the one hand and in the undefined group on the other. Second, for every respondent from the undefined group, the probability of his belonging to the defined or known group can be determined.

The tables show several figures useful in assessing results. First, correlations of the variables with the discriminant function: the higher the correlation, the more important is the variable or the indicator for discriminating between citizens in the known group and those in the group of other countries. Second, eigenvalues and canonical correlations: both high eigenvalues and high canonical correlations mean that the two groups are well separated by the given set of variables. Third, group centroids are reported. These figures are simply average scores for respondents belonging to each of the predefined groups. Fourth, we show simplified classification results. Each respondent is allocated to a group according to his greatest probability – given the set of variables for the prediction. The share of correctly classified respondents is an indicator of the goodness of fit.

Discriminant analysis allows us to assign a probability of belonging to a group that is defined a priori to represent a certain theoretical category. Although the initial score is allocated to the individual respondent, we use this variable in our analysis mainly to describe nation states by averaging the respective information.

The standard against which we determine the extent to which the societal community in specific countries is democratic is a group of countries that undoubtedly represent such a community. The countries concerned are, first, the United States and Australia, and, second, Sweden and West Germany. These are the benchmark democracies for the discriminant analysis. Table 4 shows how strongly the eight attributes of a democratic community distinguish between the benchmark democracies and the other countries. With one exception – 'confidence in governmental institutions' – all correlations of the variables with the discriminant function are statistically significant. The highest correlations are in 'support for autocracy' (-.799) at the cultural level and 'law-abidingness' (.583) at the

TABLE 4
DIFFERENTIATION BETWEEN BENCHMARK DEMOCRACIES AND OTHER COUNTRIES

	Democracies[a] r[b]	
Cultural level		
Support of democracy	.446	
Support of autocracy	-.799	
Structural level		
Support for current political system	.252	
Confidence in gov't institutions	.048[c]	
Process level		
Illegitimacy of violence	.264	
Law abidingness	.583	
Eigenvalue	.059	
Canonical correlation	.236	
Group centroids		
Groups to classify	-.121	
Democracies	.486	
Classification results		
	Group	
	1	2
1 Group to classify	.58	.42
2 Democracies	.32	.68
Correctly classified	60	

Notes:
a) Benchmark countries: USA, Australia, Sweden and West Germany
b) Pooled within-group correlations between discriminating variables and canonical discriminant function.
c) Not significant at the .001 level.

process level. 60 per cent of respondents were correctly classified on the basis of this weighted combination of characteristics.

However, our analysis is concerned with the categorisation and comparison of countries and groups of countries. For this purpose we have aggregated the results obtained at the individual level. Table 5 shows the mean of probability for respondents in a country to belong to the group of benchmark democracies as defined by the characteristics stated in Table 4. Countries are classified in terms of the geographical groups explained in the theoretical section. The name of each geographical group is given in italics over the countries, and the mean and standard deviations for these groups are also stated. The expectation formulated in the theoretical section relative to the geographical country groups postulates the following ordinal sequence in degrees of democratic community: (1) the Anglo-American and Western European countries; (2) the Central European countries; (3) the

TABLE 5
CLOSENESS OF COUNTRIES TO THE BENCHMARK DEMOCRACIES

Countries	Mean[a]	Sd[a]	N[a]
Anglo-American countries	*.552*	*(.118)*	*3,749*
USA[b]	.562	(.12)	1,235
Australia[b]	.538	(.12)	1,726
New Zealand	.565	(.11)	788
Western European countries	*.536*	*(.123)*	*4,494*
Norway	.579	(.11)	1,077
Sweden[b]	.530	(.12)	862
Finland	.493	(.13)	796
West Germany[b]	.551	(.11)	896
Spain	.511	(.12)	863
Central European countries	*.497*	*(.135)*	*4,980*
East Germany	.539	(.12)	888
Czech Republic	.512	(.13)	935
Slovakia	.482	(.13)	868
Hungary	.512	(.13)	494
Slovenia	.486	(.14)	807
Croatia	.460	(.14)	988
Baltic countries	*.436*	*(.131)*	*2,168*
Estonia	.477	(.13)	782
Latvia	.418	(.12)	894
Lithuania	.403	(.12)	492
South-Eastern European countries (mainly Orthodox)	*.468*	*(.135)*	*2,382*
Yugoslavia	.494	(.13)	1,013
Romania	.453	(.14)	804
Bulgaria	.444	(.12)	565
South-Eastern European countries (mixed-Muslim)	*.405*	*(.133)*	*2,091*
Macedonia	.429	(.12)	589
Bosnia-Herzegovina	.436	(.13)	966
Albania	.322	(.10)	536
Eastern European countries	*.374*	*(.127)*	*3,796*
Russia	.362	(.13)	1,011
Ukraine	.380	(.13)	1,008
Belarus	.382	(.12)	1,054
Moldova	.373	(.13)	723
Total	.477	(.12)	23,660
Eta2	.228		

Notes: a) Mean = Mean membership probability of respondents belonging to the group of benchmark democracies, defined by the set of eight characteristics of democratic community; Sd = Standard deviation; N = Number of cases
b) Benchmark democracies.

FIGURE 4
LOCATION OF COUNTRIES IN A TWO-DIMENSIONAL SPACE OF DEMOCRATIC COMMUNITY

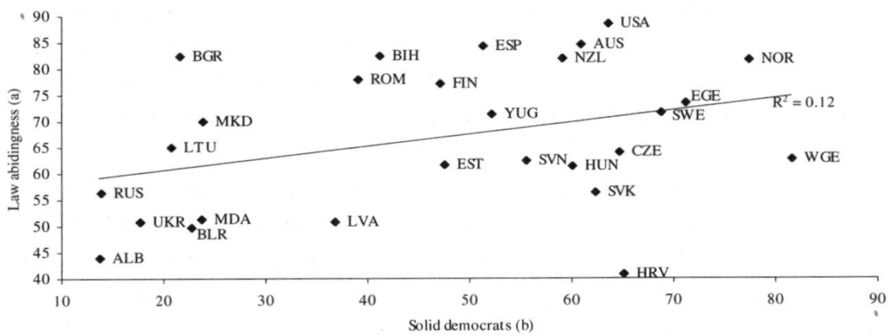

Notes: (a) Percentage of people with high degree of law abidingness; (b) Percentage of people who support democratic rule and at the same time reject autocratic rule.

Baltic countries; (4) the South-Eastern European countries; (5) the Eastern European countries.

This assumption is essentially confirmed by empirical findings. The deviant group is the Baltic countries, which rank after the Orthodox South-Eastern European countries. However, the results for individual Baltic countries differ greatly. Whilst the mean for Estonia corresponds more or less to that for Slovenia and Croatia in Central Europe, Latvia and Lithuania trail behind the South-Eastern European Muslim countries. Estonia's distinctiveness can be attributed to the country's greater modernity in comparison with the other two Baltic nations (see Table 1) and to the high proportion of the population – in comparison with all the countries under study – with no religious ties (see Table 2).

By far the greatest misclassification of a country in a geographical group is Albania. Of all countries, Albania shows the lowest mean and thus the greatest distance to the benchmark democracies. The result cannot be explained with reference to the country classification criteria. Possibly the regime of Enver Hodscha plays a role, certainly one of the most totalitarian among comparable regimes in Europe.

As we expected, the Slavic successor countries to the Soviet Union, here termed Eastern European countries, show by far the lowest mean score of all regional groups (see Table 5). They thus correspond least to the benchmark democracies. However, a majority of citizens in Moldova, Belarus and Ukraine also clearly favours democracy, while only a minority is in favour of autocracy (see Table 3). Relative distance from the benchmark democracies thus does not necessarily mean that the citizens of the country concerned do *not* form a democratic community. The relatively least support for democracy (51 per cent) and a relatively high support for autocracy (20 per cent) among Eastern European countries is to be found in Russia. Of all the countries under study, Russia, together with Albania, has the lowest mean score. These two countries are accordingly the least democratic as far as the attitudes and behaviours of their citizens are concerned.

Among the Anglo-American and Western European countries, two deviate relatively strongly from the others: Spain and, above all, Finland (see Table 5). In the case of Spain this is attributable mainly to the below average rejection of violence as a political instrument, and in the case of Finland to the below average support for democracy (see Table 3). The explanation *ex post factum* may be the tradition of violent confrontation in Spain and the geographical proximity and former dominance of Finland to Russia and the Soviet Union. Finland is the only country in Western Europe that belonged to an autocratic empire (Russia) for a longer period. These two deviant cases also explain most of the difference in the mean between the Anglo-American countries and the countries of Western Europe.

For the further analysis of the democratic community we made two simplifications in comparison with the discriminant analysis. First, we restricted ourselves to the three characteristics: ‘support of democracy’, ‘support of autocracy’ and ‘law-abidingness’. We thus leave out attitudes to the political system in the respondents’ own country, the theoretical status of which is not fully clear (see section 2). The three attributes taken into account, are, however, also those that most clearly distinguish the group of benchmark democracies from the group of other countries (see Table 4). Second, we make no a priori assumption in the form of a reference group (benchmark democracies). We localise the countries in a two-dimensional space (see Figure 4). The one dimension is the proportion of respondents that *clearly* support democracy while rejecting autocracy. These respondents are termed ‘solid democrats’.[33] The second dimension is the proportion of respondents that exhibit differing degrees of law-abidingness.

The countries are relatively widely scattered in the two-dimensional space. Although there is a significant linear relationship between the two dimensions, it is not very marked ($R^2 = .12$). Nevertheless, certain patterns can be identified that correspond to the results of the discriminant analysis. Countries with a pronounced democratic community are located in the top right-hand area of the space, the Anglo-American countries and some Western European countries. Of the Western European countries, Finland,

Spain and West Germany deviate most. Finland and Spain exhibit above average law-abidingness and an only average proportion of solid democrats. With West Germany exactly the opposite applies.

The left-hand bottom part of the space is occupied by countries whose societal community can be described as least democratic. Here we find the same countries that scored lowest in the discriminant analysis: the Eastern European countries and Albania. Combining support for democracy and rejection of democracy produces an even more marked result. In all five countries (Russia, Ukraine, Belarus, Moldova, Albania) solid democrats are a minority of less than 25 per cent. At the same time, the level of law-abidingness is below average. The Central European countries (Czech Republic, Slovakia and Hungary), although spatially somewhat apart from the North American and Western European countries, are still much closer to them than to the Eastern European countries and Albania. This finding, too, conforms to the discriminant analysis.

Types of Democratic Community

A democratic community is characterised by its members exhibiting attitudes and behaviours that meet the minimum demands of a democracy. However, a democracy can be differently realised and structured. Citizens can have differing normative ideas about this. On the basis of the democracy theory discussion, we have distinguished four normative models of democracy and the corresponding four types of democratic community (see Figure 2). Having in the preceding section empirically analysed the similarities and differences between countries with regard to the democratic community, we proceed in this section to do the same for the types of democratic community.

In Figure 3 the four types of democratic community are described in terms of characteristics that are theoretically relevant and for which indicators are available in the *World Values Survey* 1995–99. The distributions of the specific attitudes and behaviours are shown in Table 6. The distributions are not dealt with in detail; instead we turn directly to the comparison between countries.

In this comparison we proceed as with the democratic community. The statistical method used is discriminant analysis, and we define benchmark countries as the point of reference for classifying individual countries. As explained in the theoretical section 2, our definition of benchmark democracies draws primarily on the study by Lipset and a follow-up empirical analysis.[34] According to these studies, the United States is to be considered a libertarian democracy with republican elements. For the sake of simplicity, we take recourse in Table 7 and the following tables and figures only to the characterisation as libertarian democracy. Australia has structural properties similar to those of the United States (see Tables 1 and 2) and exhibits similar political attitudes and behaviours. In our analysis, Australia – in addition to the United States – therefore represents the

TABLE 6a
CITIZEN SUPPORT OF DIFFERENT TYPES OF DEMOCRATIC COMMUNITY AT CULTURAL LEVEL

Countries			Culture		
	SRE	SOL	TRU	WET	ETO
	%	%	%	%	%
Anglo-American countries					
USA	66	21	35	68	9
Australia	47	29	40	61	18
New Zealand	45	34	47	61	21
Western European countries					
Norway	37	19	65	42	22
Sweden	67	49	57	49	40
Finland	42	41	48	57	20
West Germany	41	75	40	25	45
Spain	24	67	29	55	23
Central European countries					
East Germany	19	86	24	33	35
Poland	36	61	17	32	5
Czech Republic	23	51	27	43	30
Slovak Republic	14	52	26	45	17
Hungary	12	82	22	43	13
Slovenia	24	53	15	58	20
Croatia	11	62	23	54	22
Baltic countries					
Estonia	16	56	21	57	5
Latvia	17	66	24	52	8
Lithuania	24	74	21	33	3
South-Eastern European countries (mainly Orthodox)					
Yugoslavia	16	65	29	45	4
Romania	31	63	18	63	6
Bulgaria	22	71	24	52	14
South-Eastern European countries (mixed-Muslim)					
Macedonia	16	74	7	35	2
Bosnia-Herzegovina	17	59	27	60	3
Albania	14	62	24	88	2
Eastern European countries					
Russia	16	79	23	48	3
Ukraine	14	76	29	43	3
Belarus	17	70	23	52	4
Moldova	14	75	22	54	3

Notes: SRE: Self-responsibility; SOL: Solidarity; TRU: Trust in others; WET: Work ethic; ETO: Ethic tolerance.
Cell entries are percent positive support.

TABLE 6b
CITIZEN SUPPORT FOR DIFFERENT TYPES OF DEMOCRATIC COMMUNITY AT STRUCTURAL AND PROCESS LEVELS

Countries	Structure		Process	
	PRO %	MAN %	PMO %	CIV %
Anglo-American countries				
USA	74	55	52	52
Australia	62	51	45	45
New Zealand	52	64	41	35
Western European countries				
Norway	46	34	43	25
Sweden	48	36	41	24
Finland	59	35	17	12
West Germany	61	30	55	25
Spain	34	37	17	13
Central European countries				
East Germany	37	29	47	16
Poland	31	15	27	0
Czech Republic	38	42	27	7
Slovak Republic	23	21	28	6
Hungary	40	24	24	9
Slovenia	49	22	14	8
Croatia	75	34	24	13
Baltic countries				
Estonia	33	40	26	3
Latvia	36	37	25	5
Lithuania	47	38	25	2
South-Eastern European countries (mainly Orthodox)				
Yugoslavia	42	25	21	4
Romania	55	37	21	9
Bulgaria	40	27	23	2
South-Eastern European countries (mixed-Muslim)				
Macedonia	58	37	21	8
Bosnia-Herzegovina	49	25	37	20
Albania	78	48	19	7
Eastern European countries				
Russia	14	16	23	3
Ukraine	32	23	25	1
Belarus	25	20	38	1
Moldova	20	23	23	5

Notes: PRO: Private ownership; MAN: Management of enterprise; PMO: Political motivation; CIV: Civic engagement.
Cell entries are percent positive support.

libertarian type of democracy, and the two countries form the corresponding benchmark group.

In contrast to the individualism of the United States, Western European countries have a pronounced etatist tradition. This was realised in the development of welfare states, whose functions include ensuring the greatest possible equality of opportunity for individuals competing in the markets. These welfare states correspond to the liberal model of democracy, and a societal community with the relevant attitudes and behaviours is therefore to be termed a liberal community. The benchmark countries we have chosen to represent this liberal type of community are Sweden and West Germany. Both are indubitably welfare states, but they have developed different forms.[35] By taking these two countries into account, the relevant spectrum of Western European welfare states and thus of Western European liberal democracies has been covered.

The correlations of the indicators of the discriminant function in Table 7 show how strongly the individual characteristics distinguish between the benchmark countries and the other countries. In the case of libertarian democracy, the highest correlations are for 'self-responsibility' and

TABLE 7
DIFFERENTIATION BETWEEN BENCHMARK TYPES OF DEMOCRACIES AND OTHER COUNTRIES

	Type of democracy					
	Libertarian democracy[a]			Liberal democracy[b]		
		r[c]			r[c]	
Cultural level						
Self-responsibility		.464			.513	
Solidarity with the disadvantaged		-*.504*			.095	
Trust in others		.114			*.333*	
Work ethic		.178			-*.226*	
Ethic tolerance		.012			*.722*	
Structural level						
Private ownership		*.354*			.182	
Management of enterprise (owners)		*.286*			-.035	
Process level						
Political motivation		.232			.318	
Civic engagement		*.786*			.291	
Eigenvalue		.294			.096	
Canonical correlation		.476			.296	
Group centroids						
Group to classify		-.193			-.075	
Liberal democracies		1.522			1.274	
Classification results						
		Group			Group	
	1		2	1		2
1 Group to classify	84		16	76		24
2 Liberal democracies	30		70	23		77
Correctly classified		82			76	

Notes: Benchmark countries: a) United States and Australia; b) Sweden and West Germany.
c) Pooled within-group correlations between discriminating variables and canonical discriminant functions.

'solidarity with the disadvantaged', as well as 'civic engagement'. The first two characteristics are also those with which a libertarian democracy can most strongly be identified in accordance with our theoretical assumption (see Figures 2 and 3), and 'civic engagement' is typical of republican democracies (see Figure 3). For liberal democracy, the highest correlations are for 'self-responsibility' and 'ethic tolerance'.

These characteristics, too, are to be found in the description of the liberal community in Figure 3. The proportion of correctly classified respondents is much higher for these two types of democratic community than for the democratic community in general. For 'libertarian democracy' the figure is 82 per cent, and for 'liberal democracy' 76 per cent. This indicates that the difference between the reference group and the group of other countries is relatively large. We will be dealing with this in greater detail.

The socialist community has not been included in the comparative analysis. The reason is a simple one: there is no Western country that can plausibly represent this type of community. There is also no Western country that represents the republican community in a 'pure' form. However, the United States and Australia also exhibit some republican properties. Although the benchmark group composed by these two countries predominantly represents a libertarian community, it has additional attributes.

In contrast to the democratic community in general, there are considerable differences between countries with regard to the type of democratic community. We will deal first with the *libertarian community*. Three gaps are identifiable between groups of countries (see Table 8). The first is between the Anglo-American and the Western European countries. For the first the mean is .656 and for the second .376. Since the Western European countries still have the highest mean of the European groups, the difference between Anglo-America and Europe posited by Lipset is impressively confirmed. Within the European countries, however, there are still substantial differences. The next gap in mean ranking is between Western European countries (.376) and Muslim South-Eastern European countries (.282). Right at the end of the scale come the Baltic and Eastern European countries. The mean for both groups of countries is lower than .200. The democratic communities in Europe can thus definitively not be considered libertarian but at least liberal (Western European countries), if not even socialist. There are some striking deviations within groups of countries. Among Western European countries Spain and among Central European countries Hungary have a markedly lower mean than the other countries in their groups. And among the Muslim South-Eastern European countries, Bosnia-Herzegovina has by far the highest mean. This relatively

TABLE 8
CLOSENESS OF COUNTRIES TO LIBERAL AND LIBERTARIAN TYPES OF DEMOCRACY

Countries	Libertarian democracy[a]			Liberal democracy[b]		
	Mean[c]	Sd[c]	N[c]	Mean[c]	Sd[c]	N[c]
Anglo-American countries	*.656*	*(.30)*	*3,122*	*.449*	*(.26)*	*3,122*
USA	.752	(.27)	1,016	.426	(.26)	1,016
Australia	.621	(.31)	1,528	.455	(.27)	1,528
New Zealand	.580	(.29)	578	.473	(.25)	578
Western European countries	*.376*	*(.28)*	*3,652*	*.524*	*(.27)*	*3,652*
Norway	.470	(.28)	970	.494	(.24)	970
Sweden	.431	(.28)	662	.682	(.21)	662
Finland	.334	(.26)	708	.424	(.24)	708
West Germany	.360	(.29)	604	.657	(.26)	604
Spain	.251	(.25)	708	.406	(.27)	708
Central European countries	*.240*	*(.24)*	*4,317*	*380*	*(.25)*	*4,317*
East Germany	.224	(.23)	687	.505	(.28)	687
Czech Republic	.263	(.24)	794	.413	(.23)	794
Slovakia	.199	(.20)	834	.331	(.22)	834
Hungary	.184	(.20)	467	.340	(.23)	467
Slovenia	.277	(.25)	731	.330	(.24)	731
Croatia	.274	(.25)	804	.360	(.24)	804
Baltic countries	*.191*	*(.20)*	*2,227*	*.268*	*(.19)*	*2,227*
Estonia	.200	(.20)	761	.247	(.18)	761
Latvia	.192	(.20)	844	.290	(.19)	844
Lithuania	.179	(.18)	622	.262	(.19)	622
South-Eastern European countries (mainly Orthodox)	*.225*	*(.22)*	*2,380*	*.289*	*(.22)*	*2,380*
Yugoslavia	.180	(.19)	1,073	.252	(.20)	1,073
Romania	.305	(.25)	819	.296	(.22)	819
Bulgaria	.189	(.19)	488	.358	(.23)	488
South-Eastern European countries (mixed-Muslim)	*.282*	*(.26)*	*2,193*	*.254*	*(.19)*	*2,193*
Macedonia	.223	(.22)	627	.240	(.18)	627
Bosnia-Herzegovina	.321	(.29)	917	.267	(.19)	917
Albania	.287	(.29)	649	.249	(.17)	649
Eastern European countries	*.143*	*(.16)*	*4,719*	*.247*	*(.19)*	*4,719*
Russia	.136	(.16)	1,294	.251	(.25)	1,294
Ukraine	.134	(.14)	1,381	.256	(.20)	1,381
Belarus	.146	(.15)	1,255	.264	(.19)	1,255
Moldova	.168	(.20)	789	.197	(.17)	789
Total	.297	(.23)	22,610	.352	(.22)	22,610
Eta2	.22	-	-	.09	-	-

Notes:
a) Libertarian democracy: benchmark countries USA and Australia.
b) Liberal democracy: benchmark countries Sweden and West Germany.
c) Mean = Mean membership probability of respondents belonging to the group of benchmark democracies, defined by the set of nine characteristics; Sd = Standard deviation; N = Number of cases.

greater proximity of Bosnia-Herzegovina to the benchmark democracies is, however, attributable less to the libertarian characteristics of the two countries that constitute the group than to the communitarian attribute of moral rigour (see Table 6a).

As the correlations of the *liberal community* characteristics with the discriminant function show (see Table 7), 'self-responsibility' (.513) and especially 'ethic tolerance' (.722) distinguish most clearly between the benchmark countries and the others. By the first (self-responsibility), a liberal community distinguishes itself above all from a socialist community. Thus, the results of the discriminant analysis do not inevitably fit the libertarian–liberal–socialist continuum. In the liberal community, too, there are very clear differences between groups of countries. Also in keeping with theoretical expectations, Western European countries most strongly represent the liberal community (mean: .524). The Anglo-American and Central European countries follow after clear intervals, .449 and .380 respectively. The most striking difference is apparent between the Central European countries and the other groups. Among these other groups of countries, the Orthodox South-Eastern European countries have the relatively highest mean (.289) and the Eastern European countries the relatively lowest (.247). As far as the liberal community is concerned, the major cultural dividing line suggested by Huntington does exist, separating the Western-Christian civilisation (including Central Europe) from the Orthodox-Muslim civilisation in Eastern Europe.

Since characteristics that can relate to other types have been included in the two discriminant analyses on libertarian and liberal democracy, we omit characteristics that are theoretically quite unambiguous from the following considerations. In Figure 5, countries are localised in a two-dimensional space mapping the proportion of citizens with a strong sense of self-responsibility and those with a strong sense of solidarity. The regression line shown in the figure represents the underlying libertarian–liberal–socialist continuum: strong self-responsibility and weak solidarity characterise a libertarian community, and, vice versa, a socialist community is characterised by strong solidarity and weak self-responsibility, with the liberal community located between the two. The variance of no less than 45 per cent explained by the regression shows that the assumption of this underlying continuum is justified. If we take the 50 per cent threshold in each case to ensure better orientation in the spatial classification of countries, the only country that simultaneously scores high on self-responsibility and low on solidarity is the United States. Accordingly, the United States is by far the most libertarian community, and 'American

FIGURE 5
LOCATION OF COUNTRIES ON THE LIBERTARIAN-LIBERAL-SOCIALIST DIMENSION

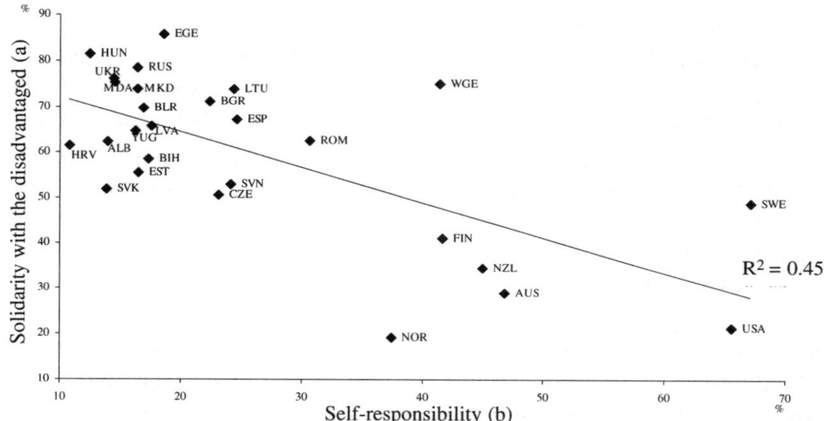

Notes: a) Proportion of respondents with high solidarity; b) Proportion of respondents with high self-responsibility.

exceptionalism'[36] is clearly in evidence. Surprisingly, an above average proportion of Swedes have a pronounced sense of self-responsibility, while evincing much greater solidarity than Americans. This high degree of Swedes' sense of self-responsibility can be ascribed to two aspects. First, the measurement of 'self-responsibility' relates to the respective country's status quo. Second, Swedes place a relatively strong emphasis on the value of self-responsibility ideologically, thus justifying the welfare state in part with the ability for self-responsibility.[37]

In the upper left-hand part of the space, which is defined by strong solidarity and weak self-responsibility, thus delimiting a socialist community, we find all the countries from Central and Eastern Europe – plus Spain as the only Western European country. Within this cluster of countries, no further differentiation by geographical region is possible. For example, two of the countries we have assigned to Central Europe – Hungary and East Germany – together with the Eastern European countries Russia, Ukraine and Moldova, form the outermost fringe of the cluster, thus representing the relatively most socialist communities. In contrast, two Central European countries – Slovenia and the Czech Republic – together with Romania are gathered at the opposite fringe of the cluster in the direction of the Western countries. The countries deviating most from the regression line are West Germany and Norway. They are average on self-responsibility, but solidarity is below average in Norway and above average in West Germany.

The two dimensions in Figure 6 relate to the constitutive characteristics of a republican or civic community. A fundamental normative concept in this type of democratic community is that the individual and not government should bear primary responsibility for the individual's affairs (see Figure 2). The same is demanded by libertarians; but, in contrast to libertarians, republicans do not assume that collective goals can be attained only indirectly through the mechanisms of the market. They stress active co-operation between citizens to realise common projects.[38] The resource on which such co-operation can draw is termed *social capital*. Social capital consists primarily in shared values and norms of reciprocity and co-operation. A consequence of the mutual assumption that such values and norms apply, and of experience with relevant action is *trust* or *confidence* in the other members of the community. Trust in others is therefore frequently used as an indicator of the social capital of a community. Co-operative values and norm orientations induce citizens to participate actively in voluntary associations, and this in its turn stabilises the social capital. Putnam therefore refers to civil or voluntary associations as 'social

FIGURE 6
LOCATION OF COUNTRIES IN A TWO-DIMENSIONAL SPACE OF REPUBLICAN COMMUNITY

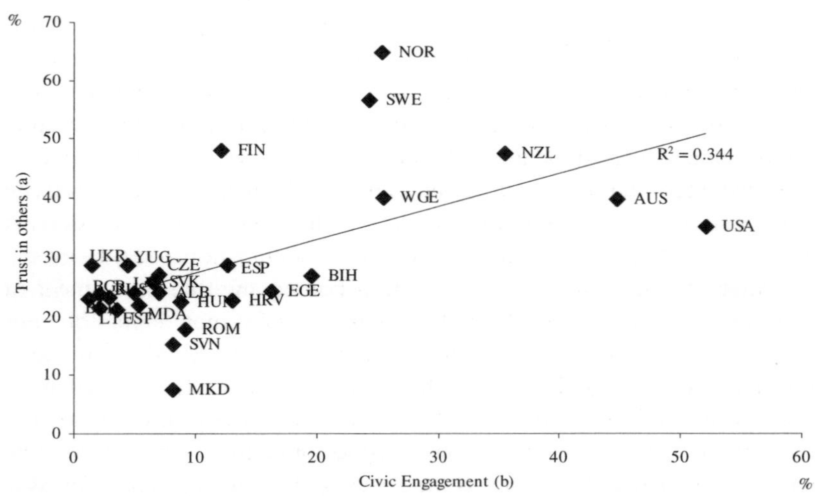

Notes: (a) Percentage of respondents who trust in other people; (b) Percentage of respondents who are active members in two or more voluntary associations.

structures of co-operation'. In Figure 6, active participation by citizens in two or more voluntary associations is termed 'civic engagement'.

The link between 'civic engagement' and 'trust in others' that Putnam posits is controversial. As the regression analysis shows ($R^2 = .344$), this assumption is confirmed by our data at least at the aggregate level of the countries under study. The classification of countries in the two-dimensional space of a republican community reveals a marked difference between Anglo-American and Western European countries on the one hand and the countries from Central and Eastern Europe on the other. The latter show less trust in others and less civic engagement. The only Western European country in the group is Spain. Taking the analysis results of this section for Central and Eastern Europe as a whole, we find a positive and a negative aspect: they relatively clearly represent a socialist community and just as clearly do *not* represent a republican community.

Among the Anglo-American and Western European countries, there is none that exhibits both strong confidence in others and strong civic engagement. Thus, we cannot identify a 'pure' case of a republican community. Two configurations among these countries are evident. First, the two Nordic countries Norway and Sweden with an average level of civic engagement and a high level of trust in others, and, second, the two Anglo-American countries Australia and the United States with an average level of trust in others and a high level of civic engagement.

SUMMARY AND CONCLUSIONS

Development towards a politically integrated and geographically more comprehensive Europe appears to be irreversible. But the general dynamic of development offers fundamental options that have yet to be decided. One is the extent of political integration through European institutions. The central issue is how strongly the competence to make binding decisions is to be transferred from the nation states to the supranational regime of the EU. Another is the matter of the eastern border, the question of which countries should belong to the EU. This is the point of reference for our study. Besides economic aspects, the question of the eastward enlargement of the EU is of strategic importance for the formation of a European demos. Every institutional arrangement of the EU needs to be legitimated, and the more strongly the decisions of these institutions directly impact the life world of the citizen, the greater is the need for legitimation. The addressee of this legitimation of a European regime and European politics is a European demos. For legitimation to be successful, a merely formal demos is presumably insufficient. Over and above legally defined membership, it should constitute a political community with a collective identity citizens can subjectively attribute to themselves and with which they can identify.

We proceed from two premises. First, that the collective identity of the European demos is grounded in subjectively perceived commonality in political values and behaviours; second, that objectively demonstrable commonality in both regards provides the potential for the formation of a collective identity. Against this background, we have attempted to answer two questions. First, the extent to which political values and behaviours are shared by the citizens of European countries; second, the extent to which there are systematic differences between Western, Central and Eastern Europe, and where possible cultural borders lie. The most important results of our analysis can be summed up as follows.

Regardless of what institutional form the regime of the EU will ultimately take, it will be a democratic form of government. Moreover, one of the key criteria for a country to join the EU is that it has a stable democracy. However, a democracy can function and survive only if the demos as the ultimate sovereign also exhibits appropriate values and behaviours. In a first step, we have therefore empirically determined the extent to which societal community in the countries under study can be described as democratic, and what differences there are between countries and groups of countries.

Differences are apparent between groups of countries, but – with one exception – they are not very pronounced. They can be mapped on a geographical west–east axis. The relatively most democratic communities are to be found in the Anglo-American and Western European countries. The countries in which the democratic community is least developed are the Muslim countries in South-Eastern Europe and the Eastern European countries. Leaving aside the Anglo-American countries and regressing the scores of individual countries for the democratic community on a geographical west–east axis, no less than 62 per cent of variance can be explained. In certain measure, this result is in keeping with Huntington's theory. However, in contrast to Huntington's assumptions, no threshold can be identified between West and East, only a continuous decline in the extent of a democratic community.

The exception mentioned above is concerned with the countries of Eastern Europe, and, in our parlance, this means the Slavic successor states to the Soviet Union plus Moldova (Russia, Ukraine, Belarus, Moldova). Albania also belongs to the group. In all these countries, 'law-abidingness' is clearly below average, and in every case there are fewer than 25 per cent 'solid democrats' among the citizenry (see Figure 4). According to our criteria, there is therefore, at least currently, no solid democratic community in these countries. Besides the longer term factors we have mentioned (religion, empire, Leninist regime and modernity), the party systems are presumably responsible for this result. In all these countries, the party system is shaped by parties that support at least the introduction of autocratic elements into the existing governmental system, if not the imposition of autocratic systems as a whole.[39] The democratic transformation of the party system, in addition to economic development, is therefore a structural prerequisite that could strengthen the democratic community in these countries.

Whilst there are relatively slight differences between the countries under study as regards the democratic community in general, this is far from being the case with the types of community. This is particularly clear if one considers the libertarian–liberal–socialist dimension. According to our analysis, the United States is indubitably a libertarian community. The vast majority of American citizens consider that not the state but the individual is responsible for his own life; at the same time solidarity with the disadvantaged is very weak (see Figure 5). *All* the countries of Central and Eastern Europe offer a contrast to the United States. In these countries strong self-responsibility is evinced by less than a third of citizens, and in most countries by even less than 20 per cent. A majority, however, exhibits strong solidarity with the disadvantaged. Thus, on the basis of these two characteristics, the countries of Central and Eastern Europe can be considered socialist communities.

The two other Anglo-American countries (Australia and New Zealand), as well as the Western European countries score between the United States and the Central and Eastern European countries on self-responsibility. On solidarity the figures are at a similarly low level as that of the United States, the only exception being West Germany. Overall, these countries can therefore be classified as liberal communities, which are, however, closer to the libertarian United States than to the socialist Central and Eastern European communities.

Following on from the studies by Putnam and Fukuyama,[40] we have operationalised the republican community by the two dimensions 'civic engagement' and 'trust in others'. The classification of countries in the space defined by these two dimensions again shows a clear West–East difference. Most republican are the Anglo-American countries, United States, Australia and New Zealand. Decidedly not republican, in contrast, are the countries of Central and Eastern Europe. 'Civic engagement' is weak, 'trust in others' is weak. The strong etatist orientation among citizens in Central and Eastern Europe is thus complemented and accordingly still further stabilised by a lack of civic society elements.

The question of the eastward enlargement of the EU can be discussed and answered from a variety of standpoints. For example, economic or geopolitical considerations can play a role. The perspective taken by our analysis is that of the implications of eastward enlargement for the development of a European demos. This, in turn, is the condition for a viable European democracy. The greater the differences are between countries, the lower is the potential for a European identity on which a European demos can be based.

Our study identifies three substantial dividing lines. The first runs between America and Europe, as already posited by Lipset.[41] For our purposes, however, this is of secondary importance. The second divides Western Europe from Central and Eastern Europe. The countries in these two parts of Europe represent different types of democratic community. At this political cultural level, Huntington's thesis of a cultural dividing line within Europe is confirmed to a certain extent.[42] According to the theoretical premises of our analysis, every eastward enlargement poses integration problems and increases the difficulty of constituting a European demos. The West–East difference we have described is concerned with differing types of democratic community. Between the countries of Europe there is little difference in the political values and behaviours that are essential to a democracy. The potential for Europeans in Western, Central and Eastern Europe to consider each other as democrats, and to integrate this understanding in their collective identity is thus considerable.

The Slavic successor nations to the Soviet Union (Russia, Ukraine, Belarus and Moldova) together with Albania are the exception. They cannot, at least not yet, be considered democratic communities, and in all the analyses we have conducted, they offer a serious contrast to the Western European countries and, to some extent, also to the countries in Central and Eastern Europe. This is the third dividing line we identify. Taking account only of political cultural points of view, the eastern border of the EU would have to be drawn before these countries. However, there is also reason to believe that democratic institutions may be supportive in creating a democratic community.

NOTES

We would like to thank Seymour Martin Lipset for his critical reading of the paper and his helpful comments. For reasons of space, an appendix including full details of the survey items and codes used in this analysis has not been included. These details are available on request from the authors.

1. M. Rainer Lepsius, 'Die Europäische Union. Ökonomisch-politische Integration und kulturelle Pluralität', in Reinhold Viehoff and Rien T. Segers (eds.), *Kultur, Identität, Europa. Über die Schwierigkeiten und Möglichkeiten einer Konstruktion* (Frankfurt a. M.: Suhrkamp 1999), pp.201–22.
2. Dieter Grimm, 'Does Europe Need a Constitution?', *European Law Journal* 1 (1995), pp.282–302; Peter Graf Kielmansegg, 'Integration und Demokratie', in Markus Jachtenfuchs and Beate Kohler-Koch (eds.), *Europäische Integration* (Opladen: Leske + Budrich 1996), pp.47–71; Fritz W. Scharpf, 'Demokratieprobleme in der europäischen Mehrebenenpolitik', in Wolfgang Merkel and Andreas Busch (eds.), *Demokratie in Ost und West. Für Klaus von Beyme* (Frankfurt a. M.: Suhrkamp 1999), pp.672–94.
3. Lepsius, 'Die Europäische Union'.
4. Dieter Fuchs, Jürgen Gerhards and Edeltraud Roller, 'Wir und die anderen. Ethnozentrismus in den zwölf Ländern der europäischen Gemeinschaft', *Kölner Zeitschrift für Soziologie und Sozialpsychologie* 45 (1993), pp.238–53.
5. Samuel P. Huntington, *The Clash of Civilizations and the Remaking of World Order* (New York: Simon & Schuster 1996); Seymour Martin Lipset, 'Conditions for Democracy', in Hans-Dieter Klingemann and Friedhelm Neidhardt (eds.), *Zur Zukunft der Demokratie* (Berlin: edition sigma 2000); William M. Reisinger, 'Reassessing Theories of Transition away from Authoritarian Regimes: Regional Patterns among Postcommunist Countries' (Paper presented at the 1999 Annual Meeting of the Midwest Political Science Association, Chicago, 15–17 April 1999).
6. Jürgen Gerhards, 'Westeuropäische Integration und die Schwierigkeiten der Entstehung einer europäischen Öffentlichkeit', *Zeitschrift für Soziologie* 22 (1993), pp.96–110.
7. Dieter Fuchs, 'The Democratic Culture of Germany', in Pippa Norris (ed.), *Critical Citizens. Global Support for Democratic Government* (Oxford: Oxford University Press 1999), pp.123–45; and Dieter Fuchs, 'Die demokratische Gemeinschaft in den USA und in Deutschland', in Jürgen Gerhards (ed.), *Die Vermessung kultureller Unterschiede. USA und Deutschland im Vergleich* (Opladen: Westdeutscher Verlag 2000), pp.33–72.
8. Christopher J. Berry, *The Idea of a Democratic Community* (New York: St. Martin's Press 1989); John W. Chapman and Ian Shapiro (eds.), *Democratic Community. Nomos No. XXXV* (New York: New York University Press 1993).
9. Dieter Fuchs and Edeltraud Roller, 'Cultural Conditions of Transition to Liberal Democracies in Central and Eastern Europe', in Samuel H. Barnes and János Simon (eds.), *The Postcommunist Citizen* (Budapest: Erasmus Foundation and Hungarian Academy of Sciences 1998), pp.35–77; Dieter Fuchs, 'Soziale Integration und politische Institutionen in modernen Gesellschaften', in Jürgen Friedrichs and Wolfgang Jagodzinski (eds.), *Soziale Integration. Sonderheft 39 der Kölner Zeitschrift für Soziologie und Sozialpsychologie* (Opladen: Westdeutscher Verlag 1999), pp.127–78; Dieter Fuchs, 'The Democratic Culture of Germany'.
10. Giovanni Sartori, *The Theory of Democracy Revisited* (Chatham, NJ: Chatham House 1987); Mogens H. Hansen, *The Athenian Democracy in the Age of Demosthenes. Structure, Principles and Ideology* (Oxford: Blackwell 1991).
11. Dieter Fuchs, 'The Democratic Culture of Germany'.
12. Hans-Dieter Klingemann, 'Mapping Political Support in the 1990s: A Global Analysis', in Pippa Norris (ed.), *Critical Citizens: Global Support for Democratic Government* (Oxford/New York: Oxford University Press 1999), pp.31–56.
13. Including Robert Nozick, *Anarchy, State, and Utopia* (New York: Basic Books 1974); Benjamin R. Barber, *Strong Democracy. Participatory Politics For a New Age* (Berkeley: University of California Press 1984); Amitai Etzioni, *The Spirit of Community: The Reinvention of American Society* (New York: Touchstone, Simon & Schuster 1993); John Rawls, *Political Liberalism* (New York: Columbia University Press 1993).
14. Chapman and Shapiro (eds.), *Democratic Community.*
15. Rawls, *Political Liberalism.*
16. Robert C. Post, 'Between Democracy and Community: The Legal Constitution of Social Form', in Chapman and Shapiro (eds.), *Democratic Community*, pp.163–90.

17. Amitai Etzioni, *The New Golden Rule. Community and Morality in a Democratic Society* (New York: Basic Books 1996).
18. Robert D. Putnam, with Robert Leonardi and Raffaella Y. Nanetti, *Making Democracy Work: Civic Traditions in Modern Italy* (Princeton, NJ: Princeton University Press 1993).
19. Ibid., p.88.
20. Huntington, *The Clash of Civilizations.*
21. Putnam, *Making Democracy Work*; Huntington, *The Clash of Civilizations*; Ronald Inglehart, 'Clash of Civilizations of Global Cultural Modernization? Empirical Evidence from 61 Societies' (Paper presented at the 1998 meeting of the International Sociological Association, Montreal, 27–31 Aug. 1998).
22. Huntington, *The Clash of Civilizations.*
23. Lipset, 'Conditions for Democracy'; Reisinger, 'Reassessing Theories of Transition away from Authoritarian Regimes'.
24. Fuchs, *The Democratic Culture of Germany*; Robert Rohrschneider, *Learning Democracy. Democratic and Economic Values in Unified Germany* (Oxford: Oxford University Press 1999).
25. Reisinger, 'Reassessing Theories of Transition away from Authoritarian Regimes'.
26. Seymour Martin Lipset, 'Some Social Requisites of Democracy', *American Political Science Review* 53 (1959), pp.69–105, and his 'The Social Requisites of Democracy Revisited', *American Sociological Review* 59 (1994), pp.1–22, and his 'Conditions for Democracy'.
27. Dieter Fuchs and Hans-Dieter Klingemann, 'A Comparison of Democratic Communities: American Exceptionalism and European Etatism' (Paper presented at the Conference 'Rethinking Democracy in the New Millennium' at the University of Houston, 17–20 Feb. 2000).
28. Huntington, *The Clash of Civilizations*; Reisinger, 'Reassessing Theories of Transition away from Authoritarian Regimes'; Lipset, 'Conditions for Democracy'. Our codes here are as follows: Religion: 1 Muslim or Orthodox, 2 Catholic, 3 Protestant or secular; Empire: 1 Ottoman or Russian, 2 Hapsburg, 3 British or none; Leninist regime: 1 yes (duration in years), 2 no; Modernity: continuous (the higher the score the more favourable to democracy and vice versa).
29. Seymour Martin Lipset, *American Exceptionalism. A Double-Edged Sword* (New York: W.W. Norton 1996).
30. Huntington, *The Clash of Civilizations.*
31. Lipset, *American Exceptionalism.*
32. Details of the indicators and indices are available from the authors.
33. Klingemann, 'Mapping Political Support'.
34. See Lipset, *American Exceptionalism*, and then Fuchs and Klingemann, 'A Comparison of Democratic Communities'.
35. Edeltraud Roller, 'Ende des sozialstaatlichen Konsenses? Zum Aufbrechen traditioneller und zur Entstehung neuer Konfliktstrukturen in Deutschland', in Oskar Niedermayer and Bettina Westle (eds.), *Demokratie und Partizipation* (Opladen: Westdeutscher Verlag 2000), pp.88–114.
36. Lipset, *American Exceptionalism.*
37. Bo Rothstein, *Just Institutions Matter. The Moral and Political Logic of the Universal Welfare State* (Cambridge: Cambridge University Press 1998).
38. Putnam, *Making Democracy Work*; Francis Fukuyama, *The Great Disruption. Human Nature and the Reconstitution of Social Order* (New York: Free Press 1999).
39. Hans-Dieter Klingemann, 'Negative Parteiorientierung und repräsentative Demokratie. Eine vergleichende Analyse', in Oskar Niedermayer and Bettina Westle (eds.), *Demokratie und Partizipation, Festschrift für Max Kaase* (Opladen: Westdeutscher Verlag 2000), pp.281–312; Hans-Dieter Klingemann and Richard I. Hofferbert, 'The Capacity of New Party Systems to Channel Discontent', in Hans-Dieter Klingemann and Friedhelm Neidhardt (eds.), *Zur Zukunft der Demokratie* (Berlin: edition sigma 2000), pp.411–37.
40. Putnam, *Making Democracy Work*; Fukuyama, *The Great Disruption.*
41. Lipset, *American Exceptionalism.*
42. Huntington, *The Clash of Civilizations.*

Culture and National Identity: 'The East' and European Integration

DAVID D. LAITIN

As political and economic forces are driving the former communist states of Eastern Europe into the web of the European Union, several questions arise as to the cultural challenges that might ensue. Do East and West have different cultural sensibilities that will act as a roadblock to further integration? More particularly, do the Eastern applicant states have political cultures that encourage people to think about the relationship of religion to the individual, the relationship of nation to the state, or the relationship between minorities (ethnic, religious, racial or those based on sexual orientation) in ways incompatible with the political cultures of EU member states? More generally, have the separate paths of west and east over the course of history forged a cultural divide, foreshadowing extraordinary difficulties in political and economic cooperation in the future?

A 'great schism' that divides the 'Euro-Atlantic Community' from the 'Euro-Asian Community' and traced back to the separation of Christianity into its Roman and Byzantine versions is commonly cited as a barrier to the real possibilities of the integration of the Eastern European states into the EU. It is hypothesised that asymmetries between East and West in regard to modernisation have deepened the schism, and, furthermore, since the end of World War II

> in the Western part of Europe historical values and traditions creating the base of the cultural and moral identity of the continent have been strengthened. In the Eastern regions of the continent, however, the strengthening of these values was hindered by the so-called socialist ideology, originating in the Western part of Europe, but in practice being connected with the Euro-Asian cultural sphere and being represented by the presence and practice of Soviet power.[1]

Based on an examination of cross-country data transcending West and East in various cultural realms – language, religion and popular culture –

this study provides some preliminary answers to the questions posed above.[2] The data show first that there exists a pan-European cosmopolitan culture that is rapidly infusing the applicant countries of the East. Second, the transcendent cosmopolitan European culture exists complementary with national cultures, which remain vibrant in the West and in the East, even in the context of an overarching continental culture. Third, the divergences of national cultures within the member states of the EU are considerable; yet on the cultural dimensions examined here, the national cultures of the applicant states fall well within the extremes set by the member states. In fact, the data present a stunning result, which of course must be taken as preliminary and still at the level of speculation: that the cultural patterns exhibited by respondents from the applicant states are somewhat closer to the patterns shown among the original six EEC members than is the case for the post-six entrants. To the degree that there is a 'catching up' process in the works, the data suggest it is occurring intergenerationally among the populations of the later entrants more so than the applicants, who are already closer to the so-called Western European norm. Fourth, the interpretation provided herein for the stunning result that the cultural practices of the applicant states are more proximate to the cultural practices of the original six EEC members than are the cultural practices of the later entrants to those of the original six is that there is often a greater motivation for those on the far periphery to assimilate into the norms of the centre than is the case for the populations close to the centre. From this point, it is concluded that the incorporation of East European states into the EU, from a cultural point of view, has greater potential for the deepening of European integration than for its erosion.

More concretely, this analysis demonstrates that the citizens of the applicant states from the East into the EU are moving towards full membership in what can be called the 2±1 cultural configuration of Europe.[3] By this is meant that all Europeans who wish to participate fully in a wide range of mobility opportunities need to be conversant with an all-European continental culture. They must also be fully integrated into the national culture of the state in which they are citizens and/or reside, and will thereby maintain the vital differences in the so-called 'mentalités' that differentiate intra-European national cultures. Thus, all socially mobile Europeans will need to participate in two complementary cultural worlds. Those Europeans whose national cultures are close to the continental norm need only be a member of a single cultural world (2-1); while those Europeans living in 'foreign' European states and those who live in regions of states with state-promoted regional cultures may need to be fully acquainted with three cultural worlds (2+1). All socially mobile Europeans will therefore have 2±1 cultural repertoires.

Taking language as the paradigm, in the emerging European quasi-state all socially mobile Europeans must be fluent in what is becoming the continental language, English. They also must be fluent in the state language in which they live. Thus bilingualism (the '2' of 2±1) is becoming a European standard. Regional cultural groups within states are getting increasing recognition by both their central states and by the EU. To the extent that their regional governments can require the languages associated with those regions as media of instruction, or as necessary tools for regional government service, residents of those regions will be required to have a third language (2+1) in their repertoires. Those who live in the UK, where English is both the European and state language, need only be equipped in one (2-1) language. Immigrants from outside the EU as of now do not get serious education in their home language, and their grandchildren, should their families remain in the EU, are likely to have language repertoires consistent with the 2±1 scheme just outlined, depending upon where they live. The relationship of language to (quasi)-state in this regard is not one of a particular language to a state, but of a particular *configuration* of languages particular to a state.[4] The suggestion here is that across cultural domains, complementary 2±1 cultural repertoires are emerging from below, and that East Europe is becoming a part of this cultural configuration.

The purpose of this study is in fact to explore this 2±1 configuration not only in language, but in religious belief and in two realms of popular culture. To the extent that the Eastern applicants are joining into this cultural configuration, we can project that the cultural barriers to political incorporation into the EU have been lowered.

STANDING AGAINST THE TIDE

There are three intuitions behind the theory of an emergent European 2±1 cultural zone that includes both East and West. First, the embeddedment of Eastern European states into some European institutions is inevitable, even if EU membership is long delayed. It appears that the material benefits for becoming part of Europe and the opportunity costs for governments failing to bring their countries into the framework of Europe are so high that governments of virtually all political persuasions will see the institutional embeddedment within Europe as unavoidable. Politics will concern the request for short-term exceptions from European institutional standards, and these politics will undoubtedly be intense, with socialist parties being the strongest advocates of states of exception. Yet inexorably, at least some East European states will become part of Europe's trans-national institutional nexus.

Second, authoritative institutions set the boundaries for cultural expression within the societies that live within those boundaries. As Susan Watkins has shown with impressive data, in the nineteenth century demographic patterns within Europe began to be explained far more adequately based upon the country of residence (where people lived under the same political institutions) than by the so-called cultural community within which a person identifies. Therefore, Spanish Basques were far closer to the Spanish mean than they were to a Basque mean, one which combined the Basque populations of France and Spain. Eugen Weber's and Abram de Swaan's separate analyses of language patterns in nineteenth century Europe show the same result. Cultural shift aligns with state institutions. And so the second element of my intuition: the more Eastern European states are embedded in European institutional structures, the more there will be a shift in cultural norms toward the European standard.[5]

Third, the natural carriers of national cultures ought not be thought of as the dominant members of the core societies around which the nations were historically constructed. In fact, elite members of the core cultures will have an interest in altering cultural norms in order to avoid the demeaning consequences of becoming indistinguishable culturally from upwardly mobile imitators of their culture. Meanwhile, aggressive and ambitious members of peripheral societies, living under the authority of a dominant culture, will have an interest in mimicking that culture in order to secure positions of responsibility within it. To an important degree, then, it is the Eastern Europeans who have a stronger interest in a utopian vision of 'Europe' as a well-defined (and easily mimicked) culture than culturally secure Europeans who are citizens of the West European states.[6]

Despite the apparent cogency of these intuitions, powerful evidence firmly grounded in field and archival research stands against the thesis propounded here. Consider the perspective on Polish Catholicism provided by Maryjane Osa. She presents rich historical data to undermine the argument that the church, because it stood on the right side of history in its opposition to communism, will lend support to the economic and political transformation that will bring Poland into the European world. In fact, she argues, the organisation of the Polish church makes it all the more likely to become a supporter of a 'new authoritarianism' in East Central Europe, where priests – and here she lends support to Jowitt's imagery – will be aligned with demagogues and colonels. She gives two reasons for her perspective. First, the church will be constrained organisationally in its search for social support, and will not easily be able to take political stands in the abstract, and ignore popular demands for social security whatever the constraints. Second, in a post-communist void of social organisations, the hierarchy and ethos of the church are (like its Leninist predecessor) against the secular individualism of the West. The church, she fears, will be on the vanguard of reaction rather than in support of integration into West European culture.[7]

Consider next the argument of Katherine Verdery, whose field research is in Romania, another of the applicant states. Verdery has, to be sure, picked up the utopian vision of Europe articulated in Romania. References to the former hegemon to the east in post-Ceaucescu Romanian discourse, she reports, exhibit fears of a renewed 'Slavic imperialism' or getting sucked into 'Bolshevist Asiatism'. Meanwhile European utopianists claim that proposed solutions to the problem of national minorities will be 'old-fashioned' until Romanians are able to discuss them 'at a European level'. This utopian discourse shows a greater confidence in 'Europe' than would be exhibited by most sectors in Europe's core, which are far more subject to 'Euro-scepticism' than is the periphery.

But Verdery claims that this utopian vision is an 'urban intellectuals' concept', one that is unconnected to village life. In the villages, she writes, a quite different story emerges, with a view of Europe that is infected by Ceauescu's indigenist ideology that has a near fascist nation-discourse. The real electoral imperative in Romania, Verdery argues, is to win political support among the anti-Hungarians living in Transylvania, who are angered by the Hungarian population's demands for autonomy, and who are uninterested in merely receiving individual rights. Second, to many rural voters, 'Europe' implies a disappearing social safety net, and the potential loss of communist-era pensions. Finally, Verdery emphasises that leading politicians in Romania, including President Ion Iliescu, were presenting to their publics a vision of Europe as filled with 'nationalised states', something that Romania must accomplish before joining into a wider Europe. This would naturally involve a form of national cleansing, Verdery fears. And this explains why, in 1993, Romania sent a delegation to Strasbourg, personally appointed by the President, for talks on joining the Council of Europe, that was filled with anti-Europeanists. While Europe is moving in a liberal direction, the implication of Verdery's sensitive analysis is that Romania is moving not towards a European utopia, but rather towards a political culture of anti-liberalism and intolerance.[8]

It would be foolhardy indeed to dismiss these two cogent – and thematically similar[9] – treatises. Yet, when compared to the 'real' Europe, the 'applicant' Europe does not look like it has been submerged in a half century of anti-liberal Leninism. To be sure, the Polish church and Romanian political parties are examples of illiberal institutions. But from the level of culture taken here, the populations of the East European applicant states look to be very much part of an emerging continental European culture; and the younger generation living in those states is quickly becoming part of it. In fact, the very division of Europe into 'East' and 'West' seems to be defunct, a product of the cold war.[10] Future research will have to reconcile the findings of Osa[11] and Verdery with those presented here; but Osa and Verdery might well have idealised Western Europe a bit too much, making the illiberal strands they saw so clearly in Eastern Europe look un-European. They may also have missed some of the broader institutional constraints implied in European membership in their focus on within-state political processes.

EAST EUROPE AND THE EMERGING EUROPEAN LANGUAGE CONFIGURATION

Although it is not publicly acknowledged, a 2±1 language configuration is consolidating itself in Western Europe. Businessmen, students and Eurocrats – virtually anyone who sees a career in a European context – must know English. Although French is the language of the European Court and it is still a preferred language in several European institutions housed in Brussels and Strasbourg, no language other than English has a claim as an all-European lingua franca. Meanwhile, state bureaucracies and school systems operate through state languages; it is not possible to survive economically or to communicate with state officials in any European state without speaking the state language. Finally, regionally based groups (with the Catalans in the lead, but the Basques, the Welsh and the Oc-speakers following) are making similar demands upon their residents, as educational texts, government memos and public pronouncements are increasingly written in regional languages. The resulting 2±1 configuration is an equilibrium because no party to it (state governments, regional activists, the European Commission, socially mobile Europeans) has an interest in deviating from it (though the French government is a partial exception). It is a self-enforcing bottom-up solution to a linguistically posed co-ordination problem.

Will the East European states become part of this language configuration? The data from the ISSP surveys, with the sample including three members of the original EEC (West Germany, Italy and Netherlands), six members of the expanded EC (Austria, Ireland, UK, Spain, Sweden and

East Germany), and seven applicant countries (Poland, Latvia, Czech Republic, Slovakia, Slovenia, Bulgaria and Hungary) suggest that the answer is 'yes'.[12] Respondents in virtually all the countries overwhelmingly report that the titular language of the country (that is, the language after which the state is named) is their home language. In this sense, all member states (with some limited exceptions) and applicants are 'nation' states in the sense of having co-ordinated on a single language for home life. Exceptions include Latvia where only 63.8 per cent speak Latvian as their principal home language (the rest mostly speaking Russian) and Spain, where 80.7 per cent claim Spanish as their first language and only 1.3 per cent more claim to speak Spanish fluently.[13] In any case, in none of the countries in the survey is there any evidence of a less than dominant role of the state language as the principal language of home life.

Second, the role of English as a lingua franca throughout Europe is becoming a fact of life. Concerning fluency in the three contenders for a European lingua franca among the original EEC members: 29.8 per cent overall claim fluency in English; 52.7 per cent in German; and 11.3 per cent in French (but note that neither France nor Belgium was part of the sample). But the data on second language learning is more telling. Among these same original EEC members, 29.7 per cent speak English as a supplementary language, while only 6.8 per cent speak German as a supplementary language, and 11.2 per cent speak French. This suggests that although German had the most first language speakers of the original EEC, English amongst this set has become the preferred second language of respondents. In the later generations of EU members (in which English as supplementary language is reduced substantially, as the UK and Ireland are two members of the sample), 7.4 per cent speak English as a supplementary language, 1.5 per cent speak German and 4.4 per cent speak French. Among the applicant countries, German (with 8.6 per cent) outpaces English (with 5.7 per cent), but French has merely 1.0 per cent. Among those under 35 years of age in the applicant countries, however, 11.7 per cent claim fluency in English as a supplementary language whereas only 10.6 per cent claim that for German. Two points are clear. First is that French may have ideological appeal to some; in reality, it is not a language of wider communication outside a few corridors of power in Brussels and Strasbourg. Second, English has already become or is becoming the widespread second language of choice in all three sets of countries. It is the language of wider communication in all of Europe.

The outlier cases concerning the multilingual repertoires of Europe are not among the applicants, but rather among the additional members after the

TABLE 1
LANGUAGE REPERTOIRES BY TYPE OF COUNTRY
(ALL COUNTRIES IN SAMPLE)

Language Situation/ Country Type	Monolinguals	Fluent in English	Fluent in Russian	Has an EU language other than English as 2nd	Has an EE language as 2nd
Original EEC	62.6	29.8	0.6	35.5	1.7
Later Member	79.1	51.1	1.0	20.0	0.2
Applicant	76.0	5.7	9.8	13.6	5.6

original six. As can be seen from Table 1, the respondents from the later members are far more likely to report being monolingual than respondents from the countries from the other two groups. This is not just due to the UK and to Ireland, which, given the 2±1 configuration, ought to be monolingual. But consider Spain, where nearly 79.2 per cent of the population reports being monolingual, and over 99 per cent of the multilinguals report speaking another language of Spain (Catalan, Galician, Basque or Castilian) as their second language. Even taking the UK and Ireland out of the sample, later members have 74.6 per cent monolinguals, considerably higher than in the original entrants yet slightly lower than the respondents from the applicant states. Therefore, if there is a non-cosmopolitan outlier set for this part of the language configuration, it is the later entrants rather than the applicants who supposedly do not belong 'culturally' in the all-European configuration.

EAST EUROPE AND THE RELIGIOUS BELIEFS OF ITS CITIZENS

In 1991, ISSP sponsored an earlier study, with a somewhat different sample of countries, that focused on religion and religious belief. Among the original six, West Germany, Netherlands and Italy were included. Among the later entrants, samples from Great Britain, Northern Ireland, Ireland and Austria are included in the data base. Among the applicant countries, there was Hungary, Slovenia, Poland and (with a different coding for 1991 than it received in 1995) East Germany.[14] The data also show what was indicated in the national identity survey about language: that there is a greater level of common cosmopolitanism, multilingualism and here secularism among the original members and present applicants than there is among the later members. If there is an intergenerational trend, it is towards the later members catching up to the secularism of the original members and the present applicants.

The findings should be no surprise once it is recognised that the Ireland and Northern Ireland samples are extremely religious (on most questions more so than the Poles), while the East Germans and Hungarians are extremely secular. Consider the question (v26) of whether those who do not believe in God are unfit for public office. Of the country samples, the two highest scores are among the later entrants, Ireland and Northern Ireland where 22.7 per cent and 29.6 per cent respectively either agreed or strongly agreed. Among the two lowest scores are Netherlands (3.6 per cent) and East Germany (3.9 per cent). On the question of respondents' belief in the Devil (v35), again the highest scores were from Ireland (48.6 per cent) and Northern Ireland (68.1 per cent), and the lowest both from the applicant states, East Germany (6.5 per cent) and Hungary (11.3 per cent). On the question of respondents' beliefs about heaven (v36), 90.3 per cent of the Northern Ireland respondents and 87.2 per cent of those from Ireland answered that there is definitely or probably a heaven. Compare this with the five lowest scores: 20.1 per cent in East Germany, 28.2 per cent in Hungary, 40 per cent in Netherlands, 42.3 per cent in Slovakia and 42.7 per cent in West Germany. Meanwhile, all four of the later entrants are among the six countries with the highest percentages – after the two Irelands, Great Britain as 54.3 per cent and Austria 45.9 per cent.

Five questions examined the degree to which religious criteria should play a role in public authority. The questions are: (1) Whether R agrees that politicians who do not believe in God are unfit for pubic office (v26); (2) Whether R agrees that religious leaders should have no influence on how people vote in elections (v27); (3) Whether R agrees that there ought to be more people with religious beliefs in public office (v28); (4) Whether R agrees that religious leaders ought to have no influence in government decisions (v29); and (5) Whether R agrees that religious organisations have too little power (v30). Each of the answers were on a five-point scale, and they were recoded so that a 5 represented views that government ought to be highly influenced by religious values and leaders, and a 1 represented views that government ought not be so influenced. The sum of the five answers was divided by five, giving an index ranging from one to five. The sample was then weighted such that there were the same percentage of respondents for each country, based on country population.

Again with the weighted sample a regression model was run with the index for religious influence in governmental affairs as the dependent variable. Age was controlled for, as well as whether the mother of the

TABLE 2
REGRESSION MODEL WITH APPROPRIATE LEVEL OF POWER FOR RELIGION IN GOVERNMENT AS DEPENDENT VARIABLE, COMPARING ORIGINAL EEC MEMBERS, LATER ENTRANTS AND PRESENT APPLICANTS, WITH CONTROLS

Variable	
Dummy for Later Entrant	**.224098** (12.351)
Dummy for Present Applicant	**.105763** (5.903)
Education	5.26170E-04 (1.149)
Age	**.006985** (12.351)
Dummy for Mother Roman Catholic	**.080282** (5.139)
Sex	**.105775** (7.524)
Constant	**1.617763** (46.984)
R squared	.04901

Notes: Bold indicates p<.01. T-ratios are in parentheses.

TABLE 3
MEAN LEVELS OF POWER FOR RELIGIOUS BELIEFS AND INSTITUTIONS AS APPROPRIATE FOR GOVERNMENT (1=LOW LEVELS OF RELIGIOUS INFLUENCE ARE APPROPRIATE; 5=HIGH LEVELS OF RELIGIOUS INFLUENCE ARE APPROPRIATE) AND CHANGE OVER GENERATIONS

Mean Level of Religious Power Appropriate in Society	All Respondents	Old (> 35 years)	Young (< 35 years)	Change in mean
Original EEC	2.1438	2.1959	2.0567	.1392
Later Member	2.3309	2.3722	2.2583	.1139
Applicant	2.2424	2.2660	2.2029	.0531

respondent were a Roman Catholic, respondent's sex, level of education, and then dummies for each of the three stages of membership in the EU. The model in Table 2 shows the results of an equation that enters both the applicant and later dummies, which in effect compares each of them with the original members. The result shows that the average respondent from a later entrant country will have a score on the religious power index that is twice as far (in the more religious sense) from the average respondent from an original member country than the average respondent from an applicant country.

Table 3 shows these differences as comparative means. Here we see the differences among the three categories of states; and as well for two sub-populations – those under 35 years old and those 35 years or older. The final column shows that from an intergenerational point of view, it is the young populations of the later entrants who are moving more quickly to the religious culture of the original six than the young populations in the applicant states. One might interpret these data as showing that the later entrants adjusted culturally from one generation to the next in light of EU membership; but that such a cultural shift is not as necessary for the populations of the present applicant countries.

The list of religions – as the ISSP study differentiated among 29 religious denominations – was recoded to a list of five: (1) Catholic, (2) National Christian Church, (3) Protestants and those who called themselves Christians with no denomination, (4) Non-Christian and (5) No religion. Tables 4 and 5 present data on correlation coefficients among respondents' reports of religious affiliations of themselves (themselves as children) and close family members. No clear trends emerge, but there are two interesting results. First, rather surprisingly on two measures, religious similarity of mother and father, and religious similarity of respondent and spouse, the respondents in the later entrant countries show a far more cosmopolitan bent than either the respondents from the original six or from the applicant countries. Since on other measures the later entrants were the non-cosmopolitans, this suggests that there is not a single 'cosmopolitan' factor when it comes to culture. Second, there is a vast difference among respondents from the applicant countries in reporting their religion as a child and their current religious affiliation. Reports on religion as a child suggests that under communist rule there was little attention to religious membership in family life. Reports on the current religion of the respondent suggests that after the fall of communism, people began to accept their ascribed religious labels as part of their identity, even if they report being atheists, and marry within their ascribed groups. In fact, there is far greater religious endogamy (computed as in Table 5 rather than the low level as computed in Table 4) among the respondent populations of the applicant states than the other two sets.

It may be argued that the same levels of secularisation indicated by the data have vastly different meanings in the West and the East, as the East did not experience the history of the Enlightenment, nor was its secularisation the cumulative impact of individual agnosticism. Rather the secularisation in the East was due to intense religious delegitimisation by the agents of Soviet communism. Data do not allow a rejection of this interpretation. But

TABLE 4
CORRELATIONS BETWEEN RELIGIOUS IDENTIFICATION AMONG FAMILY MEMBERS (WEIGHTED)

Relationship/ Country Type	R (as child) and Mother	R (as child) and Father	R (as child) and Spouse	Mother and Father
Original EEC	.8322	.6885	.6187	.7301
Later Member	.6327	.2159	.1954	.2538
Applicant	.3062	.2636	.4010	.7784

Note: These are correlation coefficients based upon v50–v53 in ISSP religion survey.

TABLE 5
CORRELATIONS BETWEEN RELIGIOUS IDENTIFICATION AMONG FAMILY MEMBERS

Relationship Country Type	Respondent and Mother	Respondent and Father	Respndent and Spouse	Mother and Father	Respondent now and Respondent as a child
Original EEC	.6264	.6120	.6244	.7836	.6698
Later Member	.4486	.4514	.3855	.6780	.2336
Applicant	.7953	.7802	.8292	.8545	.0362

Note: These are correlation coefficients based upon my recoded and compressed values based upon v50–v53, and v106.

how could the Soviet rulers have been so successful in achieving secularisation from above when they could not instill socialist values from above? East European secularisation could therefore be accepted as individual and reflective of the same Enlightenment processes that pushed citizens in the original six towards secular, cosmopolitan world views.

Overall, then, the religious surveys point to an Eastern Europe that is quite close to the norms of the original EEC members in regard to beliefs and values concerning the role of religion in public life. And they are closer in fact than respondents from the later entrants, and now members of the EU. It would be difficult, with these data on the table, to argue that there are religious cultures in Eastern Europe that are reinforced by the hierarchical values of Leninism, and which support anti-liberal values.

The data are consistent with the cultural configuration notion of the emergent European quasi-state. There is an emerging secular religious culture throughout Europe, one that sees religion as inconsequential for political life. There is, complementary with this secular religious culture, a high level of membership in and identification with nationally based churches, within which there is considerable endogamy. Thus two religious cultures are in simultaneous existence within many European respondents. There are of course many minorities who develop separate religious traditions alongside the secularisation of Europe and possible connection to the national churches, making for a 2+1 religious culture: most European citizens will be highly influenced both by a universalist secularism as well as by an identity connected with the church associated with the dominant population (the 2 religion formula). Religious minorities will be affected by both these religious traditions, but will be free to participate in rituals of their own religion (2+1). Of course, there will remain a class of true secular cosmopolitans, with no connection to any national church (2-1). This (2±1) multiple religious configuration is in equilibrium, not in tension, with itself, and reflective of both West and East.

EAST EUROPE AND POPULAR CULTURE

Popular culture (here film and music) has two profiles. On the one side, its products are industrial commodities pervading markets all over the world, no different from detergents. On the other side, its products help reproduce local, national and/or transnational cultures. The French government seeks to compete with 'Titanic' the movie and 'Tide' the detergent for an overlapping set of reasons. One reason why they want to respond to the former (and not a reason to respond to the latter) is a fear that a globalised artistic industry would reduce the symbolic space that encompasses 'Frenchness'. In any event, thinking of its cultural profile, the data on film and music, *faux de mieux*, show Eastern Europe and members of the EU to be part of a common global regime, in film dominated by United States' production and distribution hegemony, and in popular music by a West European/North American duopoly.

Film

In the film industry, hegemony is found in Hollywood. Consider Table 6, on the 'top ten' films in four recent years reported from four of the original six (Germany, Netherlands, France and Italy), two of the later entrants (UK and Spain) and four applicant states (Hungary, Latvia, Poland, and Slovakia). The first remarkable fact is that in none of these ten countries, and in all four sample years, are fewer than half of the 'top ten' US productions. There are a few reasons why all Europeans are attracted to the same internationalist

TABLE 6
THE 'TOP TEN' FILMS: SELECTED COUNTRIES, SELECTED YEARS
[FIGURES REPRESENT THE PERCENTAGE IN THE COUNTRY, FOR EACH YEAR]
[PERCENTAGES: DOMESTIC, OTHER EUROPEAN, AND US FILMS]

Country	1992	1995	1996	1997
Original six EEC members				
Germany	10, 0, 90	10, 0, 90	20, 0, 80	30, 20, 50
Netherlands	10, 0, 90	20, 0, 80	0, 0, 100	0, 10, 90
France	40, 0, 60	30, 0, 70	40, 0, 60	40, 10, 50
Italy	10, 0, 90	30, 0, 70	20, 0, 80	30, 20, 50
Later EC entrants				
Spain	0, 0, 100	0, 0, 100	0, 0, 100	10, 20, 70
United Kingdom	0, 0, 100	0, 0, 100	10, 0, 90	20, 0, 80
Applicant states				
Hungary	0, 0, 100	0, 0, 100	NA	20, 20, 60
Latvia	NA	NA	0, 0, 100	10, 10, 80
Poland	NA	0, 10, 90	0, 0, 100	30, 10, 60
Slovakia	0, 0, 100	0, 0, 100	0, 0, 100	0, 30, 70

Sources: Derek Elley, *Variety Movie Guide '97* (London: Hamlyn 1996); European Commission, *Panorama of EU Industry 95/96* (Brussels: Office for Official Publications of the European Communities 1995), pp.27.1–27.22; *International Motion Picture Almanac* for years, 1991, 1992, 1995, 1996, 1997, 1998 (Chicago: Quigley Publishing Co.); *Screen International Euroguide* (London: British Film Institute 1996); and *Variety International Film Guide for 1994* [for data on 1992] and 1998 [for data on 1996] (Los Angeles, Silman-James).

movie culture. First, big-budget US films are better produced and technically superior, for example with respect to special effects and animation, and thereby attract wide audiences throughout the world. Second, the European film industries are poorly funded, save for UK, Spain, Italy and France. In the Eastern European countries, the political and economic turmoil in the past decade vastly reduced the production of films. Thus there has been no serious 'European' alternative, though the figures for 1997 suggest a counter-trend. Third, some of the best European directors are being attracted to Hollywood, and help produce American films. Fourth, success at the box office requires control over distributional networks, from producers to theatres, and this system is now fully dominated by a handful of massive distribution chains, all with close ties to the Hollywood majors. In Spain, for example, 96 domestic feature films were produced in 1996, and film attendance is rising. Yet only 38 of the 96 domestic films, due to lack of a local distributor, received at least one public showing. The enormous new growth of multiplex theatres in Europe (with 120 in Spain, 40 in Germany, 25 in Netherlands, and 98 in the UK in 1997) plays into the hands of the distributional giants. Despite the enormous growth of screens, by putting the best screens under control of the giants, the result may actually lower the chances for a screening of domestic films.

A second fact illustrated by Table 6, perhaps even more astonishing than the first, is that in none of the countries does any film produced outside the US or Europe make it into the 'top ten'. This means that Russian, Australian, Hong Kong and Indian films (the latter two having extraordinarily large film industries) did not penetrate into the upper levels of box office success among the member countries of the original six, the later entrants, or the applicant states. The cultural influence of films from these countries has been negligible in the realm of European popular culture.

A third important fact that comes out of Table 6 is the relative weakness of European films outside their home countries. In the data from 1992, 1995 and 1996, not one European film made it to the 'top ten' in another European country. The data from 1997 suggest that a pan-European audience for European films is perhaps emerging. The leading film for 1997 in all countries of the sample was 'Mr Bean', based on a BBC TV series that is in the genre of comedic pantomime. This film did not make it into the US 'top ten', suggesting at least some autonomy of European movie tastes from Hollywood blockbusters. Overall, the West European film industry, notably in the Netherlands and Germany, has achieved somewhat of a renaissance in the late 1990s, as young film directors, often working through film divisions of state-owned TV networks, have made more films on issues that affect young people. European joint ventures is a related route towards competition with America. From 1993 to 1996, for example, Latvia had not produced a feature film, and its market was heavily dominated by US productions. The first new film in 1996 was a co-production with a West European consortium.[15] Joint ventures with the US industry offer another route to quasi-autonomy. One of the European productions in 1997 that made it to three 'top tens' outside France, where it was produced, was 'La Femme Nikita'. This was a joint French/US production in reality (distributed in the US under the name 'The Fifth Element') and it starred the American actor Bruce Willis. It was not among the US 'top ten' for 1997.

Another (albeit small) spark to the European film industry is 'Euroimages', formed under the aegis of the Council of Europe in 1988. Since its creation, with a mean support figure of about 12 per cent of budget, Euroimages has co-produced some 460 feature films and documentaries. Presently, all six of the original EEC members are members of Euroimages, as are eight later members (Austria, Finland, Denmark, Greece, Ireland,

Portugal, Spain and Sweden, with the UK recently leaving), and six applicant countries (Bulgaria, Czech Republic, Hungary, Poland, Romania and Slovakia).[16] It seems clear that to the extent that there is competition vis-à-vis the American film industry in both West and East Europe, it will be films from Europe itself (and virtually nowhere else) that will move into a second position in domestic markets.

A fourth fact that comes out of analysis of Table 6 is that the applicant states share with the rest of Europe a common movie culture. The dominance of American films has been clear. Until 1997, in fact, there was only one film that was not American in the four applicant states. This was 'Priest', produced in the UK, which *Variety* described as 'an absolutely riveting, made-for-BBC slice-of-life drama that's a controversial look at incest, gay-life and the Catholic Church'. The movie was seen by approximately 430,000 Poles and generated just under a million US dollars in revenue. As with the rest of Europe, the applicant states had only fledgling domestic products. Also, as with the rest of Europe, the popularity of films made in other European countries (apart from 'Priest') appears only in 1997. Most interesting, given the so-called legacy of the socialist past, among applicant states no non-American or non-European films made it onto any 'top ten' list.

Thus, one might say there is a European 2±1 film regime in early stages of development: American films dominate throughout Europe; some state film industries are either strong (as in France and Italy) or re-emerging (Germany, UK, Poland) which will represent an alternative film culture. Finally (and this component is different from the language regime), trans-state European films are developing their own markets within the EU and outside their national borders. Outside American films, only European films seem to have the power to capture a limited share of trans-European markets. All other national film industries (and film industries from the regions within European states) will play only to boutique markets. In this sense, both West and East Europe are part of the same film culture.

Popular Music

In the world of popular music, the applicant states to the EU are part of a global music regime that is commensurate with the film industry. An English-language internationalist popular music is the dominant seller. Each country has its own national version of international pop that sells well domestically. Finally, European countries sell their top records to consumers in other European countries. The data show that the applicant states to the EU are very much part of this configuration.

The international music business today is one in which the United States and five EU countries share a duopoly. Three major EU companies (Thorn EMI in the United Kingdom; PolyGram in Netherlands; and BMG in Germany) account for about 40 per cent of the world market in sales, on par with sales from US companies. In many respects, West European youth culture has begun to surpass the Americans in setting standards for musical trends. The result is a powerful global pop music culture that pervades Western Europe. In Eastern Europe especially, but in Western Europe as well, there are three musical cultures: first, the global pop music culture that arrives in the Eastern European states with a marked time delay; second, the remnants of national pop music cultures that have not been entirely erased by the global market; and, finally, a healthy market of European pop that sells quite well throughout the EU and Eastern Europe. Therefore, one could call the European pop culture configuration a 2±1 outcome (as the UK's English language pop is both titular and pan-European).

Popular music has become so global in the past generation that the national origin of popular music and the artists who produce it are blurred and difficult to code. In the early post-World War II generation, Americanisation was clear.[17] Radio Luxembourg (as well as the US Armed Forces Radio Network) brought American rock and roll to Europe in the 1950s. The 1960s–70s saw the supposed 'Americanisation of youth culture'. In fact, the so-called 'British Invasion of America' was really a moment of recognition in the UK that their artists' true market was in the US, and contracts with US recording companies the criterion of success.

But a European disco culture grew from semi-obscurity to world dominance from the 1970s to the 1990s. In the early 1970s, a genre of 'Euro Pop' – a combination of Eurovision song contest entries and the disco-dance sound from holiday dance clubs in Ibiza – began to develop on its own, outside American direct influence. ABBA, a Swedish disco act, went beyond the confines of Europe, and brought this chirpy singalong music to international audiences. As the genre developed, it hit the gay disco scene, and influenced the German/Italian disco sound called 'Eurobeat' in which high quality technology gave the music a sheen that assured club and radio play. With the American disco scene fading away, British companies began producing not for the Americans, but for Europeans, as Europe's sales growth was far more robust. The marriage of Britain to Europe made Europe a genuine challenger to the US for the definition of an international youth music.

The 'international pop' that constitutes the first part of the 2±1 formula is largely English in language (as would be expected from the data on language use) but multicultural in form. A significant proportion of EU hits originate in the UK and Ireland, but even those originating from Germany, the Netherlands, Sweden, Austria and Denmark (and sometimes Spain as well) feature English titles and texts. While most of the lyrics for these songs are so primitive that it seems generous to call them 'language', the words tend to be English ones. In Table 7, we see that in ten selected countries for 1999, only in France (and of course the UK) do a majority of titles in the 'top twenty' appear in the titular language. For 1999, taking the mean percentage of original six countries (Germany, Netherlands, France and Italy – where only the 'top ten', not 'top twenty', are recorded), later members (only Spain, as in the UK the titular language and English are the same), and applicants (Hungary, Latvia, Poland and Slovakia – where only 1998 data are available) reveals an already familiar pattern. The mean figure is 73.8 per cent of English language titles for the original six and 70 per cent for the later member (here only Spain). Thus the mean figure for the applicant states (at 75 per cent) shows closer connection to the original six than does the figure for the later member. As a rule, foreign language titles, other than English, rarely make it into individual country charts, the figure never going over ten per cent. In a data base going back to 1992 (not shown), occasionally a German language title hits the Dutch charts, or a Portuguese song the Spanish, or a French and/or Italian song receives general European interest. For example, in 1998, a Russian song appeared successfully in the Latvian charts. But in general, apart from English, foreign language titles do not reach the top of the popular music charts in the European cultural configuration.

The dominance of the English language is attenuated by attempts to cultivate a sexy multicultural image. A good example of this is Sash!, a German disc jockey (Sascha Lappessen) who employs various vocalists to sing in different European languages. He has had five 'top five' hits from 1997 to 1998 ('Encore un Fois', 'Ecuador', 'Stay', 'La Primavera' and 'Mysterious Times') with titles in three languages, none of them German. In the February 1999 listing of the 'top ten' or 'top twenty' from the nine countries for which we have data, there were 170 different titles, but of the 22 that appear on the lists of more than one country, only one of these titles was not in English.

The second part of the expression 2±1 refers to music that plays mostly, or primarily, to domestic audiences. For example, the EU Industry Guide of 1995 reports that EU markets typically have 60 per cent of sales for 'international pop'. Domestic artists for domestic audiences contribute around 30 per cent. Classical recordings account for the final ten per cent.

TABLE 7
LANGUAGE OF SONG TITLES IN THE 'TOP TWENTY' POP MUSIC CHARTS IN 1999 BY COUNTRY

Country	English	Titular	Other
Original six EEC members			
Germany	80	15	5
Netherlands	80	10	10
France	35	55	10
Italy	100	0	0
Later EC entrants			
Spain	70	30	0
United Kingdom	100	(100)	0
Applicant states			
Hungary	70	30	0
Latvia	85	15	0
Poland	70	30	0
Slovakia (1998)	75	15	10

Sources: The 1997 data are from *Variety Film Guide International* (London: Faber and Faber 1999), pp.64–74; The 1999 raw music data were downloaded from:
Germany = http://www-info6.informatik.uni-wuerzburg.de/~topsi/deu_040299.html.
Hungary = http://www.externet.hu/mahasz/slagerkis.htm.
Latvia = http://www.lanet.lv/news/airplay/1999/990214lv.html.
Holland = http://www.radio538.nl/charts/top40.html.
Poland = http://www.radom.top. pl/radio/listaprz.htm.
Spain = http://www.Cadena40.es/scripts/40w3/lst.asp.
UK = http://www.dotmusic.com/charts/top20singlesyr_print.asp.
Italy = http://www.televisual.net/telemusic/sp.html.
France = http://www.ifop.fr/actualit/top50/top50.htm.

In Greece, Italy and France, the second category – domestic pop – is somewhat stronger, accounting for 40–60 per cent of the markets. In regard to language, as shown in Table 7, titular language songs have a grip in virtually all the European markets, with France, Poland, Spain, Hungary and (of course) the UK being the strongest. On the charts of 'top twenty' for February 1999, there are ten songs with French titles; but in no other country besides France are these songs in the 'top twenty'. Although some of these songs are from a French Canadian popular musical then playing in Paris and from French-singing North Africans, it is fair to say that while English language songs play internationally, French language songs play well only in Francophone countries.

Table 8 paints a complementary picture, and one that helps draw out the pan-European aspect of the 2±1 configuration. It computes the percentage of the 'top twenty' for 1999 by the country in which the song was produced.

TABLE 8
PERCENTAGE OF 'TOP TWENTY' POP SONGS BY NATIONAL ORIGIN BY COUNTRY AND YEAR

Origin/Country	Domestic	EU-other	US/Canada	Other	Unknown
Original six EEC members					
Germany	25	10	25	0	40
Netherlands	10	15	45	0	30
France	35	5	35	5	20
Italy	0	20	40	0	40
Later EC entrants					
Spain	25	30	35	10	0
United Kingdom	10	0	55	0	35
Applicant states					
Hungary	35	25	30	0	10
Latvia	15	25	45	0	15
Poland	35	30	35	0	0
Slovakia (1998)	20	30	40	0	10

Sources: See Table 7.

Unlike the case of film, every country in the sample (with Italy the major exception) has a marked national presence in the top sellers. Also unlike film, EU productions sell widely beyond their national boundaries, and compete successfully with American productions. Taking the means of the three sets of countries in the samples, we see that for the percentage of 'top twenty' hits that are of domestic (national) origin, of the original six, the mean figure is 17.5, and for the later members it is also 17.5, with the applicants at 23.8. And showing the greatest pan-European support, the applicants have the highest percentage of other EU at 27.5 per cent, with the original six having a mean percentage of 12.5 and the later members a mean percentage of 15. It is clear from these data that the Eastern European applicant states included in this sample are very much part of the 2±1 music configuration that marks the countries already members of the European Union.

IS THIS ALL THERE IS TO CULTURE?

One might object and ask whether language repertoires, beliefs about the political relevance of religion and popular exposure to movies and music are all there is to 'culture', or whether the data presented here are indicators of 'culture' at all.

Consider the discussion concerning language repertoires. Two questions about the interpretation of these data speak to the core concerns of this study. First, is the 2±1 configuration in any way unique to Europe, or is it a function of globalisation that is affecting all states? The answer to this is that while there are elements of globalisation that are reflected in the European configuration (for example, the dominance of English is a global phenomenon), the specificity of the repertoires is distinctly European. Consider the following cases. Germans working in France will expect their children to have a sound education in German (as well as English and French), yet Algerians working in France will regard Arabic as a language of the home, and not a language of instruction in their schools. This is because German is a language of Europe while Arabic is not. The concessions given to Catalan in the EU quickly get incorporated into political programmes in other minority language regions, on a premise that all European regions have equal rights to full cultural expression. It is the case that 2±1 repertoires may become more common in other regions of the world, and no doubt English will continue to play a larger role; but the elements of these configurations will differ across regions. In this sense the European configuration will be unique.

Second, to what extent do languages used for specific domains represent something 'cultural' and not just functional? This question can be addressed by an analogy between changing one's language repertoire with religious conversion. As demonstrated by Nock, religious converts almost never imbibe the cultural ethos of the religion; rather they take advantage of the instrumental benefits that accrue to 'believers' of their adopted religion. It is only in successive generations, when for example the children of converts get educated at the hands of the religious virtuosi, that a cultural shift takes place.[18] This mechanism could well operate with language repertoires. In the present generation of Languedocians born after World War II, reliance on English may be thought of as purely functional, and reliance on Occitan may be purely recreational. But their children may well see this multilingual repertoire as constitutive of their identities (combining the cosmopolitan and the local in a unique way), and appeal to it with pride. To the extent that a language repertoire becomes constitutive of social identities, it is properly conceived of as cultural. And so the data cannot demonstrate that the emerging 2±1 European repertoire is a fully developed aspect of culture; but intergenerationally it is likely to become one.

But even if the three realms analysed here are cultural, and even if the interpretation of the long term implications of the data are correct, are there not other, perhaps 'deeper', elements of culture that divide East from West? Ralf Dahrendorf raised this issue in a poignant way when an earlier version of this paper was presented to the European Committee of Reflection in

September 1998. In particular, he asked, would the audience of books and newspapers, as opposed to films and music, show the same global culture? He thought not, as reading is far more national than continental. But more important, he insisted, there is in the heart of Europe a common element or value, one that respects the rule of law, carries with it a desire for social democracy and reflects 'a combination of a desire to be a successful part of the global economy, but to also conduct policies that favor cohesion and justice'. This value is not (now) shared in the East, he fears, and he sees this as ominous for the EU should its core values be diluted by too quick entry of the applicant states into the EU.

On Dahrendorf's first point, it might be noted that what constitutes 'real' or 'deep' culture cannot so easily be discerned. Worse, looking ever deeper for culture subverts any attempt at the systematic analysis of the effects of culture. This is so because if we have an intuition that Xs and Ys are different in a deep way, any evidence that they share cultural traits will be written off as 'shallow'. Since it is always possible to dig a bit deeper, the intuition cannot be scientifically undermined. All that is claimed for the data presented here is that evidence of a cultural divide between members of the EU and applicants from the East is lacking in three domains of culture. Those who wish to examine other realms are welcome to do so; and if they find a cultural divide between East and West, as might have been expected from the research of Verdery and Osa, the findings here would need to be revised. But as yet there are no systematic data, only vague impressions.

Dahrendorf also claims that in *political* culture, those in the East may not have the same social democratic values and concern for the rule of law as do the populations of nearly all of the present members of the EU.[19] This may well be true, but trivially so. This study has postulated a range of cultural variables as independent, and asked whether different values on these variables for new members would negatively impact the common political venture of the EU, which is the dependent variable. But if you want to collect data on 'respect for the rule of law' or 'the value of social democracy', you need to observe political behaviour, which is more or less the same information that will inform the coding on the dependent variable. Dahrendorf's claim therefore verges on tautology. His thesis in caricature is that there would be a clash of political values were the eastern applicant states admitted into the EU because they have different political values. My thesis is that if the applicant states fail to integrate into the European political community, it would not be because of cultural difference.

My suspicion is that the thesis of cultural difference is a canard, upheld by concerned citizens and political leaders who fear, for other reasons, the consequences of joining East to West. It may be the case that for other reasons – economic differentials, non-institutionalised systems of justice, non-consolidation of democratic elections – the attempted integration of eastern Europe into the EU would entail heavy costs. But there is no systematic evidence that for *cultural* differences the costs would be any heavier than the incorporation of Britain, Ireland, Austria and the other later entries. Some positive evidence has been presented here that those costs might be lighter than the incorporation of the already integrated later entrants.

IMPLICATIONS FOR A DEEPENING OF THE EU

This study has made three claims, and provided data from three cultural realms to give support for these claims, all of which are in some tension with popular understanding of the dynamics of the deepening of the EU and of the implications of Eastern European incorporation into the EU for that deepening.

The first claim is that despite the still and ever-vibrant national cultures that constitute the member states (and associated nationalities) of the EU, there is an emergent cultural configuration in Europe that represents a common cultural (and proto-national) zone. Although there is significant cultural diversity between nations and between states within Europe, that diversity is contained within a coherent cultural system, such that most Europeans have a set of cultural repertoires which enables them to act appropriately (that is, according to local standards) throughout the EU. For language, there is an emerging lingua franca, a continued vibrancy of state languages, and a subsidised system to protect minority languages. The norms for which languages are to be used in which contexts are well internalised. It is the internalised norms of the cultural system that constitute the common cultural zone. In religion, there is an EU-wide consensus in support of a secular Christianity, a respect for national churches that do not meddle in political life, and a recognition as well of minority religious groups as long as the religious expression of these groups is contained within that community. In popular culture, Europe participates in an international popular film and music system (the latter in which it is a duopoly producer) that is dominant in each realm, but each has a small but viable national production of film and music that is made for domestic audiences and for other Europeans. Europeans therefore have a common matrix for the production and consumption of popular culture.

The second claim is that the applicant states from Eastern Europe are far closer to the European cultural system than is popularly understood, or even recognised, by leading social scientists who have observed the cultural life of these states with great perspicacity. In fact, the preliminary data show that in the cultural realms of language and religion the applicant states are somewhat closer to the original six in a common cosmopolitanism (multilingualism in language; secularisation in religion) than are the later entering states into the EU. In aspects of popular culture as well, the applicant states appear on some dimensions to be nearly as international as the sample from the original six, and more internationalist than the sample from the later EU entrants. These findings are so counter-intuitive that they demand future analysis. Of course it cannot be ruled out that in other cultural realms the East/West divide might be a deep one. But there is no evidence in the wide-ranging sets of data that went into this analysis that the cultural configurations of Eastern Europe pose a threat to the emerging cultural system of the current member states.[20]

The third claim is more of an interpretation than a finding. It is that in dynamic national projects (as Europe has become), there is greater interest in promoting a national culture in the periphery than in the centre. A particularly good example of this is to think of middle class Jewish culture in post-emancipation Europe.[21]

The Eastern Europeans today, in significant numbers, seek to become part of a European national culture that is clearer to them than it is to everyday West Europeans. To be sure, it might be argued, along lines suggested by Bourdieu, that peripheral peoples are 'pretenders' with a negative (even cynical) view of the centre. They could well be emulating the centre purely for instrumental gain, while in fact they are more nationalistic in their apparent cosmopolitanism.[22] This would be more in line with the perspective presented earlier from Verdery and Osa. The fact, however, is that the emulation, in seeking to learn English, in wanting secular rule, in listening to 'top ten' songs and watching 'top ten' films, is not a result of an effete class of social climbers (as was perhaps the case with German Jews). Rather it is a mass phenomenon, belying a notion of cynical adaptation.

There is yet another important difference. Unlike the situation of post-Enlightenment Jewry, West Europeans are not seeking to escape from a European mould to keep a distance from those seeking to assimilate. The 'Catch-22' of the Eastern Europeans becoming 'Europeans' while the actual EU members become something else is not therefore likely. The more likely outcome is that the pressures of peripheralisation will induce East Europeans self-consciously to promote a deepening of a European culture that West Europeans themselves have less motivation to foster. Rather than eroding a common EU culture, the data in this study suggest that East European entry into the EU will contribute to its deepening.

NOTES

Research assistance by Brett Klopp is gratefully acknowledged. Peter Katzenstein and Gary Herrigel provided useful comments on an earlier draft. Comments provided by members of the Reflection Group on the EU's Eastward Enlargement at a meeting organised by the European University Institute and the European Commission's Forward Studies Unit in September 1998 are also acknowledged

1. Here (with italics omitted and other small changes made in the quoted texts) is Kálmán Kulcsár's characterisation of a position that he argues must be overcome to achieve the goal of building upon what he considers 'the growing awareness of the common elements of European culture'. See his 'East Central Europe and the European Integration', in Máté Szabó (ed.), *The Challenge of Europeanization in the Region: East Central Europe* (Budapest: Hungarian Political Science Association 1996), quotes from pp.12–16.
2. The cross-country data for language and religion are calculated from surveys conducted by the International Social Survey Program (ISSP), and the data are supplied by the Zentralarchiv für Empirische Sozialforschung, in Köln, Germany, and distributed by the Inter-university Consortium for Political and Social Research, Ann Arbor, Michigan, USA. While sampling procedures differed in each of the countries, the overall attempt was to get country-wide stratified samples, with total number of respondents ranging from about 1,000 respondents in Italy to 2,700 in Russia. Full details of the surveys are available from ICPSR at http://www.icpsr.umich.edu.
3. David D. Laitin, 'The Cultural Identities of a European State', *Politics & Society* 25/3 (Sept. 1997), pp.277–302. As I discuss later, the cultural configuration for popular music is 1+1.
4. On language configurations, see Abram de Swaan, 'The Evolving European Language System: A Theory of Communication Potential and Language Competition', *International Political Science Review* 14/3 (1993), pp.241–55.
5. Susan Watkins, *From Provinces into Nations* (Princeton: Princeton University Press 1991); Eugen Weber, *Peasants into Frenchmen* (Stanford: Stanford University Press 1976); and Abram de Swaan, *In Care of the State* (New York: Oxford University Press 1988).
6. This is a central argument in Peter Sahlins, *Boundaries* (Berkeley: University of California Press 1989). I develop this theme in Laitin, 'Cultural Identities'.
7. Maryjane Osa, 'Pastoral Mobilization and Symbolic Politics: The Catholic Church in Poland, 1918–1966' (Ph.D. Thesis, Department of Sociology, University of Chicago 1992). The speculations about the future are on pp.1–5. Her reference is to Ken Jowitt, *New World Disorder: The Leninist Extinction* (Berkeley: University of California Press 1992). For a similar analysis, see Wodek Anio *et al.*, 'Returning to Europe: Central Europe between Internationalization and Institutionalization', in Peter J. Katzenstein (ed.), *Taming Power: Germany in Europe* (Ithaca: Cornell University Press 1997), pp.200–204. They make the excellent point that in the post-Franco era, the Spanish Catholic Church (unlike the Polish Church after communism) reconciled itself to Spain's 'European vocation'. Thus the challenge for Poland to become part of Europe will be more difficult than it was for Spain.
8. Katherine Verdery, 'Civil Society or Nation? "Europe" in the Symbolism of Postsocialist Politics', chapter 5 of her *What was Socialism, and What Comes Next?* (Princeton: Princeton University Press 1996).
9. Verdery, as with Osa, relies upon and has been influenced by Jowitt, *New World Disorder.*
10. For a refusal to put the Visegrad states in the 'East', yet an unwillingness of most elites of those states to become part of a 'Central European' alternative, see Anio *et al.*, 'Returning to Europe', esp. p.195 n.1, and pp.196, 250.
11. In an article consistent with both Osa and the position taken herein, Ewa Morawska, 'The

Polish Roman Catholic Church Unbound: Change of Face or Change of Context?' in Stephen E. Hanson and Willfried Spohn (eds.), *Can Europe Work? Germany and the Reconstruction of Postcommunist Societies* (Seattle: University of Washington Press 1995), pp.47–77, argues that the Polish Catholic Church is indeed a bastion of reaction. However, she argues that its position in regard to both public and private spheres is one 'that the majority of Polish society perceives today as detrimental to the satisfactory functioning of the democratic nation-state' (p.48). She concludes that when Poles observe the 'naked requirements for a concrete Christian ethos ... the negative perceptions of the church as 'meddling' and encroaching upon people's lives are enhanced' (p.68). This is very much in line with West European orientations toward national churches.

12. As with the religion data, when I report percentages for all cases, or for the set of cases of either the original EEC members, the later entrants, or the applicants, I assign a weight to each respondent, the same for all respondents in each country, such that there is an equal percentage of respondents as a function of the population of the country.
13. My guess is that the 210 respondents who claimed Basque, Galician or Catalan as their first home language but did not report Spanish as a language they knew well were giving surveyors political rather than linguistic knowledge.
14. The reasoning on Germany is as follows. It would be too early to consider a poll done in 1991 to reflect East Germany as anything but an applicant to the EU. But by 1995, it is fully part of a country that was an original member.
15. Data on the film industries of Europe come from the sources cited at Table 6.
16. Information on Euroimages has been downloaded from the world wide web. See: http://culture.coe.fr/Eurimages.
17. The following discussion is based upon the analysis of Simon Frith, 'Euro Pop', *Cultural Studies* 3/2 (1989), pp.166–72.
18. A.D. Nock, *Conversion* (London: Oxford University Press 1933).
19. See also Fuchs and Klingemann (this volume).
20. Perhaps there is a not-so-East set of countries close to the EU norm (the Visegrad and Baltic states) and a 'real' East that is far from that norm (e.g. Romania, Bulgaria). My data do not allow me to address this possibility, but I am sceptical that new data would demonstrate such a cultural boundary.
21. As described by Zygmunt Bauman, 'Entry Tickets and Exit Visas: Paradoxes of Jewish Identity', *Telos* 77 (1988), pp.52–5: 'The Jews who took the Enlightenment on its word and identified emancipation with refinement of manners and, more generally, with self-cultivation, had become cultural fanatics. In every Western nation they were the ones who treated national cultural heritage most seriously … Trying to excel in the complex and often elusive task ahead, they sung the praises of national monuments and masterpieces of national art and literature, only to find that the audience comprised mostly people similar to themselves. They read avidly and voraciously, only to find they could discuss what they read only with other *aspiring* Germans or Frenchmen like themselves. Far from bringing them closer to assimilation, conspicuous cultural enthusiasm and obsessive display of cultural nobility set them aside from the native middle class and, if anything, supplied further evidence of their ineradicable *foreignness* ... The self-destructive tendency of assimilation also effected occupations[;] legal or medical careers ... offered particular attractions to assimilating Jews ... The unplanned outcome ... was ... an overrepresentation of Jews in the professions, and a new set of arguments to prove the Jews' permanent distinctiveness. The abandoning of traditional Jewish occupations, which from the assimilants' viewpoint meant *Entjudung* (de-judaisation of 'men as such') appeared to the baffled native public more like the process of *Verjudung* (judaisation of heretofore gentile areas). This was a 'Catch-22' plight [for which] there was no guaranteed escape'.
22. Pierre Bourdieu, *Distinction: A Social Critique of the Judgement of Taste* [trans. Richard Nice] (Cambridge, MA: Harvard University Press 1984), chapter 6.

Discomforts of Victory: Democracy, Liberal Values and Nationalism in Post-Communist Europe

VLADIMIR TISMANEANU

The purpose of this analysis is to identify the main threats to post-communist liberal democracies, especially those perils related to the weakness of pluralist traditions, institutions and values, and the rise of movements and ideologies rooted in cultural and political malaise, *ressentiment* and disaffection. But despite this attention to the perils, listed in the latter half, it must be made clear that the purpose here is not to put forward apocalyptic scenarios for post-communist societies, but rather a diagnosis of the main vulnerabilities of Eastern Europe's post-communist states in order to evaluate prospects for further democratic consolidation and risks for the rise and affirmation of ethnocratic parties and movements. To be sure, most of the pessimistic forecasts uttered in the aftermath of Leninism's collapse in East-Central Europe and the former USSR have not come true. Twelve years after that series of world-historical events, more than one possible future can be reasonably canvassed, and the likelihood for the worst-case scenario, one of a slide into regional ethno-nationalist anarchy, remains somewhat dubious.[1] Understanding the post-communist political and cultural situation, including persistent isolationist, anti-globalisation, populist and nationalist trends, is therefore of critical importance for interpreting the main directions these countries will pursue in their efforts to join the European Union institutions.

The new European democracies have avoided the rise to power of staunchly illiberal forces and, in spite of widespread cynicism and corruption, there is a growing consensus regarding the desirability of markets, free media and pluralist institutions. True, the situation differs from country to country, and from region to region. In South-East Europe (often designated as the Balkans), the transitions turned out to be more difficult and problematic: if we think of Romania, the results of the November–December 2000 elections have brought back to power a political formation and a personality (Ion Iliescu and his Party of Social Democracy, after June 2001 renamed the Social

Democratic Party of Romania) with a long record of opposition to radical reforms. In Bulgaria, former King Simeon has become prime minister after his political formation won the elections in June 2001 on a populist platform promising everything to everybody.[2] But even in these countries, nobody within the political mainstream questions the necessity, indeed the imperative of joining Euro-Atlantic institutions. The magnetism of united Europe (or perhaps the political myth of unified Europe) has thus played a decisive role in preventing anti-democratic forces taking the lead and subverting the democratic institutions. Many of the encouraging trends in recent years, including the signing of treaties between Hungary on one hand and Slovakia and Romania on the other, as well as the institutionalisation of political guarantees for minorities in most of these countries, are directly related to the pressure exerted by the European Union and its affiliated organisms on the political elites of the new democracies. Western Europe is clearly tired of the long history of strife, exclusiveness and bickering that made the continent's twentieth century history such a bleak one, and the candidates for acceptance into the European Union realise that they have to come to terms with expectations of genuine commitment to human rights as well as a demystification of past experiences, including atrocities related to Fascism and Communism.[3] Obviously, these are challenges that will take time to deal with, but the important fact is that the new political elites have accepted the inevitability of integrative processes and seem increasingly inclined to come to terms with the implications of globalising processes, including a reduction of nation-state prerogatives. The decision of the Serbian government to extradite Slobodan Milosević for trial in The Hague under charges of crimes against humanity indicates that the democratic *Zeitgeist* has an enormous contaminating effect: any European government that wants to be treated as part of the emerging unified structures needs to go beyond parochial, self-serving nationalist demagoguery and recognise the need to address lucidly the shameful moments of their countries' past.[4]

The typology of the post-communist transitions can be briefly (and somewhat simplistically) described as follows: (a) the Central European successful democratic experiments (Poland, Czech Republic, Hungary, Slovenia, Baltic states), where markets, political parties, free media, legal-constitutional structures and dynamic civil societies have developed relatively smoothly and with palpable positive results; (b) the protracted, middle-of-the-road transitions (Bulgaria, Romania, Croatia) where the presence of former communists and neo-populists, and the weakness of pluralist forces have prevented the rapid economic, legal and political reforms; and (c) the quasi-democracies with strong authoritarian potential, continuous attempts to limit the freedom of the media by either political or financial operators, strong neo-Communist formations and a beleaguered judiciary system (Russia, Ukraine, Moldova, to some extent Albania, certainly Belarus, and until recently Serbia).[5] In this respect, we have to consider the importance of political-cultural traditions in the shaping of the new democratic communities: some of these countries have more of a usable liberal-constitutional past than others. In understanding the role played by civil society in the democratic transitions, we have to take into account the role of historical legacies, pre-communist and communist as well. Whatever the self-idealising rhetoric of local cultural elites may claim, these societies have a long record of illiberal, anti-modern, often xenophobic and exclusive behaviour.[6] In other words, the appeals to a pre-communist Central European identity that would presumably be based on tolerance, civility and trust, as opposed to the collectivistic-authoritarian model imposed by Sovietism, tends to neglect the heterogeneous nature of these political cultures, in which democratic and non-democratic, pro-Western and anti-Western, modern and traditionalist values and discourses have long competed with each other.[7] The important thing, however, is the general liberal trend in European and international affairs, and the disrepute of oppressive and repressive forms of political organisation. No less significant, the globalisation of civic networks, including those committed to the defence of human rights, has been a favourable element during the transitions.[8]

While there are many disturbing factors in post-communist politics, including a decline of moral standards and a demobilisation of civil society, there is no reason to declare the failure of the democratic transitions. At the same time, we should avoid the temptation of liberal triumphalism and admit that the situation in the post-Communist East-Central Europe is still fluid, and while the democratic forces, at least in Central Europe, have prevailed, it is not certain that new fundamentalisms (militaristic, fascist, ultra-clericalist, and so on) will not try to subvert the pluralist arrangements. After all, the democratic institutions (especially the party system and widespread corruption) have recently been under attack in Western Europe as well, anti-immigration actions have intensified, and populist politicians such as Jörg Haider or certain members of Silvio Berlusconi's coalition have successfully campaigned using xenophobic rhetoric.[9] Such forces can capitalise on political and social anxieties, especially among those strata that experience transitions, acceptance of European Union norms and regulations, and cultural globalisation, as a traumatic loss of identity and status. Furthermore, as some countries will join the EU earlier than others, populist ethnocentrism will play on feelings of abandonment, rejection and humiliation among the 'forgotten' nations. European enlargement should therefore be a process that ought not to allow for any marginalisation ('essentialisation') of one part of Eastern Europe as inherently backward, dominated by irrational passions and irretrievably tribalistic.

Moreover, even among those who will be the first to 'join the club', the discussion is not closed regarding the nature of political and national community: will Poland and Hungary accept multiculturalism as a foundation of their new identity, or will they rather favour an Austrian-style model of ethno-cultural homogeneity and by implication rejection of the other? Even if we think of the Czech Republic, often seen as one of the most successful cases of democratic transition, there are quite a few alarming trends: for instance, the Zeman minority government has stayed in power with former premier Václav Klaus's party support, in exchange for not looking into the latter's record of corruption; several years ago, when the Czech Philharmonic hired a conductor from Hamburg, he was fired for being German and thus presumably lacking a 'Czech' soul for 'Czech' music; and the notorious walls and violence against Roma as means to 'solve the Gypsy problem'. In the same vein, though the Baltic states have often been presented as models of non-violent, civic-driven democratic transitions, their 'singing revolution' has recently gone sour during the feud between Lithuania and Latvia over ownership of folk songs. As a journalist put it: 'Inter-Baltic cooperation was meant to be a rehearsal for EU and NATO membership. But if the Balts can't sing together in their own little trio, then how they will manage when they join the big choirs?'[10] The debate is going on, and it is much too early to advance any forecast about its conclusions. For reasons which are both psychological and cultural, many politicians and intellectuals in East-Central Europe have reservations about the supranational, cosmopolitan, globalised vision of the European Union and share French Premier Lionel Jospin's opposition to the German proposal for a radical reduction of national sovereignty: 'I want a Europe, but I remain attached to my nation', said Jospin, who added, 'making Europe without unmaking France, or any other European nation – that is my political choice.'[11]

The Milosević-style expansionist chauvinism has not been emulated outside the borders of the former Yugoslavia, although similar outbursts of hatred and intolerance have accompanied the breakdown of the Soviet Union, especially in the Caucasus. In much of the post-communist world, the landscape is one of disenchantment, uncertainty and cynicism. The initial times of post-communist euphoria are obviously over, and this applies also to the more advanced states in terms of democratic capitalist reforms. However, the post-revolutionary discomfiture is more intensely felt in South-Eastern Europe, where democratic transitions have been slow and half-hearted, therefore allowing for the rise of new collectivisms, marginalisation of the former heroes and, more recently, return of the former communists. Romania's elections in 2000 offer a clear example: Corneliu Vadim Tudor, the former court-poet of the Ceaușescu regime, and his 'Greater Romania Party' became a major voice of the opposition. Ironically, Ion Iliescu, the former apparatchik who succeeded Nicolae Ceaușescu in December 1989, appeared to many in the country as the guarantor of democracy and civic rights.[12] Adam Michnik's term for this general trend is 'the velvet restoration'.[13] The term 'velvet counter-revolution' is proposed to indicate the direction of this phenomenon, especially in the rise of strong anti-intellectual and illiberal trends.[14]

The search for new political myths is simply more visible in the East, where all social contrasts are exacerbated and where the individual senses these tragic breakdowns of old identities with more acuity (Katherine Verdery writes about an ongoing cosmic re-ordering).[15] But the phenomenon is worldwide: the return of myth is part of the universal uneasiness with the cold, calculated, *zweckmässig* rationality of the iron cage: prophets and demagogues (often the same persons) do have audiences in the East as well as in the West. The latter is, however, better protected: institutions function impersonally, procedures are deeply embedded in the civic cultures. In the post-communist world they are only incipient. This study looks into these uncertainties and the psycho-ideological responses to them: they may be considered fantasies in that they give a wishful image of reality, rooted in imagination, approximation and magic thinking. Things are of course extremely complex: there is indeed a feeling of exhaustion, of too much rhetoric, a sentiment that politicians are there simply for cheating. Corruption seems to be universal, and most of these societies are closer to Latin America (or Southern Europe) than to any Anglo-Saxon model of pluralism. On the other hand, it is precisely this exhaustion of traditional worldviews, this post-modern syndrome of repudiation of grandiose teleological constructs in favour of mini-discourses, that is conducive to ennui and yearning for alternative visions which would not be scared of boldness and inventiveness. This is a secularised world, but the profane substitutes for traditional mythologies still have a future. Fascism as a phenomenon is not simply linked to one personality or the specific conditions in Italy or Germany in the 1920s and 1930s: its roots are to be found in the readiness of desperate masses to follow highly self-confident individuals.

After the extinct period of 'legitimation from the top' (through ideological rituals of simulated participation, mobilisation and regimentation), it seems that in most of these countries nascent, legal-procedural legitimation is paralleled (or countered) by something that, echoing Eric Hobsbawm's insightful analysis of the new discourses of hatred, could be called *legitimation from the past.*[16] The more inchoate and nebulous this past, the more aggressive, feverish and intolerant the proponents of the neo-romantic mythologies. The following myths are the ideological foundation, the intellectual cement that tends to become prevalent in these societies: redemptive, vindictive, scapegoating and neo-utopian.[17] This study uses the term 'myth' in the broadest sense, indicating the world of fantasies, illusions, expectations and yearnings, rooted in anguish, doubt and uncertainty, and often rationalised as political messianism and other radical discourses. The rise of nationalism as a compensation for perceived failure and externally imposed marginality, as flight from the complexities of modernity into the politics of collective salvation, is linked to this ambiguous Leninist legacy of distorted modernity and dictated human needs, and to the pre-Leninist ethnic-oriented cultural forms in the region. In other words, the discomfiture with democratic challenges and the prevailing constitutional pluralist model is not only linked to the transition from Leninism, but to the larger problem of legitimation and the existence of competing visions of common good, as well as the coalescence of movements and parties around different and frequently rival symbols of collective identity. To put it simply, the post-communist wave of primordial passions and the appeals of the new exclusionary discourses remind us that neither the premises nor the outcomes of modernity have been universally accepted. This point was raised by S.N. Eisenstadt in a path-breaking analysis of the revolutions of 1989:

> These problems, however, do not simply arise out of the breakdown of "traditional" empires, the transition from some "pre-modern" to fully modern, democratic society, or from a distorted modernity to a relatively tranquil stage which may well signal some kind of "end of history." The explicit and/or latent cultural tensions evident in Eastern Europe today bear witness to some of the problems and tensions inherent in modernity itself, attesting to the potential fragility of the whole project of modernity.[18]

For this very reason, then, one cannot see the Eastern part of Europe as the only candidate for embracing these ethnocentric follies. We deal with a resilient, persistent form of barbarism that, again, is situated in the very heart of modernity. Radical nationalism is the absolute exacerbation of difference, its reification, the rejection of the claim to a common humanity and the proclamation of the ethno-national distinction as the primordial fact of human existence.[19]

The following sections introduce and briefly examine nine threats to fledging democracies. There are, of course, many other threats, including external ones, that have been ignored. The purpose is to show why, in achieving the overthrow of Sovietism, many (but not all) of the countries in Eastern Europe and the former Soviet Union have not achieved liberal democracy or political stability. While arguments can be made that democratic stability cannot happen without massive inflows of Western economic aid, a lack of capital is not the determining factor in the region's future.[20] As Haider's party advances in the Austrian elections demonstrate, a nation's wealth is no guarantee of its citizens' liberal-democratic sensibilities. There are several complex internal factors that make the fall of communism in Eastern Europe an uncomfortable victory and they will certainly affect the emergence of united Europe as a political, economic and cultural entity. In identifying them, it is not argued that they will pre-empt these countries' access into the Union, but rather that they can delay and/or distort this process.

NINE THREATS

1. The Leninist Debris or Waiting for Peron

Of all the authors who acclaimed the breakdown of communism in Eastern Europe, Ralf Dahrendorf has turned out to have been the most prescient in pointing to the many perils marking the road to an open society, especially in the light of the not-so-solid, that is, quite problematic, personalistic, individualistic and democratic traditions in the region.[21] After all, it was Karl Marx who so clearly indicated that any new society will carry for a long time its birthmarks, in this case the habits, mores, visions and mentalities (*forma mentis*) associated with the Leninist faith.

At first glance, democratic institutions have emerged, democratic elections have been held, and the malediction called 'Balkanisation' so far has plagued only ex-Yugoslavia, but looms large in areas of the former Soviet Union. Furthermore, as Karen Dawisha has argued, 'electocracies' should not be automatically regarded as liberal democratic communities.[22] Thus, in reality, constitutionalism remains marred by its very universalistic formalism (its coldness, and its often decried tediousness) and the subsequent failure to adjust to pressures resulting from collective efforts aimed at reverting, subverting and obliterating the project of modernity (by which is tentatively understood the substantive construction of politics in anti-absolutist, individualistic and contractual way). In many of these countries, reasserted presidentialism, indigenism, dirigism and statism are reminiscent of Latin American (Peronista-style) experiments in corporatism and authoritarian party hegemonism.[23] Corporatism, after all, has had a long tradition in the region. Mihail Manoilescu, a Romanian economist, was among the most influential theorists of revolutionary-nationalist corporatism. Such ideas seem to come back with vengeance in the discourse of fundamentalist populists of various stripes (extreme left or right). Their appeal, like fascism's in the 1930s, is linked to their ability to 'combine resentful nationalism with a plausible theory of economic development that emphasised authoritarianism, mass mobilisation of the population, and the retention of supposedly traditional, pure, non-western values'.[24] But the 'return of the repressed', real and often disturbing, does not exhaust the picture. Indeed, with all the predicaments and setbacks, the spiritual *situation* in Europe (and in Eastern Europe in particular) remains fundamental for the attempted *reinvention of politics*.[25] The point here is to highlight the uncertainties of this political drama, the possible fractures, delusions and ordeals, but also the still untested freedoms and new forms of human solidarity.[26]

Concurrently, the Leninist decline has led to a general breakdown of the established framework of political arrangements, compromises, mutual coverages and accepted 'rules of the game' in the West as well. In this respect, the rise of Jörg Haider's Freedom Party is a response to deep-seated discontent with the corrupt status quo rather than a mere expression of residual fascist nostalgia.[27] Foreseeing these new waves of rage, Gianni De Michelis (Italy's foreign minister until 1992) wrote in 1993 that the Perot phenomenon in the US was like an overall revolt against conventional party politics (in Italy and elsewhere). The current crisis transcends the simple 'sweeping away of the scoundrels' and bears upon a genuine political 'great transformation': 'we are witnessing the explosion of a long-obsolete model of liberal democracy that can no longer accommodate our dynamic, complex societies with their sophisticated electorates of vast diversity and highly differentiated interests.'[28] It is thus tempting to assume that the major difficulties in the articulation of ideologically differentiated political platforms in Eastern Europe are connected not only to the absence and/or weakness of clear-cut interest groups and lobbies, but also to increasing atrophy of the Western sources of inspiration ('models') for such endeavours. The famous law of political synchronisation (of the East to the West) may this time play against the revival of ideological politics.[29]

The growing political appeals and uses of myths and the omnipresent selective memory (and forgetfulness) have led to the resurrection of historical phantoms (for example, Horthy in Hungary, Codreanu and Antonescu in Romania, Mgr. Tiso in Slovakia, Ante Pavelić in Croatia). Obsessive self-pity and the absence of empathy, the inability to mourn with the others and to understand their plight, is indicative of a general collective self-centredness that erects fences around the in-group and elaborated, manufactured inhibiting images about the 'Other'. In Michael Ignatieff's terms, this is a latter-day expression of what Freud called the 'narcissism of minor differences'. But, once again, is this phenomenon uniquely East European? Are not these new (or not so new) fantasies part of a more widespread need to redefine identity and authority in a post-Leninist world? Are not the outcomes of the 1994 and 2001 elections in Italy as disturbing as the populist, potentially fascist revival in the East? Daniel Chirot argues that the absence of legitimising signals from the West, the presumed reconciliation between Western intelligentsia and liberalism would diminish the chances for the Eastern neo-fundamentalists to really enjoy a second life.[30] But this seems to have been utterly revised by the Austrian, Swiss and Norwegian new waves of xenophobic populism. In other words, ethnocentric radicalism still has a future in Europe (and not only there).[31]

In the East, the landscape is, of course, utterly puzzling and evanescent. The achievements cannot be simply dismissed: during the last ten years, East-Central European societies have evolved from authoritarian, ideologically monistic, extremely centralised and bureaucratically corrupt regimes towards democratic forms of political and economic organisation. To focus exclusively on their difficulties during the transition period is to miss the drama of social and political experimentation in that region. To deny these dangers is on the other hand myopic and in the long run disastrous. Furthermore, what is at stake is the validity and the very possibility of the liberal democratic paradigm in traditionally authoritarian societies. What do Mill and Tocqueville have to say to the denizens of the post-Leninist world? Second, we have to assess the meaning of the great transformations unleashed by the cataclysmic events of 1989: are the newly awakened societies propitious to pluralism, or may the upper hand eventually belong to illiberal, anti-modern demagogues? Can the revolutionary promises, that at least during the first stage were predominantly civic and 'cosmopolitan', be, to use Bruce Ackerman's term, constitutionalised?[32] What are the chances for these countries to build up a constitution of liberty, to rid themselves of their legacies of autarchy, obscurantism, 'tribalism' and resentments, and safeguard the recently acquired areas of autonomy?[33] Formulated in this way, the issue bears upon the future of the region, of Europe and international security.[34]

2. The Power of Magic Thinking

Intellectual stupor, moral disarray and yearning for the 'magic saviour' are symptoms of the post-communist culture of disillusionment. The ideological extinction of Leninist formations left behind a cultural chaos in which syncretic constructs emerge that draw from the pre-communist and communist authoritarian, often irrational, heritage. We deal with a shapelessness of political commitments and affiliations, or better said with the breakdown of a political culture (that Leszek Kolakowski and Martin Malia correctly identified as Sovietism) and the painful birth of a new one. The moral identity of the individuals has been shattered by the dissolution of all the established values and 'icons'. There are immense continuity gaps in both social and personal memory. There is very little public trust and only a vague recognition of the need for a shared vision of the public good. Individuals are eager to abandon their newly acquired sense of autonomy on behalf of different forms of protective, pseudo-salvationist groups and movements. Václav Havel emphasised this peril when he wrote:

> In a situation when one system has collapsed and a new one does not yet exist, many people feel empty and frustrated. This condition is fertile ground for radicalism of all kinds, for the hunt for scapegoats, and for the need to hide behind the anonymity of a group, be it socially or ethnically based.[35]

Assumed responsibility for personal actions, risk taking and questioning of institutions on the base of legitimate claims for improvement are still embryonic.[36]

Leninist regimes kept their subjects ignorant of the real functioning of the political system. The chasm between the official rhetoric and the everyday reality, the camouflaging of the way decisions were reached, the anti-elective pseudo-elections and other rituals of conformity neutralised critical faculties and generated a widespread scepticism about the validity of politics as such. Add to this that anti-communism tended to be just another supra-individual, non-differentiated form of identity. The problem now is that the aggregation of social interests needs a clarification of the political choices, including an awareness of the main values individuals do indeed advocate. Is after all Václav Klaus the conservative economist he pretends to be? As Martin Palous has noted: 'The most important and most dynamic factor in post-totalitarian politics has to do with the way people in post-communist societies perceive and conceptualise the social reality and political processes they are a part of.'[37] The difficulties and ambiguities of the left–right polarisation in post-communist regimes are linked to the ambiguity and even obsolescence of the traditional taxonomies: Marxism or Leninism ceased to be exhilarating ideological projects, and the references to the 'Left' (in its radical version, at least) are rather opportunistic gestures than expressions of genuine commitment. As Adam Michnik once put it: 'The issue is not whether one is left or right of center, but West of center.'[38]

Liberal values are thus seen by some as left-oriented simply because they emphasise secularism, tolerance and individual rights as against different varieties of radicalism (including 'civic' or 'ethical' clericalism or even theocratic fundamentalism). At the same time, as shown by new radical-authoritarian trends (often disguised as pro-democratic) in Russia, Ukraine, Bulgaria, Romania, Slovakia, and so on, lingering reflexes and habits inherited from Leninist and pre-Leninist authoritarianisms continue to exist: intolerance, exclusiveness, rejection of any compromises, extreme personalisation of the political discourse and the search for charismatic leadership. These Leninist psychological leftovers can be detected at both ends of the political spectrum (the 'right' and the 'left') and this explains the rise of the new alliances between traditionally incompatible formations and movements. In Russia, this takes the form of the Stalino-nationalist coalition, with its own tradition of national-Bolshevism. Political corruption, economic frustrations and cultural despair are the ingredients for the rise of anomic mass phenomena of panic, millennial expectations, pseudo-chiliasms and sectarian magic – as for instance could be seen in the pyramid scams in Albania and Romania.

3. Remembrance of Things Not Quite Past or Nonexistent

Less paradoxically than at first glance, there is a growing nostalgia for the old regime and the revival of 'reactionary rhetoric'.[39] One should seriously examine the fallacy of a discussion in terms of neo-communism: for such a development to take place, ideological zeal and utopian-eschatological motivation are needed. Snegur, Brazauskas, Zyuganov, Iliescu, Meciar and Milosević are not simply neo-communists. Obviously, there are fundamental distinctions between truly reconstructed ex-communists (Alliance of Democratic Left in Poland, Hungarian Socialist Party) and hard-core Leninist nostalgics (Communist Party of Bohemia and Moravia).[40] Between recantation and impersonation, the successor formations to the Leninist parties have to cope with a widespread sentiment of disaffection with traditional socialist rhetoric.[41] The cases of the Serbian socialists and Corneliu Vadim Tudor's 'Greater Romania party' are emblematic for the current trend toward the co-operation between radical nationalist forces and nostalgics of bureaucratic collectivism. The foundation of this trend is the ideological vacuum created by the collapse of state socialism, with populism being the most convenient and frequently the most appealing ersatz ideology. And populism is neither left, nor right. Uprootedness, status loss and identity uncertainties are fertile ground for paranoid visions of conspiracy and treason: hence, the nationalist salvationism as a substitute for what Freud described as the 'oceanic sentiment'. Simply marching with Stalin's portrait is not an expression of Stalinism, but rather one of disaffection with the status quo, perceived as chaotic, anarchic, corrupt, politically decadent and morally decrepit. Especially in Russia, where this disaffection (*desencanto*) is linked to the sentiment of imperial loss, the cultural despair can lead to dictatorial trends. Exaggerated as they may be, references to 'Weimar Russia' capture the psychology of large human contingents whose traditional set of collectivistic values has dissipated and who cannot recognise themselves in the often contradictory new ones based on individual action, risk and intense competition. Similar trends exist in Bulgaria, Poland and Hungary (for example, István Csurka's 'Hungarian Life and Justice Party').[42]

4. Protean Politics: Fluidity of Political Formations

With a private sector and entrepreneurial class still in the making, political liberalism and the civic culture associated with it are under attack from different directions: nationalist, neo-Leninist, clericalist, anti-modern traditionalists and authoritarian pro-big business populists.[43] Political parties in most of these countries are coalitions of personal and group affinities rather than collective efforts based on the common awareness of short- and long-term interests: hence fragmentation, divisiveness, political convulsions and instability.[44] One reason for the rise of populist, potentially fundamentalist movements is the presence of the paternalistic temptation, the need for protection against the destabilising effects of the transition to market and competition. Another significant factor is the perception that the civic-romantic stage of the revolution is over and that currently the bureaucracy is intent upon consolidating its privileges. One also notices the transformation of initially self-described liberal formations into conservative, big business friendly, often authoritarian-populist ones (see the case of Hungary's FIDESZ and its leader, Viktor Orban).

5. Tyranny of the Majority

Political reform in all these post-communist societies has not gone far enough in creating and safely protecting the counter-majoritarian institutions (independent media, market economy, political parties) that would diminish the threat of new authoritarian experiments catering to the subliminal, but powerful egalitarian-populist sentiments.[45] The main dangers are the formulae linked to statism, clericalism, religious fundamentalism, ethnocentrism and militaristic fascism. These themes appear clearly in the discourse of the ethno-religious fundamentalism in countries like Romania, Serbia and Russia.[46] The key question therefore is linked to the risks for further political fragmentation ('Balkanisation') in the region, with the more developed cases (Poland, Hungary, Baltic states, the Czech Republic) developing a culture of impersonal democratic procedures (a genuine civic culture), whereas the Southern tier becomes increasingly beset by what Jowitt refers to as movements of rage.[47] Here the role of Euro-Atlantic institutions is paramount: South-East European countries need to be integrated in various international structures that would encourage the democratic trends and deprive the illiberal forces of their political and symbolic ammunition ('the West despises us', 'we truly do not belong to the West' and so on). Passive attitudes and indifference of Western powers to political and economic developments in the less successful part of post-communist Europe can result in the failure of precarious but nonetheless real pluralist experiments.

6. A Crisis of Values, Authority and Accountability

The weakness of the political parties is primarily determined by *the general crisis of values and authority* and the no less widespread scepticism regarding a *culture of deliberation*. There is a need for 'social glue' and the existing formations have failed to imagine such ingredients for the consensus needed in order to generate 'constitutional patriotism'. Instead, there is the feeling of a 'betrayal of the politicians' and a quest for 'the new purity'. What is the meaning of the left–right dichotomy when the ex-communists often carry out programmes as inclement for their supporters as the execrated free marketeers? In the words of a disaffected Polish citizen: 'I voted for the communists, but they cheated and lied to us. It's much worse under the former communists than it ever was under the center-right governments.'[48] We deal with the same impotent fury against the failure of the state to behave as a 'good father', part of a patrimonial legacy that is characteristic, to different degrees, of all these societies (less so perhaps in Bohemia). Peter Reddaway labelled this a yearning for the state as a 'nanny'.[49] For instance, it is not for Ceaușescu that Romanians are expressing their regrets, but rather for the age of predictability and frozen stability, when the party-state was taking care of everything. For many, the jump into freedom has turned out to be excruciatingly painful. What has disappeared is the certainty about the limits of the permissible, the petrified social ceremonies when the individual anticipated exactly his or her life itinerary. The former prisoners are now free to choose between alternative futures, and this choice is difficult for many of them.

7. No Peace without Justice

The ideological syncretism of 'Stalino-fascism' ('red-brown') has capitalised on the delays in the exercise of political justice. In reality, the moment for such an approach was universally missed, even at the level of a genuine historical debate.[50] In Russia, the much ado about the 'trial of the old party' has not resulted in anything significant, beside the initial perverse effect of Vladimir Zhirinovsky's collecting the votes of the banned Leninists and later the rise of Gennady Zyuganov's national Bolshevik Communist Party of the Russian Federation – Zyuganov's national Bolshevism. Demagogy, overblown rhetoric, the continuous indulgence in scapegoating, as well as fictitious boundaries between 'martyrs' and 'criminals' undermine the legitimacy of the existing institutions and allow the rise of ethnocentrism. This repression of a public discussion is bound to fuel discontent and frustrations, thus encouraging yet more demagogues and mafiosi.[51] Instead of lucid analyses of the past, new mythologies are created to explain the current predicament: foreign conspiracies, the 'endangered national interest', and vindictive references to the need for 'purification through retribution'.

8. The Fragility of the Political Class

Delays in the coalescence of a political class are linked to the weakness of a democratic core-elite: political values remain still very vague, programmes tend to overlap and corruption is rampant. Think of the short life expectancy of most political parties in the region. In fact, most of the parties that were dominant in the first five years after the collapse have either lost electoral significance (for example, Hungary's Magyar Democratic Forum, or, after the elections in November 2000, the National Peasant Christian and Democratic Party, once the pillar of Romania's anti-communist coalition), or significantly altered their orientations and allegiances (such as FIDESZ). This is particularly dangerous in Russia where there is a conspicuous absence of political competition between ideologically defined and distinct parties (after all, Vladimir Putin's background says nothing about his preferences for one or another Russian political party). In Peronista-style politics, Putin (but also other post-communist leaders) can migrate from one to another political formation in terms for electoral needs rather than because of genuine ideological affinities.

9. The Individualistic versus Communitarian Values Split

The political space is still extremely volatile, and the ideological labels conceal at least as much as they reveal. The urgent choice is between personalities, parties and movements that favour individualism, open society, risk-taking, as against those who promise security within the homogenous (and mythological) environment of the ethnic community. Politically, the most important sectors to be reformed are the legal and the military ones: as long as property rights are not fully guaranteed, economic reforms cannot really succeed. Strategy is as important as tactics, and the will to reform is as important as the articulation of concrete goals. The conflict takes place between the advocates of the homogenising (mythologically instituted and constructed) nation/state, aiming to create an ethnically pure community, and those who believe in the right to diversity, the right to think and act differently.

CONCLUSION

Post-communist democratic transitions have ushered in an ambivalent situation: on the one hand, a state of confusion and uncertainty; on the other, a strong need to be accepted into the 'club' and redesign the contours of what we call Europe. As noted above, some countries have managed to construct credible liberal institutions and viable markets. Others, and arguably most, have not transcended their historical legacies: democratic forms (institutions, discourses, practices) have emerged, but they are still perfunctory. This is not a cultural deterministic argument, but rather a recognition of the enduring power of symbolic, political and moral traditions, as well as an admission of the fact that so far the West has not made the great economic efforts that could speed up the growth of local middle classes and with them the consolidation of liberal values (think of the gigantic support for Greece, Portugal and Spain in the late 1970s).[52] East European political cultures remain thus heavily indebted to the ideological age: symbols, myths, rationalised miracles, liturgist nationalisms and teleological pretence have developed after the short-lived 'post-modern' interlude of the revolutions of 1989. And with them, the politics of emotion, unreason, hostility, anger and unavowed, unbearable shame. This is indeed the politics of rancorous marginality, 'cultural despair' and convulsive impotence that the nascent democratic (dis)order can barely contain. The fate of Yugoslavia thus tells much about the infinite capacity of elites in these societies to reinvent their past fallacies and restore them to the rank of new national religions in the attempt to maintain and expand their hold on power. As Slovene social philosopher Slavoj Zizek argues, the issue is who and under what circumstances will be accepted as part of the 'West': 'what is at stake in contemporary post-socialist states is the struggle for one's own place: who will be admitted – integrated into the developed capitalist order – and who will be excluded?'[53]

It is therefore better to look into the real pitfalls and avoid them, rather than simply fall back on the comforting notion of an 'ultimate liberal triumph'. Indeed, what we deal with is both the gains, but also the fragility and vulnerability of liberalism in the region; the backwardness, delays and distortions of modernity, and the rise of majoritarian, neo-plebiscitarian parties and movements.[54] Against this background, one can easily imagine the advent of political demagogues whose unique loyalty would be to their own luck, glory and power. The versatility and free convertibility of political beliefs can assure individual fame and power, but it can never construct legitimate institutions and civic virtues.

The good news is that the ongoing transitions take place simultaneously with the reinvention of Europe, and that the ideal of a united Europe is one of the most contagious and magnetic models these countries have ever dealt with. At the same time, one does not need to be a Eurosceptic in order to agree with the following realistic assessment:

> If Europe is to work, if Eastern Europe and Russia are to be brought into the modern world, if Germany is to remain integrated as a peaceful and harmonious part of Europe, then something more than the mere repetition of a few stock phrases – privatisation, democratisation, let markets work, abandon inefficient industries – will be required. What will be needed, as Havel wrote recently, is faith in the morality of the original Western liberal ideal. ... If Western Europe as a whole does not join in a great and self-confident effort to ensure the triumph of liberal values and policies, then Europe will not work.[55]

As it enters the twenty-first century, Europe finds itself at a crossroads: after many decades of division, fragmentation, bloody ethnic, civil and ideological wars, the continent has finally the chance to overcome these troubling legacies and move in the direction of peaceful co-operation and integration. Resurrecting the demons of the past and engaging in the destructively venomous politics of ethnic or religious feuds could destroy these promising prospects. More than ever, it is up to the political elites and the civic forces of both the emerging and consolidated democracies to stand up against populist forces and defend the values that inspired the revolutions of 1989: freedom, dignity and a united European destiny.

NOTES

A draft of this paper was initially presented at the session on 'Nation, Democracy, and the State', of the Reflection Group on 'Diversity and Unity in the Enlarged European Union: What Influences the Process of Transition and Adaptation in Central and Eastern Europe', jointly organised by the Robert Schuman Center. European University Institute, Florence, and the Forward Studies Unit, European Commission, Brussels, 1–2 March 2001. The author is grateful to the members of the Reflection Group for extremely thoughtful and stimulating suggestions. Special thanks to Professor Judy Batt, University of Birmingham, UK, for her excellent comments. Professor Ilya Prizel, University of Pittsburgh, kindly read the revised version of the text and made helpful suggestions. I completed the text during my stay as a Public Policy Scholar at the Woodrow Wilson International Center for Scholars in Washington, DC, in the summer of 2001. Special thanks to my assistant Luke Murry for research and editorial help.

1. See Jan Urban, 'Europe's Darkest Scenario', *Washington Post*, Outlook Section, 11 Oct. 1992, pp.1–2; G.M. Tamás 'Post-Fascism', *East European Constitutional Review* 9/3 (Summer 2000), pp.48–56; G.M. Tamás, 'Victory Defeated', *Journal of Democracy* 10/1 (Jan. 1999), pp.63–8. For a less pessimistic approach to the legacies of 1989, see Vladimir Tismaneanu, 'Reassessing the Revolutions of 1989', *Journal of Democracy* 10/1 (Jan. 1999), pp.69–73.
2. See John Tagliabue, 'On Top in Bulgaria: New Premier is the Old King', *New York Times*, 15 July 2001, p.A4.
3. In the apt words of Roger Cohen, one of the best observers of the emerging trends in the post-Cold War European political and cultural landscape, 'the journey from Bosnia to Berlin to The Hague is an education in how tired Europe really is of war, tired of the trampling of people and their displacement, perhaps tired altogether after the havoc of the last 100 years. If this weary continent is now able to muster an aim, an idea, a vision, it is to put an end to conflict, division and ethnic oppression on its soil'. See Roger Cohen, 'From Bosnia to Berlin to The Hague: On a Road to a Continent's Future', *New York Times*, 15 July 2001, 'Week in Review' section, p.7.
4. In this respect, the Polish soul-searching discussion on the Jedwabne massacre in July 1941, and the readiness of the top political elite to admit responsibility for that tragic moment in the history of Polish–Jewish relations, suggest that a democratic environment is a premise for a much-needed demystification of the past. See Ian Fisher, 'At Site of Massacre, Polish Leader Asks Jews for Forgiveness', *New York Times*, 11 July 2001, p.A1 and A4. Not everybody in Poland has been so forthcoming as President Aleksander Kwasniewski in recognising collective responsibility (not collective guilt). High-level figures of the Catholic clergy have spelled out positions reminiscent of the old anti-Semitic 'Judeo-Communist' stereotype. As a whole, however, the Polish political and historical discussion linked to Jedwabne has been strikingly mature and free of innuendo and prejudice. See Istvan Deak's excellent analysis, 'Heroes and Victims', *New York Review of Books*, 31 May 2001, pp.51–6.
5. See Jacques Rupnik. 'The Post-Communist Divide', *Journal of Democracy* 10/1 (Jan. 1999), pp.57–62.
6. For the indulgence in a politics of redemption and the uses of political hysteria in pre-communist East-Central Europe, see István Bibo, 'The Distress of the East European Small States', in *Democracy, Revolution, Self-Determination: Selected Writings* (Boulder, CO: Social Science Monographs, distributed by Columbia University Press 1991), pp.13–87.
7. The main proponents of this vision of Central Europe in the 1970s and 1980s were Milan Kundera (on 'The Tragedy of Central Europe') and György Konrád (on *Antipolitics*); both views are discussed in my *The Crisis of Marxist Ideology in Eastern Europe: The Poverty of Utopia* (London: Routledge 1988).
8. See Benjamin R. Barber, 'Globalism Nightmare or Global Civil Society', in *Freedom in the World: The Annual Survey of Political Rights and Civil Liberties, 2000–2001* (New York: Freedom House, and New Brunswick, Transaction Publishers 2001), pp.17–25; for the impact of political and cultural past experiences on the post-communist transitions, see Beverley Crawford and Arend Lijphart (eds.), *Liberalization and Leninist Legacies: Comparative Perspectives on Democratic Transitions* (Berkeley: University of California Press 1997); on prospects for liberalism in the region, with a special focus on Poland, see Jerzy Szacki, *Liberalism After Communism* (Budapest: Central European University Press 1997).

9. See Alexander Stille, 'Making Way for Berlusconi', *New York Review of Books*, 21 June 2001, pp.73–4.
10. See Philip Birzulis, 'Out of Tune: Latvia and Lithuania Feud Over Folk Songs', *Business Central Europe* (July/Aug. 2001), p.41.
11. See Suzanne Daley, 'French Premier Opposes German Plan for Europe', *New York Times*, 29 May 2001.
12. See Vladimir Tismaneanu and Gail Kligman, 'Romania's First Post-Communist Decade: From Iliescu to Iliescu', *East European Constitutional Review* 10/1 (Winter 2001), pp.78–85.
13. See Adam Michnik, 'The Velvet Restoration', in Vladimir Tismaneanu (ed.), *Revolutions of 1989* (London: Routledge 1999), pp.244–51.
14. See Vladimir Tismaneanu, *Fantasies of Salvation: Democracy, Nationalism and Myth in Post-Communist Europe* (Princeton, NJ: Princeton University Press 1998).
15. See Katherine Verdery, 'What Was Socialism and Why Did It Fall', in Vladimir Tismaneanu (ed.), *The Revolutions of 1989* (London and New York: Routledge 1999), pp.63–88.
16. See Giuseppe De Palma, 'Legitimation from the Top to Civil Society: Politico-Cultural Change in Eastern Europe', *World Politics* 44/1 (Oct. 1991), pp.49–80; Eric Hobsbawm, 'The New Threat to History', *New York Review of Books*, 16 Dec. 1993, pp.62–4.
17. One might say that the real problem about East-Central Europe is the desperate search for and manufacture of ideology rather than ethics. Ironically, the blatant amorality of the Leninist age was followed by a widespread distrust of ethical values, a flight from individual responsibility and a repudiation of genuine political commitments. Thus, and paradoxically, those who are the beneficiaries of the new freedoms (the successful business people) who are politically apathetic.
18. See S.N. Eisenstadt, 'The Breakdown of Communist Regimes', *Daedalus* 121/2 (Spring 1992), p.35, reprinted in Tismaneanu (ed.), *The Revolutions of 1999*, pp.89–107.
19. For an excellent discussion on nationalism see Tzvetan Todorov, *On Human Diversity: Nationalism, Racism and Exoticism in French Thought* (Cambridge, MA: Harvard University Press 1993).
20. External support for democratic developments has been crucial in the case of Russia, however, and the West's failure to launch a Marshall Plan initiative hampered the much-needed transition from the plundering of the state resources through nomenklatura privatisation into what George Soros calls legitimate capitalism. See George Soros, 'Who Lost Russia?', *New York Review of Books*, 13 April 2000, pp.10–18. For faltering (failed) transitions, see the special section edited by Kazimierz Poznanski, *East European Politics and Society* 15/2 (2001).
21. See Ralf Dahrendorf, *Reflections on the Revolution in Europe* (New York: Random House 1991) and his *After 1989: Morals, Revolutions, and Civil Society* (New York: St Martin's Press 1997).
22. See the special issue of *East European Politics and Societies* 13/2 (Spring 1999), especially pieces by Valereie Bunce, Daniel Chirot, Grzegorz Ekiert, Gail Kligman, Katherine Verdery; and Sorin Antohi and Vladimir Tismaneanu (eds.), *Between Past and Future: The Revolutions of 1989 and Their Aftermath* (Budapest: Central European University Press 2000).
23. Think of former Croat president Franjo Tudjman, Romania's Ion Iliescu, or Ukraine's Leonid Kuchma. For Latin American disillusionment with leftist radicalism, see Jorge Castañeda, *Utopia Unarmed: The Latin American Left After the Cold War* (New York: Knopf 1993).
24. See Daniel Chirot, *Modern Tyrants: The Power and Prevalence of Evil in Our Age* (New York: Free Press 1994), p.251.
25. Julia Kristeva is thus right to insist: 'The problem of the twentieth century was and remains the rehabilitation of the political. An impossible task? A useless task? Hitler and Stalin perverted the project into a deathly totalitarianism. The collapse of communism in Eastern Europe, which calls into question, beyond socialism, the very basis of the democratic governments that stemmed from the French Revolution, demands that one rethink that basis so that the twenty-first century not be the reactionary domain of fundamentalism, religious illusions, and ethnic wars.' See Julia Kristeva, *Nations Without Nationalism* (New York: Columbia University Press 1993), pp.68–9.
26. For the concept of uncertainty, see Valerie Bunce and Maria Csanadi, 'Uncertainty in the Transition: Post-Communism in Hungary', *East European Politics and Societies* 7/2 (Spring 1993), pp.240–75.

27. See Tony Judt, 'Tale From Vienna Woods', *New York Review of Books* 47, Issue 5, pp.8–9; also Marc Howard's contribution to the symposium on 'Post-Cold War European Populism', *East European Politics and Societies* 15/1 (Spring 2001).
28. De Michelis quoted in Nathan Gardels, 'From Machiavelli to Zeffirelli', *Washington Post* (Outlook Section), 10 April 1994.
29. This 'synchronisation' was the thrust of inter-war Romanian liberal theorist Eugen Lovinescu's approach to the country's modernisation.
30. See Daniel Chirot, 'Liberty or Prelude to New Disasters? The Prospects for Post-Revolutionary Central and Eastern Europe', paper presented at the conference 'Legacies of the Collapse of Marxism', organised by the International Institute, George Mason University, Fairfax, Virginia, and Institute for European, Russian and Eurasian Studies, George Washington University, Washington DC, 22–25 March 1992.
31. See Roger Griffin (ed.), *International Fascism: Theories, Causes and the New Consensus* (London: Arnold 1998); and Sabrina Ramet (ed.), *The Radical Right After Communism* (University Park: Penn State University Press 1999).
32. See Bruce Ackerman, *The Future of the Liberal Revolution* (New Haven: Yale University Press 1992).
33. About tribalism as the barbaric component lying at the core of modernity, see Hannah Arendt, especially in *The Origins of Totalitarianism* (New York: Meridian Books 1958), and the whole critique of Enlightenment by Frankfurt School theorists Theodor W. Adorno and Max Horkheimer – see Wolf Lepenies, 'The Future of Intellectuals', *Partisan Review* 1 (Winter 1994), pp.111–19. This argument is important in the light of the widespread tendency to posit a distinction between the dark, unpredictable, South-Eastern Europe, almost inherently irrational and violent, and Central Europe, presumably more able to articulate and internalise the discourse of reason.
34. Here we have to remember Ken Jowitt's apposite warning: 'Liberal capitalist democracy has aroused a heterogeneous set of opponents: Romantic poets, Persian ayatollahs, the Roman Catholic Church, and fascists. For all the real and massive differences that separate these oppositions, one can detect a shared critique. Liberal capitalist democracy is scorned for an inordinate emphasis on individual materialism, technical achievement, and rationality … [and] for undervaluing the essential collective dimension of human existence [and the] human need for security.' See Ken Jowitt, 'The New World Disorder', *Journal of Democracy* 2/1 (Winter 1991), pp.16–17, and his *New World Disorder: The Leninist Extinction* (Berkeley and Los Angeles: University of California Press 1992).
35. See Václav Havel, 'Post-Communist Nightmare', *The New York Review of Books*, 27 May 1993, p.8.
36. See John Rawls' discussion of criteria for assessing civic freedom and the idea of a well-ordered society in *Political Liberalism* (New York: Columbia University Press 1993), pp.30–40.
37. Martin Palous, 'Post-Totalitarian Politics and European Philosophy', *Public Affairs Quarterly* 7/2 (April 1993), pp.162–3.
38. Personal interview with Adam Michnik, Warsaw, May 2000.
39. See Albert Hirschman's analysis of the 'perversity argument' in his *The Rhetoric of Reaction: Perversity, Futility, Jeopardy* (Cambridge, MA: Harvard University Press, 1991).
40. Focusing on Latin America, Jorge Castañeda captures well this post-Cold War dilemma: 'The left found itself in a no-win situation. Either it stuck to its guns – which were not really its own, but were foisted on it – and defended the indefensible; a state-run, closed, subsidised economy in a world in which such a notion seemed totally obsolete; or it turned around and supported the opposite, apparently modern, competitive, free-market course. In that case it ended up imitating – or being assimilated by – the right and losing its raison d'être.' See Castañeda, *Utopia Unarmed*, p.247.
41. For the former communists, see Andrew Nagorski, *The Birth of Freedom: Shaping Lives and Societies in the New Eastern Europe* (New York: Simon and Schuster 1993), pp.55–91, and Georges Mink and Jean-Claude Szurek, *La grande conversion: Le destin des communists en Europe de l'Est* (Partis: Ed. du Seuil 1999).
42. See Ilya Prizel, 'Nationalism in Post-Communist Russia: From Resignation to Anger', in Antohi and Tismaneanu (eds.), *Between Past and Future*, pp.332–56.
43. For the latter trend, see the transmogrification of FIDESZ in recent years. The most important point about this new blending of economic liberalism and political

authoritarianism is that it jeopardises the still precarious pluralist institutions. For an analysis of party evolutions in the region, see Paul G. Lewis, *Political Parties in Post-Communist Europe* (London and New York: Routledge 2000).

44. For the global impact, in terms of norms definition, see James N. Rosenau, *Turbulence in World Politics: A Theory of Change and Continuity* (Princeton: Princeton University Press 1990).
45. See Andrew Arato, 'Revolution, Restoration and Legitimization: Ideological Problems of the Transition from State Socialism', in Michael D. Kennedy (ed.), *Envisioning Eastern Europe: Post-Communist Cultural Studies* (Ann Arbor: University of Michigan Press 1994), pp.180–246.
46. For the revival of radical right in Romania, see Vladimir Tismaneanu and Dan Pavel, 'Romania's Mystical Revolutionaries: The Generation of Angst and Adventure Revisited', *East European Politics and Societies* 8/3 (Fall 1994), pp.402–38; for the rehabilitation of the former Iron Guard doctrinaires, see Vladimir Tismaneanu, 'The Ecstasy of Nihilism: E.M. Cioran's Transfiguration', in Edith Kurzweil (ed.), *A Partisan Century: Political Writings from Partisan Review* (New York: Columbia University Press 1996), pp.383–92.
47. Jowitt, *New World Disorder*.
48. See 'Poles Hold March Over New Budget', *New York Times*, 10 Feb. 1994. This was one of the many voices protesting the austerity budget in February 1994 in what turned out to be the largest anti-government demonstration since the collapse of communism (about 30,000). For the cultural and ideological confrontations in post-communist Poland, see Marcin Frybes and Patrick Michel, *Après le communisme: Mythes et légendes de la Pologne contemporaine* (Paris: Bayard Editions 1996).
49. See Peter Reddaway, 'Russia on the Brink', *The New York Review of Books*, 28 Jan. 1993, pp.30–35. Reddaway notices a multi-layered feeling of moral and spiritual injury related to loss of empire and damaged identity: 'Emotional wounds as deep as these tend to breed anger, hatred, self-disgust and aggressiveness. Such emotions can only improve the political prospects for the nationalists and neo-communists, at any rate for a time.' Needless to add, in the meantime, Reddaway has become even more pessimistic. See Peter Reddaway and Dmitri Glinski, *The Tragedy of Russia's Reforms: Market Bolshevism Against Democracy* (Washington, DC: US Institute of Peace 2001).
50. See Arpad Göncz, 'Breaking the Vicious Circle', *Common Knowledge* 2/1 (Spring 1993), pp.1–5; see also 'Cette etrange epoque postcommuniste: Adam Michnik s'entretient avec Vaclav Havel', in Georges Mink and Jean-Charles Szurek, *Cet etrange post-communisme: Rupture et transition en Europe centrale et orientale* (Paris: Presses du CNRS/La découverte 1992), pp.17–48.
51. The immense power of these new mafiosi has become a challenge second to none to the establishment of the rule of law in Russia: see K.S. Karol, 'Moscou sous la loi des gangs', *Le Nouvel Observateur* (Paris), 17–23 March 1994, pp.36–7, and Steven Handelman, *Comrade Criminal: Russia's New Mafiya* (New Haven: Yale University Press 1997).
52. See, for the current reservations regarding the financial burden of EU Eastward enlargement, William Drozdiak, 'Another Wall for East Europeans: Admission to EU Faces New Obstacles as Members Express Concern About Cost', *Washington Post*, 27 May 2001, p.A24; for the connection between economics and politics in the European enlargement process, see Laurentiu Stefan-Scalat, 'Romania – A Litmus Test for European Eastward Enlargement', paper presented at the conference 'Quo Vadis, Europa? The Vision and Frontiers of Europe', organised by the Institute for European Studies, Hebrew University, Jerusalem, 22–23 April 2001.
53. See Slavoj Zizek, 'Ethnic Danse Macabre', *The Guardian*, 22 Aug. 1992; for the impact of nationalism and ethnic turmoil on the democratic transitions, see J.J. Brown, *The Grooves of Change: Eastern Europe at the Turn of the Millenium* (Durham: Duke University Press 2001).
54. See Georges Mink's distinctions between 'partis consensuelists, tribunitiens et querelleurs', in his 'Les partis politiques de l'Europe centrale post-communiste: etat des lieux et essai de typologie', *L'europe centrale et orientale en 1992*, Documentation française, pp.21–3.
55. See Daniel Chirot, 'Introduction', in Stephen Hanson and Wilfried Spohn, *Can Europe Work? Germany and the Reconstruction of Post-Communist Societies* (Seattle: University of Washington Press 1995), pp.11–12.

Making Institutions in Central and Eastern Europe, and the Impact of Europe

DARINA MALOVÀ and TIM HAUGHTON

The end of communism in Central and Eastern Europe offered a unique opportunity for institutional redesign. At the heart of much of the initial institutional change in the region was a desire to build modern democratic states, invariably, though not exclusively, following West European templates. Throughout the course of the 1990s, however, a more influential mechanism emerged stimulating institutional convergence in Central and Eastern Europe: the European Union (EU). The desire of countries in Central and Eastern Europe (CEE) to join Europe's best and wealthiest club helped engender the replication of Western European institutions in CEE, reminiscent of the process of institutional unification which took place in non-Communist Europe after World War Two. The process of institutional convergence in CEE countries has not been encouraged and undertaken to achieve institutional uniformity, rather the aims have been the establishment of democratic forms of government and democracy as the only game in town, allowing room for institutional diversity within a democratic framework.

Even a cursory examination of constitutional changes in Central and Eastern Europe reveals several commonalties in overall institutional design. The prevailing institutional model involves parliamentary democracy, a proportional representation electoral system, multiparty systems, coalition governments and constitutional review. During the last decade several applicant countries have shifted towards this pattern, even if their constitutions and electoral laws originally provided for some forms of mixed types of government, such as semi-presidentialism and mixed electoral formulae. The adoption of the West European institutional model has been helpful in the process of democratic consolidation in CEE countries by promoting the necessary values and habits such as self-limitation, bargaining, reciprocity and feedback.[1]

After a brief discussion of the EU's membership criteria, this study will chart the process of institutional development in CEE in the past decade, particularly with regard to the separation of powers. Europe has played an important role in institutional development, although it is wise to bear in mind Helen Wallace's distinction between 'Europeanisation' (the adoption of West European models) and 'EU-isation' (changes driven by the desire for EU membership).[2] The whole gamut of institutional change (incorporating the separation of powers, changes in the forms of executive leadership, parliamentary reform, the introduction and modification of electoral systems, judicial review and the development of informal rules), however, has also been driven by other factors such as domestic political concerns.

THE REQUIREMENTS FOR THOSE WHO WISH TO JOIN THE CLUB

Before embarking on an attempt to chart the progress of institutionalisation in CEE countries, it is worth reviewing briefly the EU's membership requirements. To join any club applicants have to demonstrate they are suitable members. The EU is no exception. At the Copenhagen European Council in June 1993, the EU outlined the political criteria for membership. Applicants were required to demonstrate the 'stability of institutions guaranteeing democracy, the rule of law, human rights and respect for and protection of minorities'.[3] The criteria were broad and did not prescribe any particular institutional model. Indeed, given the variety of institutional forms between different EU member states such as France, Germany and the United Kingdom, it would have been distinctly odd for the EU to have demanded that applicant nations conform to a specific institutional model.

The EU's criteria therefore provided ample room for institutional variation, allowing CEE countries to establish democratic institutions in accordance with their own political traditions and culture. Initially, a range of different formal institutions and political rules emerged, but a decade on from the revolutions of 1989 many commonalities in the general political set-up among the applicant countries are discernible. Moreover, the key state institutions have come to resemble those of Western Europe. This process of institutional convergence is likely to contribute to overall democratisation and stability on the continent, because it increases predictability, that is, political actors in CEE are increasingly expected to behave at the state level according to the democratic rules of the game. At the same time, this convergence provides sufficient room for institutional diversity at lower levels.

The requirements for joining the EU in the current decade differ from previous enlargements, most notably the Southern European enlargement of the 1980s, because membership clearly depends not just on economic factors, but on political conditions which have become explicit requirements of entry. In the cases of Greece, Portugal and Spain, European Community membership was considered part of the process of democratic consolidation rather than a reward for achieving consolidation.

MAPPING THE PROCESS OF INSTITUTIONALISATION IN CENTRAL AND EASTERN EUROPE

Although political actors formulate policies and make decisions, they do so through institutional frameworks. Political institutions matter because they provide agency with formative incentives and disincentives that shape both the strategies pursued and the goals achieved.[4] Nonetheless, it should be emphasised that institutional frameworks are not conjured out of thin air, they are created by political actors and are the product of bargaining and negotiation. A major shift in power relations may therefore lead to modifications, changes or even a drastic overhaul of an institutional framework. Throughout Central and Eastern Europe in the past decade there has been a decrease in the occurrence of major institutional change, which has allowed the constitutional arrangements to acquire stability and value. What change there has been has resulted in a trend of institutional framework convergence across the region.

In order for a social arrangement to be called an 'institution', two conditions have to be met. First, institutions play a socialising role in that they prescribe desirable and proscribe undesirable behaviour. In other words, they restrict modes of actions (negative part) and reward preferable activities (positive part). Second, institutions not only perform the role of 'congruent socialisation'[5] but they should also function correctly, that is, they should be able to solve problems they were created to cope with. In short, institutions impose obligations upon actors as well as produce policy outcomes.

The initial constitution making process in CEE yielded a wide variety of constitutional structures. This diversity was a product of the inputs into the decision making process. Inherited structures, historical experiences, political actors' preferences during the transition, deal sweeteners during the round-table talks, a concern for historical continuity – in Central and Eastern Europe's case, 'the European inheritance of parliamentarism'[6] – and the pull of the European Union all played their part. The output of each constitution making process was determined by the differing mix of these ingredients in CEE countries. The constitution makers were not operating on a *tabula rasa*, however: constitutions had existed before 1989, even if, under communist rule, they were reduced to little more than extensions of Communist party programmes designed to lend a 'veneer of legality to monocratic rule'.[7] In framing the institutional structure politicians looked to three models: the 'distant past', the modern West and the 'accomplishments of the immediate past of the state socialist system'.[8]

The largely formal and empty texts of the communist times have been replaced with democratic constitutions on the Western model. Concepts at the heart of all democracies such as the division of powers and human rights were enshrined in these documents. The constitutions established the guiding principles regulating the rules and procedures through which actual policy outcomes are reached. These rules of the game are enshrined in the constitutions and invariably require specific procedures such as constitutional assemblies and extraordinary majorities in order to be changed. Although the desire to construct democracies was at the heart of much constitution making in CEE in the early 1990s, it is worth reiterating that these constitutions were drawn up not by saints, but by politicians driven in part by their own personal political interests. Framers may have offered impartial arguments based on concepts such as the public good, individual rights or democracy, but the motivation may have had much to do with their own self-interest and 'the position in which politicians find themselves at the time of design'.[9] As an outcome of a bargaining process, constitutions therefore 'resemble bundles of compromises rather than acts of legal professionalism'.[10] Nevertheless, despite their human frailties political players have been able to solve institutional conflicts under valid rules of the game – a sign of their commitment to democratic procedure.

The Separation of Powers

Many CEE countries began the process of the institutionalisation of democracy with vaguely drafted constitutions. The provisions specifying the separation of powers in particular tended to be ambiguous.[11] Such ambiguity, allowing varying interpretation, allied with weak checks and balances, was a recipe for outcomes not conducive to the consolidation of democratic polities. Hence, some constitutions, instead of being capable of solving political crises, themselves became the source of political conflicts. The position, role and powers of the presidency, for instance, have led to countless controversies. In part this may be a legacy of the communist tradition of (at least nominal) collective leadership. With the exception of Czechoslovakia and Romania a single head of state was, to some extent, an institutional novelty.

Poland has witnessed significant shifts in the relative positions of president, government and parliament throughout the 1990s.[12] With at least half a nod towards Poland's institutional history, but also an outcome of the bargaining process, the 1989 round table discussions created a strong, but indirectly elected president. The head of state was accorded powers to veto legislation with a two-thirds override requirement for both houses of parliament, to dissolve the legislature, and gave the office holder executive control over defence and foreign policy ministerial appointments. Because of Lech Walesa's desire to increase his power he pushed for a more powerful presidency. Parliament rejected Walesa's constitutional plans which envisaged a shift in power in favour of the head of state. In fact the balance of power shifted in the other direction. Under first the so-called 'Little Constitution' in 1992 and then more significantly the 1997 Constitution the powers of the cabinet and the prime minister increased at the expense of the president. The president retains veto power, but can be overridden by a majority of three-fifths of MPs, not two-thirds, as in the previous constitution. The presidential power to dissolve parliament was also curtailed. S/he can do so only when parliament fails to enact the budget within four months and when the government is unable to form a cabinet. In addition, presidential power over the nomination of ministers was curtailed. Polish constitutional development, therefore, provides a good example of a shift from a hybrid system towards a more clear-cut parliamentary democracy. Although Poland ended up with a balance of power between president, prime minister and parliament typical of many EU members, the cause appears more likely to be found in personalities and internal political debates and arguments than in any attempt to adopt a European model.

Slovakia's hastily drafted constitution of 1992 incorporated countless vague and contradictory rules. Although most of the provisions were typical of parliamentary democracies, several unclear powers, typical of semi-presidential systems, were vested in the presidency. Thanks in part to the lack of constitutional clarity, but also to an almost visceral hatred between the two office holders, President Michal Kovac and Prime Minister Vladimir Meciar, Slovakia experienced tense relations between prime minister and president in the mid-1990s. In January 1999, the new parliament passed an amendment to the Constitution, which not only provided for direct elections of the president, but also limited the head of state's power. The president, for instance, lost his/her power to preside over cabinet meetings and to intervene in the process of forming a government, and may impose a veto only on regular laws, not on constitutional laws –

that is, laws passed by a three-fifths majority in parliament. As in the Polish case it is hard to argue that the motivation for these constitutional changes was exclusively the EU. The constitutional amendment passed in 1999 had more to do with the outcome of the coalition formation discussions in late 1998 and a desire to avoid a repeat of the Slovak parliament's failure to elect a new president after Kovac's term had expired in March 1993, leaving the country without a president.

A process of constitutional convergence is discernible across the region. Most CEE constitutions now have a weak head of state, even where the president is directly elected, who plays mostly a symbolic role and intervenes in politics only in explicitly defined cases to limit institutional conflicts. A notable exception to this trend is Romania, which retains a semi-presidential system based on the French model. Under the 1991 constitution, for instance, the president and not the legislature nominates the prime minister. The lack of clear constitutional rules concerning the dismissal of the prime minister has led to political disputes. While the 1991 dismissal of Petre Roman by President Illiescu did not raise controversy, the 1999 removal of Prime Minister Radu Vasile by President Constantinescu has provoked institutional disagreement, which the Constitutional Court refused to interpret. Nonetheless, a more typical development has been that witnessed by Romania's southern neighbour Bulgaria. Through institutional trials and tribulations in the early 1990s, particularly the severe tensions between President Zhelyu Zhelev and Prime Ministers Philip Dimitrov and Ljuben Berov,[13] Bulgaria appears to have found a balance of power through a process of simultaneous learning.

Executive Leadership

In general, constitutions in CEE give little guidance about the organisation of cabinets. Usually constitutions state that decisions are to be taken collectively or they assign a particular role to the prime minister. This situation is not, however, unique to CEE polities. Cabinet decision making in Western Europe is often more a matter of practices than of constitutional rules. Parliaments play an important role in cabinet formation thanks to the fact that in most CEE countries newly formed cabinets have to pass some form of parliamentary investiture.[14]

Dependent as it is on the constitutional positions of the president and parliament and the nature and strength of parliamentary parties, the position of prime minister in the matrix of power differs significantly throughout Central and Eastern Europe. Most CEE constitutions provide for a weak prime ministerial leadership, although both the Hungarian and Polish constitutions include provisions strengthening the position of the prime minister. Not everything, however, is down to the wording of the constitutions. The relatively strong position of the premier in the Czech Republic seems to have less to do with the constitutional arrangement and more to do with the political context, particularly the relative stability of the party system, the cohesion and party discipline of the ruling political parties and inter-party co-operation. Moreover, the former Slovak Prime Minister Vladimir Meciar was not averse to ignoring the provisions of the constitution to increase his control over political system.

In addition to constitutional limitations, prime ministers in CEE are also hampered by political limitations on their power. The cabinets they chair are invariably not of their own making. They do not have a free hand to 'hire and fire' ministers. Many CEE prime ministers can be forced to accept parliamentary decisions on the dismissal and appointment of individual ministers. More significantly, the selection of cabinet members is often the result of bargaining between coalition partners rather than a purely prime ministerial decision. In the post-fascist democratic transition in Germany and Spain constitution crafters designed the position of prime minister carefully to help promote stability in the polity, most notably through the introduction of the constructive vote of no-confidence. In contrast, the constitutional arrangement of the executive, and in particular the position of the premier in CEE did not receive as much attention as in the German and Spanish case. Indeed, the relative neglect of the premier's position marks a clear deviation from the Western European model. The failure to devote adequate attention to the position of the prime minister could have significant implications for the future of CEE countries. Stable executives not only assist applicant countries in their quest for EU membership, but they also strengthen the position of member states within the EU structures. Although a sweeping generalisation, it appears clear a strong and united government can achieve more within European structures than a weak and divided one.

There is a general agreement about the poor performance of CEE executives in general.[15] Among the reasons for this dissatisfying functioning of the executive is not so much their weak constitutional powers as a general lack of experience on the part of new ministerial elites. The very structure and organisation of cabinet has been under constant review. Almost every new government has changed the structure of ministers and ministries, the committee systems, and some have also altered procedures of decision making. Such tinkering is not unique to CEE. Western Europe has also indulged in similar amendments, but not to the same extent or with the same frequency.

The nature of coalition government has also complicated cabinet formation and operation. Fragmented and unstable party systems, often accompanied by high polarisation, have hampered the rule of the executive. Moreover, lack of trust among coalition partners has necessitated detailed coalition and policy agreements. Such documents often include not just a description of the spoils of office – which party gets control of which ministry – but also outline policy. Detailed agreements can form the basis of stable government, but as the current (1998–) Slovak government has demonstrated, both differing interpretations of these texts and problems not explicitly dealt with in the documents can cause tensions and difficulties between the coalition partners. In order to resolve difficulties between coalition partners, pre-cabinet bodies such as coalition councils have been instituted. Even the existence of such institutions, however, does not preclude cabinet meetings from degenerating into opportunities for parties to criticise the policies of their partners in government. The Czech Republic has employed an unusual mechanism for promoting stability, the so-called opposition agreement, between the Social Democrats (CSSD) and the Civic Democratic Party (ODS). After the 1998 elections CSSD fell short of an overall parliamentary majority. Rather than form a regular minority government, CSSD leader Milos Zeman signed a pact with his sworn enemy, ODS leader Vaclav Klaus, allowing CSSD to govern in return for policy guarantees and control of important parliamentary bodies. Although the agreement provoked strong hostility among the smaller parties excluded from even a sniff of power, and has at times been awkward for both sides, it has achieved its overriding aim of providing Czechs with a stable government.

In most CEE countries cabinet meetings tend to be lengthy and time consuming procedures, with the exception of Hungary, where a sophisticated hierarchical and multi-level system of government was established, and it is evident that the complicated procedures and relations among coalition parties can work to undermine the administrative capacity of the executive. It may well be that the CEE countries could benefit from assistance or advice from the EU in this regard, particularly in that the political context and the party system cannot be subject to institutional engineering

Executives are dependent on bureaucracies to implement policy. The concept of a 'neutral' state bureaucracy was not prevalent in CEE in the early 1990s. The boundaries between political and administrative appointments have been established only gradually. In the first half of the 1990s, the general pattern of the ruling political parties was to replace as much staff as possible in the state administration, which undermined the overall performance of the government. In response to the constant chopping and changing of bureaucrats, one of the top priorities of the National Accession Partnership Programmes was to pass civil service-related legislation to limit the high turnover of personnel in the state administration and to stabilise the positions and competencies of officials. The aim of such legislation is to foster political independence and reduce the scope for political intervention in the appointment of officials. The EU deserves praise in this regard. Without the EU's pressure it is not clear, most notably in the Czech and Slovak cases, whether political parties would have been willing to pass such legislation. Reform of the state administration aimed at achieving a politically impartial and rationalised bureaucracy is hampered by two factors, however. Firstly, the existing terms and conditions of those officials currently in place; and, secondly, the comparatively low levels of salaries in the public administration compared to the private sector are not attractive for well-educated young people. Low salaries also reinforce the incentives for increased corruption in the state sector.

In contrast to Western Europe, some CEE countries incorporated NGOs in the process of the government, taking over public administration functions normally performed by the government. In Bulgaria, for example, the training of governmental staff was organised by NGOs and not by the state institutions. In Slovakia, some bills were drafted with the assistance of NGOs. The fact that some institution building was undertaken by NGOs suggests that when the state is weak, civil society may take over its functions and act as a democratic consolidator.

The Place of Parliaments

The new constitutions in Central and Eastern Europe tend to accord a greater role for legislatures than most of the recent Western European constitutions, such as the 1949 German Constitution, the 1958 French Constitution or the 1978 Spanish Constitution.[16] The more elevated status of parliaments is in part a product of the legacy of communist rule, when, theoretically at least, the constitutions invested all power in parliament, but part of the explanation is also to be found in the process of democratic transition. In the initial stages of transition parliaments served a dual purpose, not just as an *ordinary* legislature, but also as a constituent assembly. Thanks to their 'institutional self-interest' the constituent assemblies crafted institutions with a more powerful role for the legislature.[17] At the beginning of institutional crafting, for example, the Polish and Romanian parliaments were given the power to override the rulings of the constitutional courts. Whether the relatively exalted status of CEE parliaments compared to their legislative cousins in Western Europe is desirable or a portent of troubles ahead in an enlarged EU is an open question. There are so many variable factors, not least the personalities and party programmes of future parliamentary deputies, that it would be unwise to predict an outcome. The EU would, however, be well advised to think through possible scenarios and either prepare contingency plans and nip possible future problems in the bud.

The choice between a unicameral and bicameral parliament was rather contingent. In so far as a pattern can be observed, it follows that which has been noted in the rest of Europe, with unicameral legislatures existing in countries with small populations. Two of the region's largest countries, Poland and Romania, opted for bicameral legislatures. The decision of the Czechs to institute a Senate had less to do with concerns of size than with historical traditions, institutional self-interest and political bargaining. Slovenia's upper chamber, with its advisory function and recruitment by appointment, appears to be more the legacy of the self-governing regime in the former Yugoslavia than the outcome of considered institutional choice. Whether bicameral or unicameral, parliaments are powerful actors in the political process in CEE, although the extent of their power varies from country to country. Parliaments in CEE countries tend to enjoy many powers over the establishment, replacement and suspension of the executive, judicial bodies and their incumbents. Although the institutional framework creates the parameters of the parliaments' power, the extent to which parliaments can use this power is dependent on non-institutional factors such as the composition of parliament, the party system and party discipline and cohesion.

Thanks to fractious parliaments and unstable coalitions, the legislative process can be long and drawn-out. One might expect unicameral systems to have speedy legislative processes. According to the European Commission's annual reports, the legislative process in most applicant countries has been rather slow, even in those with one chamber parliaments. The reasons vary from country to country. One of the most important is the existence of parliamentary rules and procedures. In most CEE countries, for example, standing orders usually require three readings to adopt any piece of legislation. Each reading takes time.

Absorption of the EU's body of laws, the *acquis communautaire*, is a prerequisite for entry into the club. Incorporating the EU's laws, which run to around 80,000 pages and have been built up over decades, could be a long and laborious process if normal procedures were used. Not only would it demand enormous amounts of legislative time, depriving the countries of CEE of the time needed to deal with domestic laws, it would also put a brake on fulfilling accession aspirations. CEE countries have resolved this problem by instituting shortened procedures for *acquis*-related laws.

In Bulgaria, for example, the National Assembly set up a Council on European Integration, chaired by the Speaker to consider all draft laws related to the adoption of the *acquis*. It is made up of three members from each of the five parliamentary groups, which are represented on an equal and non-proportional basis. Where the Council members agree there is consensus on a draft law, the Council can replace the committees and send a draft law straight to the plenary for a vote, thus speeding up procedures. However, should one parliamentary group object, the draft law must go through the normal procedures. Such a procedure appears wise and well thought-out, enabling rapid incorporation of *acquis*-related laws where general consensus exists, but where initial agreement is absent consensus is valued higher than raw speed. In a similar vein, the Czech Republic's lower chamber has amended its rules of procedure to introduce a fast-track possibility for EU-related laws. Prior to the submission of legislative drafts by the government to the parliament, ministers discuss the matter with the Committee for European Integration.

Slovenia's parliament also treats EU-related laws as a legislative priority and has used extraordinary sessions to speed up their adoption. The European Commission remained critical, complaining that 'the legislative process is still slow and no progress has been made in streamlining the parliamentary process',[18] because every law still requires three readings and *acquis*-related laws are not allowed to jump the legislative queue. All laws are dealt with in the order they are submitted to parliament. Criticism of the slow pace of legislation has stimulated the Slovenes to introduce an accelerated procedure for adopting EU-related laws, where three readings were held within a few days. To legitimise these procedures the ruling political parties pushed for the adoption of a new parliament standing order, which would shorten the current three-reading procedure, and limit the speaking time of parliamentarians. Due to difficulties in obtaining a two-thirds majority in parliament, this attempt to change the current standing order has so far been unsuccessful.

More drastic tactics have been adopted in Romania, where the fragile ruling coalition in the highly fragmented parliament was able to pass only 59 of the 453 bills in 1999. The government has tried to circumvent a parliament with more than its fair share of un-cooperative MPs by issuing extraordinary decrees, which immediately enter into force and need only retrospective approval by parliament. However, the frequent use of this governmental procedure, although backed up by the constitution, may distort the institutionalisation of democratic legislature and weaken the state administrative capacity.

Fast-tracking for EU-related laws also has important consequences for the institutionalisation of democratic norms. Attracted by the lure of joining the club that flows with milk and honey, applicant nations have cast aside the norms typical of democratic legislatures. Regular parliamentary procedure, which provides for several steps in making legislation, ensures that all political forces in the parliament can provide input into the legislative drafting process, but slows down the process. The speedy procedures for the *acquis*-related legislation run the risk of reducing parliaments to little more than rubber stamps and may undermine the overall institutionalisation of parliaments and weaken their legitimacy. In particular, the consolidation of the committee system may suffer, in that fast-tracking tends to bypass committees. Committees play an important role in fostering habits of political bargaining and cross-party co-operation. Fast-tracking will therefore hamper the emergence of such a procedural culture.

The institutional effectiveness of parliament depends in part on the men and women who sit in the chambers. Many of the new parliamentarians in the early 1990s were, by and large, inexperienced in parliamentary affairs. Although the situation has in general improved over the past decade, as the recent Lithuania example showed, the number of inexperienced newcomers can still be high. In the early post-communist days deputies were also hampered by the lack of support staff and general resources, a situation much improved in the past ten years or so. The performance of the parliaments is also dependent on the political context. Parliamentary party discipline and cohesion, or their absence, have complicated matters by sometimes blurring the distinction between government and opposition. Fluid party systems and weak party loyalty amongst deputies result in shifting coalitions and changes in government, a pattern which appears to be particularly prevalent in smaller polities such as the Baltic States and Slovenia.

Parliaments throughout Central and Eastern Europe have begun increasingly to resemble their sister institutions in Western Europe. Legislative effectiveness, organisational articulation and rule abiding patterns of behaviour have been or are being acquired. In terms of organisation, membership and procedures, the institutional capacity of parliaments has been gradually increasing, and this has helped the institutionalisation of democracy in the region.

Electoral Systems

The choice of electoral system is important because it helps to shape a country's party system[19] and consequently also its institutional framework, that is, the composition of the parliament, the form of executive, and the overall profile of executive–legislative relations. The chosen electoral system plays a significant role in explaining the degree of fragmentation of parliaments and thus influences the creation and durability of governments which depend on the enduring confidence of a parliamentary majority. In creating the electoral system a number of choices need to be made. The most obvious choice is that between majoritarian, proportional or mixed formulas, but other issues such as open versus closed party lists, preference voting, thresholds, assembly size, district magnitude and different mechanisms employed to count the votes (Hagenbach-Bischoff/Droop, D'Hondt, STV, Imperiali and so on) are important and can be of significance.[20]

In accordance with the prevailing norms in Western Europe, CEE countries have tended to opt for proportional representation electoral systems rather than using the plurality formula. Hungary and Lithuania with their mixed PR/plurality systems are exceptions to this general trend. Even within PR, however, there are variations. Just as Western European systems differ as to the number and magnitude of constituencies, the existence and type of party list and the methods for counting votes and remainders, so the PR systems instituted in CEE differ from each other. As the Polish experience shows, the introduction of thresholds, for example, can have a 'reductive effect'[21] on the number of parties in parliament and therefore increase governability, but it can also nullify the votes of a significant portion of the electorate. Indeed, in elections in the early 1990s around a quarter of Czechs, Slovaks and Bulgarians voted for parties which failed to cross the respective thresholds. This fact highlights an important broader point. Whatever the constraining effects of the electoral systems might be, these may be mitigated by the degree of institutionalisation of the party system.[22]

The initial decision to opt for PR was in part a desire to emulate Western European democracies, but it was also the product of political traditions, the political bargaining process, an aversion to the idea of one-party rule and the desire to foster political pluralism.[23] With the exceptions of Poland and Bulgaria (which will be discussed below), none of the applicant countries seriously considered a plurality electoral system as a possible solution, although conventional political science wisdom asserts that this arrangement is more likely to enhance political stability in the form of government durability than proportional electoral formulas.

Despite the fact that Poland's 1989 electoral law provided for a plurality system it was soon abandoned. Thanks to the fracture of both major party groupings a new round of electoral system negotiation began. Given the fact that in a fragmented party system no individual actor could hope to benefit from plurality voting rules, most Polish legislators favoured and adopted a party list PR system. The upshot of this new arrangement was a proliferation of parties in parliament and the inability to create a stable government. In response, most legislators backed the introduction of a threshold requirement typical of Western European democracies. One of the unexpected outcomes of this attempt at 'institutional engineering' was the elimination of several post-Solidarity parties who had backed the threshold's introduction from the parliament.

Initially Bulgaria opted for a mixed electoral system combining multi-member district proportional representation with a four per cent threshold and single-member district majoritarian representation. After the Bulgarian Socialist Party (BSP) began losing support, however, the BSP led a successful reform of the process resulting in a closed list, multi-member district proportional representation system which favoured larger parties to the detriment of the smaller splinter parliamentary parties. In both the Polish and Bulgarian examples the decision to move towards proportional systems was largely due to the power balance concerns of domestic politics.

Judicial Review

CEE polities have copied Western European models by instituting judicial review, but they have accorded it a stronger position in their polities. Both constitutional courts and the very concept of constitutional review are almost completely new phenomena in CEE. Only a few of the countries in the region, such as inter-war Czechoslovakia, had pre-communist experience with constitutional courts. Even in the Czechoslovak case, however, it did not play a major role in the political system.

In Western Europe judicial review is a rather contested institution, as it makes non-elected judges politically influential, although there is no mechanism for holding those judges accountable. Why did the CEE political elite and legal experts allocate so much power to small groups of lawyers without instituting any mechanism of accountability? The answer probably lies in the communist experience and the desire for an independent and neutral arbiter. Czechoslovakia's Charter 77 provides an illustrative example. That particular dissident movement was founded explicitly (although other ulterior motives were also present) to highlight the fact that the communist government was not obeying its own laws on human rights. More broadly, emerging from 40 years of communism and into a fluid and uncertain political environment, CEE countries were keen to see the emergence of a body which could solve conflicts about the interpretation of the rules of the game and at the same time protect human rights, including minority rights, which had been neglected and violated in the past.

Although all applicant countries have furnished their polities with a constitutional court, there are some variations. Constitution drafters in several countries perceived the concept of judicial review as contrary to the main idea of popular and parliamentary sovereignty. Poland and Romania, for example, somewhat reluctantly included the constitutional courts in their constitutional designs, and limited their actual powers by allowing a special parliamentary majority the right to overturn the courts' decision.

The stronger version of constitutional courts in CEE has played a prominent role in the consolidation of democracy, as many political and legal disputes between ruling parties and opposition have been settled by constitutional jurisdiction. Their binding decisions have established a minimum but necessary certainty of the rules of the game. Political elites throughout the region have not always agreed on the interpretation of constitutional provisions and have at times tried to use the constitutional courts to resolve arguably non-constitutional political disputes, but throughout Central and Eastern Europe a general acceptance of the courts' rulings has prevailed.

Informal Rules and Unwritten Agreements in the Institutional Framework

The importance of informal rules in the institutional framework has been alluded to earlier, but before concluding it is worth reiterating. Thanks to the multi-party systems and fragmented parliaments in CEE countries, problems are resolved by means of coalition bargaining, including the establishment of informal coalition bodies and formal coalition agreements, cabinet reshuffles and, if all else fails, early elections. Prior to 1989 these processes were mostly unknown in the region and have needed to be learned. However good an institutional structure, informal rules between political actors are essential for the successful functioning of a democratic polity, because not all conflicts can be managed through formal structures. Successful democratic institutionalisation requires an unwritten understanding that the change-over from one government to another will not harm the stability of the democracy and that the new government will continue along the same democratic path.

Towards Even Greater Convergence?

Adoption of the *acquis* is not just significant in terms of its procedural effect. The incorporation of the EU's body of law into the domestic laws of the applicant states is also having a substantive effect on the social and economic policies implemented in CEE. Beyond the elements of what we could dub the first-level institutional design (the meta-rules of the constitution), we may see more convergence on a second level in order to address social and economic problems in accordance with EU law and procedure. Other factors may also play their part here, of course, not least the motive force of 'Europeanisation' (rather than 'EU-isation') to adopt Wallace's terminology again.

We would be wise, however, to add a note of caution on the speed of institutional convergence in CEE. The West European model, for instance, is built on the idea of strong political parties representing the interests of voters and acting as bridges between state and society. In CEE, however, there has been a greater prevalence for parties to articulate an agenda dominated by entry into Western and West European clubs (and the necessary membership requirements) rather than pursue any ideological agenda and/or represent clearly defined sectional interests. More broadly, adopting the West European institutional model involves an adaptation to the values necessary for such a framework to function properly and effectively. Such value adaptation takes time and may require the introduction of unusual short-term solutions.

CONCLUSIONS

Central and Eastern Europe has witnessed significant institutional change since the end of communism. Both Western European models and the EU have played an important role in the process of institutional development, but domestic political factors and the institutional histories of the countries in the region have also been significant. The prevalent institutional model in CEE consists of parliamentary democracy, a proportional representation electoral system, multi-party politics, coalition governments and constitutional review. All applicant states with the exception of Romania have opted for some form of parliamentary system of government, even if their presidents are directly elected. This framework, as Linz and others predicted, has lessened stakes in politics, minimised zero-sum outcomes, and contributed to the consolidation of democracy.[24] Moreover, the adoption of proportional voting systems has limited the chances of majority rule and the emergence of a more adversarial type of politics. It has helped to promote consensus and has taught political leaders of the need to craft and maintain coalitions, even if they have to be embedded in formalised coalition contracts. The reality of the last decade in Central and Eastern Europe has shown that in spite of a plethora of problems the main political actors have, with a few exceptions, demonstrated their respect for democracy and the rule of law, making their countries reliable partners for EU accession. A paradox at the heart of the EU enlargement process, however, is that some institutions established to hasten the adoption of EU-related laws may harm the institutionalisation of parliamentary democracy and also the national interests of candidate countries. The Bulgarian solution to this problem (as outlined above) appears to be a good solution, combining as it does a desire to fulfil the aspiration of EU membership, whilst ensuring the desire to follow the procedures of a consensual democracy are not thrown into the institutional rubbish bin.

The impact of fast-tracking is a symptom of a deeper problem. Effective governance requires some degree of flexibility and institutional diversity. Pressure towards uniformity can, if taken too far, be inimical to efficacious governance. Just as golfers are allowed to pick which 14 clubs they play with, so the states of the enlarged EU should have the right to choose whether to pick the institutional equivalent of the sand wedge or another driver to suit their circumstances, traditions and needs. There is, as Wallace argues, 'in the more mechanical process of EU enlargement' the need to recognise the value of indigenous practice and preference.[25]

The emerging CEE institutional pattern has significant consequences for their respective polities. As Lijphart suggested, institutional frameworks which promote consensus tend to yield parliaments and governments where sometimes fractious coalitions are more likely to predominate and where mustering the requisite majorities to pass legislation can be difficult.[26] The institutional framework in CEE has helped to hinder effective cabinet government, particularly in those countries where former communist or new nationalist forces do not sufficiently support democratic values. The obstacles in the way of effective executive decision making, although theoretically beneficial to the fostering of a pluralist democracy, may therefore undermine the institutional and organisational ability of the state to implement the social, economic and administrative reforms necessary to build a modern democratic state on the Western European model.

Enlargement is a challenge not just for the applicant states of Central and Eastern Europe, but also for the institutions of the EU itself. At the Nice European Council, EU leaders hammered out a deal aimed at reforming the

EU's decision making procedures to enable effective governance in an enlarged Union encompassing up to 28 states. The provisions of the Nice Treaty, should it be finally accepted, and particularly the extension of qualified majority voting, might help to ensure more effective decision making, but effective governance may also require further reform. Coping with diversity by centralisation may not be the answer. Effective governance in the enlarged EU therefore requires a balance to be struck between a workable institutional framework for the EU and a recognition of diversity and complexity across the European continent.

Despite what the Eurosceptics tell us, particularly in Britain, the most important decision making bodies in the EU remain those which are constituted of member states' executives: the Council of Ministers and the European Council. Given the relatively weak position of CEE executives and their greater dependence on fragmented parliaments, it may be wise, therefore, for CEE countries to consider strengthening their executives in order to ensure better representation and articulation of their national interests within the EU decision making framework and hence increase their bargaining power. The relatively weak executive leadership in CEE has been partly replaced by EU conditionality and other external pressures. The reliance on the desire to please external actors, particularly the EU, may therefore lead to a decrease in the legitimacy of the state and its institutions. One means of restoring or enhancing the legitimacy of the state may lie in strengthening the position of the executive, and the procedures adopted by CEE legislatures to pass EU-related laws highlight the benefits and drawbacks of such systems. But while the *national aspiration* to join the EU can be pursued more easily and effective governance can be increased, this could nevertheless hinder the emergence of the necessary democratic values including consensus. In politics, where good arguments exist on both sides of the debate, balances have to be struck. It may be wise for CEE countries to place all the arguments back on the scales, weigh up the options and strike a new balance.

NOTES

1. The terms are those of Schöpflin: see G. Schöpflin *Politics in Eastern Europe 1945–1992* (Oxford and Cambridge: Blackwell 1993), pp.256–300.
2. H. Wallace, 'The Domestication of Europe and the Limits to Globalisation', paper delivered to IPSA Congress, Quebec, Aug. 2000.

3. Council of the European Union, *Presidency Conclusions: Copenhagen European Council* (Brussels: European Union 1993); J. Gower, 'EU Policy to Central and Eastern Europe', in Karen Henderson (ed.), *Back to Europe: Central and Eastern Europe and the European Union* (London: UCL Press 1993), pp.3–22, particularly pp.7–8.
4. S. Haggard and M.D. McCubbins (eds.), *Presidents, Parliaments, and Policy* (Cambridge: Cambridge University Press 2001); S. Steinmo, K. Thelen and F. Longstreth (eds.), *Structuring Politics: Historical Institutionalism in Comparative Analysis* (Cambridge: Cambridge University Press 1992); A. Przeworski, 'Democracy as a Contingent Outcome of Conflicts', in J. Elster and R. Slagstad (eds.), *Constitutionalism and Democracy* (Cambridge: Cambridge University Press 1988), pp.59–80; J.G. March and J.P. Olsen, *Rediscovering Institutions: The Organizational Basis of Politics* (New York: Free Press 1989); J. March and J. Olsen, 'The New Institutionalism: Organizational Factors in Political Life', *American Political Science Review* 78/3 (Sept. 1984), pp.734–49.
5. C. Offe, 'Designing Institutions in East European Transitions', in J. Elster, C. Offe and U.K. Preuss, *Institutional Design in Post-communist Societies: Rebuilding the Ship at Sea* (Cambridge: Cambridge University Press 1996), pp.199–226.
6. M.S. Shugart, 'The Inverse Relationship between Party Strength and Executive Strength: A Theory of Constitutional Choices', *British Journal of Political Science* 28 (1998), pp.1–29 at p.28.
7. K. Williams, 'Constitutional Choices and Separation of Powers in East Central Europe' (unpublished lecture, School of Slavonic and East European Studies, UCL, 29 Nov. 2000).
8. Elster *et al.*, *Institutional Design*, p.15.
9. Shugart, 'The Inverse Relationship', p.2.
10. S. Holmes, 'Conceptions of Democracy in the Draft Constitutions of Post-Communist Countries', in B. Crawford (ed.), *Markets, States and Democracy* (Boulder: Westview 1995), pp.71–81 at p.73.
11. J. Zielonka, 'New Institutions in the Old East Block', *Journal of Democracy* 5/2 (1994), pp.87–104; S. Holmes, 'Back to the Drawing Board', *East European Constitutional Review* 2/1 (1993), pp.21–5.
12. G. Sanford, 'Parliamentary Control and the Constitutional Definition of Foreign Policy Making in Democratic Poland', *Europe-Asia Studies* 51/5 (1999), pp.769–97.
13. V.I. Ganev, 'Bulgaria', in Robert Elgie (ed.), *Semi-Presidentialism in Europe* (Oxford and New York: Oxford University Press 1999), pp.124–49.
14. J. Blondel and F. Muller-Rommel (eds.), *Cabinets in Eastern Europe* (Houndsmills: Palgrave 2001); J. Blondel and F. Muller-Rommel (eds.), *Cabinets in Western Europe* (Houndsmills: Palgrave 1997).
15. Zielonka, 'New Institutions'; R. Taras 'The Politics of Leadership', in S. White, J. Batt and P.G. Lewis (eds.), *Developments in Central and East European Politics 2* (London: Macmillan 1998), pp.103–25.
16. J.-E. Lane and S. Ersson, *The New Institutional Politics: Performance and Outcomes* (London and New York: Routledge 2000).
17. Elster *et al.*, *Institutional Design.*
18. European Commission 'Regular Report' 2000 on Slovenia posted at europa.eu.int/comm./enlargement/slovenia.
19. M. Duverger, *Political Parties: Their Organization and Activity in the Modern State* (New York: Wiley 1954); R. Taagerpera and M.S. Shugart, *Seats and Votes: The Effects and Determinants of Electoral Systems* (New Haven and London: Yale University Press 1989).
20. Elster *et al.*, *Institutional Design*; M. Gallagher, 'Comparing Proportional Representation Electoral Systems: Quotas, Thresholds, Paradoxes and Majorities', *British Journal of Political Science* 22 (1992), pp.469–96.
21. G. Sartori, *Comparative Constitutional Engineering: An Inquiry into Structures, Incentives and Outcomes* (Houndsmills, Basingstoke: MacMillan 1997), p.32.
22. R.G. Moser, 'Electoral System and the Number of Parties in Postcommunist States', *World Politics* 51 (April 1999), pp.359–84 at p.360; T. Haughton, 'The Institutional Framework of Slovak Politics' (unpublished paper, School of Slavonic and East European Studies, UCL, London University, 2001).

23. B. Geddes, 'Initiation of New Democratic Institutions in Eastern Europe and Latin America', in A. Lijphart and C.H. Waisman (eds.), *Institutional Design in New Democracies* (Boulder: Westview Press 1996), pp.15–42.
24. J.J. Linz, 'The Perils of Presidentialism', *Journal of Democracy*, 1 (Winter 1990), pp.51–69; J.J. Linz, 'The Virtues of Parliamentarism', *Journal of Democracy* 1 (Fall 1990), pp.84–91.
25. Wallace, 'The Domestication of Europe'.
26. A. Lijphart, *Democracies* (New Haven: Yale University Press 1984).

Making Markets and Eastern Enlargement: Diverging Convergence?

LASZLO BRUSZT

MARKET MAKING AND EUROPEANISATION

The 1990s was the decade of market making in both parts of Europe. This was the decade of the radical extension of the internal market and the creation of the conditions for the European Monetary Union in the Western part of Europe. This was also the decade in which the former communist countries undertook to transform their economies, to create functioning market economies, and, as of the second half of the decade, to build up the conditions for entry into the EU internal market. Market making in the former communist countries was influenced in several ways by the other part of Europe. In undertaking to transform their economies, the political elite in these countries used the ideology of 'Europeanisation' extensively, and the promise of potential EU accession played a considerable role in shaping political cleavages and the political agenda within these countries. As of the early 1990s, the EU also played a considerable role in setting the criteria for Europeanisation in the economic transformation for these countries, and actively participated in building up capacities to meet these criteria.

This study discusses the broad question of the extent and content of 'Europeanisation' of Central and Eastern European (CEE) countries at the level of market making. It argues that, for the most successful CEE countries, Europeanisation at the level of market making meant the emergence and the strengthening of a state with strong capacities to preserve and regulate markets, while having at the same time increased administrative and transformed planning capabilities. By the end of the 1990s, those CEE countries that had such states had come close to meeting the EU's demanding convergence criteria. Countries that did not have such states diverged both from the successful CEE countries and the EU. However, even the most successful CEE countries 'converged' on a moving target. While undertaking to meet the Copenhagen criteria of *national-level* market making they were 'converging' on EU member countries that themselves were busy diverging from these criteria in order to meet the Maastricht criteria of *supranational* market making. The content of these criteria diverged, and so did the consequences of meeting them.

The Copenhagen criteria of national-level market making that were the official compass for the CEE countries coupled neo-liberal policy prescriptions aiming at the rapid exposure of these countries to supranational markets with considerable demands on establishing domestic market order by way of building the institutional capabilities of national states. The Maastricht criteria of transnational market making, on the other hand, coupled domestic level policy demands with the transfer of basic domestic state capacities to the supranational level. The most successful CEE countries met the criteria of Europeanisation at the level of market making with relatively strong regulative states that were busy (re)creating, transforming and further strengthening their planning capacities. Within the EU, at the same time, national states were losing a large part of their capabilities to manipulate economic processes. Substantial parts of the economic powers of the national states were transferred to the supranational level and the placing of the domestic governments within a Europe-wide competitive regime further decreased their scope of action.

On the other hand, and largely as an unintended side-effect of supranational market making, organisations of non-state actors and their co-operative institutions became considerably stronger in several of the EU member countries. This development led in several EU countries to the partial mitigation of the social consequences of supranational market making being undertaken in the absence of supranational welfare state making. During the 1990s, however, non-state actors and various co-operative institutions in the CEE countries remained weak or were even further weakened.[1] As a result, those CEE countries that are achieving most progress in Europeanisation at the level of market making diverge considerably from the newly emerging EU 'model' of capitalism itself, consisting as it does of different sub-types of 'embedding' markets. This emerging EU model of capitalism mixes elements of supranationally regulated markets with weakened national states and, in most of the member countries, relatively stronger non-state actors with co-operative institutions that seek to maintain competitiveness and to alleviate the social consequences of increased competition. While several of the CEE countries have well functioning market economies, most of the institutions that could make markets more inclusive, and/or support the process of catch-up growth of these economies, are weak or absent.

The emerging capitalism in CEE countries looks like an institutional desert, at least in comparison to the form(s) of capitalism evolving within the European Union. Institutions that would improve the market power of the different categories of economic actors and allow for the emergence of 'win–win' forms of co-operation among them are lacking. All in all, the good news from Central Europe is that the countries most developed in market making have relatively strong states. The bad news is that in most of these countries only the state is strong, while all other major economic actors, such as domestic business, labour or the local and regional self-governments, are weak.

The configuration of strong states and weak social and economic actors might have afforded the leading CEE countries a relatively calm arrival at the gates of the EU. Yet this configuration might also become the biggest liability for these same countries during the next stage of Europeanisation, that is, once they are within the EU and approaching the semi-periphery of Europe. The major argument of this study is therefore that while progress in state making was the *sine qua non* of Europeanisation at the level of market making, the constellation of forces noted above might become the major obstacle facing these countries in their efforts to cope with the social and economic problems of participation in the next stage of supranational market making.

The next section gives a sketchy general overview of the processes of convergence and divergence among the CEE countries, as well as between these countries and the existing EU member states at the level of market making. The following section then discusses the specifics of national-level market making in the CEE countries, focusing on the factors that explain divergence in Europeanisation at this level. The final part discusses the 'diverging convergence' between the CEE and EU member countries at the level of the organisation of economic actors and their co-operative institutions.

CONVERGENCE AND DIVERGENCE

In assessing developments during the last decade at the level of market making from the viewpoint of the highly demanding EU performance criteria, we can see considerable *convergence* between the two parts of Europe. According to the regular reports on the progress towards accession, the five leading reform countries of the region basically meet the so-called

Copenhagen criteria, that is, they have a 'functioning market economy with the capacity to cope with the competitive pressure and market forces within the Union'.[2] According to the same reports, several other countries are also on their way to meeting these criteria in the medium term. The degree of economic integration that these countries have achieved with the Union even prior to accession, as measured by the volume and range of products traded with EU member states (the evidence used by the EU of the ability to take on the obligations of membership) is also impressive. The CEE countries have doubled their exports since the beginning of the 1990s, and by the end of the decade almost 80 per cent of these exports went to the Western countries. In terms of the structure of the regulations taken over from the EU, and in terms of the structure of their trade, finances, organisation and ownership, the leading reform countries have already integrated into the EU economy even before the actual accession.[3]

Behind these indicators of convergence there are several processes of considerable *divergence*, which, although not challenging the processes of convergence noted above, might still impose important constraints on the longer term European integration of the economies in the region. The first of these is the serious divergence in economic developments within the region itself. Following nearly a decade of experimentation with economic reforms, we find signs of the consolidation of the market order and competition only in the leading reformist countries in the region. In many of the post-communist countries that have rapidly undertaken the liberalisation of prices and trade and the privatisation of property, we find anything but signs of the emergence of a functioning market order. The most important difference between the two groups of countries is perhaps that while the latter have states with the capacity to uphold economic freedoms, to maintain the rule of law, to resist state capture and to regulate relations among economic actors, the former do not have such states. The constitution of a market making state in several of these countries was blocked by the dominance of a nationalistic political agenda and/or the presence of strong economic groups that captured the state.[4] The creation of states with the capacity to constitute and preserve the market order is therefore a task that still lies ahead for several countries in the region.

In accounting for this type of divergence, as will be discussed later, legacies of the past, the characteristics of constitution making and bad economic policies played the major role. The EU itself could play only a partial, albeit non-negligible role in re-making states in the region. The criteria of Europeanisation of the CEE economies, the so-called Copenhagen criteria, include several elements of state making as conditions of creating functioning markets, and through various programmes, the EU directly participated in the upgrading of the administrative and institutional capacities of several of these states. The EU also played a role in influencing the formation of national political agenda in several of the South-Eastern European countries through various incentives. However, in addressing the problem of state capture, the anti-corruption measures and policies suggested by the EU proved inadequate. Unlike corruption itself, which is a general problem in both parts of Europe, state capture can be linked to a specific power structure within the state, and cannot be cured without considerably changing the structure of representation.[5]

The second process of divergence can be observed between the EU member countries and the leading CEE reform countries at the level of building institutions of economic development. Market making in both parts of Europe was strongly and directly linked to the (re)making of the state and to the strengthening of the institutional capacities of the (supra)national state to preserve and regulate markets. Within the EU the strengthening of the regulative capacities of the supranational quasi-state went hand in hand with preserving and, in several cases, with strengthening various non-market institutions of economic governance at the national, regional, local and workplace levels. Linking diverse groups of non-state actors with diverse metrics of success in economic development, these co-operative institutions facilitated combining the creation of the conditions to improve competitiveness with a wider range of developmental goals, and so allowed diverse actors to frame markets in a socially and economically less exclusive way.[6] Examples include the renewal of national level social pacts, the extension of social dialogue at national, subnational and supranational levels, the (re)emergence of various institutions of developmental partnerships at sectoral and regional levels, or the new forms of cross-border collective bargaining.[7] In the other part of Europe, institution-building efforts were concentrated on strengthening solely the capacities of central state agencies. The different organisations of labour, business or local self-governments are weak, and the diversity of co-operative institutions characteristic of the EU, albeit sometimes formally present in the region, do not play any significant role in framing markets in a more inclusive way. This type of divergence from the 'European model' can largely be explained by domestic conditions, including the weakness of diverse non-state organisations, their problems of legitimacy, or the largely exclusionary policies of national governments.[8]

In the emergence of this type of divergence, however, problems of the 'self-definition' of the EU as a distinctive model of economic development also played a considerable role. Putting it briefly, while the strengthening of regulative state capacities is part of the evolving neo-liberal 'European model', the diverse co-operative forms of economic governance largely form the 'optional' part of the model, and as something that is mainly seen as a matter of the domestic business of the member states.[9] To be sure, the struggle within the EU to 'Europeanise' such institutions, that is, to make them part of the 'model', has achieved some success, but, perhaps reflecting the ongoing fight for the redefinition of the model, EU pressure on the new applicants to take over such institutions has been weak.[10] While the EU put strong pressure on the applicant countries to modernise the administrative, regulative and developmental planning capacities of their states both at the national and local level, its pressure on the applicants to extend the scope of co-operative institutions that could frame markets in a more inclusive way proved rather lukewarm.[11]

Largely related to this institutional void, the third process of divergence could be observed inside the non-EU member countries in the form of growing disparities across regions, sectors and social groups, as well as between the 'internationalised/Europeanised' parts and the rest of the economy. As argued below, the co-operative institutions might well play a central role in the reduction of such disparities. Finally, at least in the first decade of economic transformation, there was not much evidence of convergence at the level of aggregate indicators of economic development and quality of human life conditions between even the best performing CEE countries and the EU member countries.[12] While the EU did include a country such as Portugal, with relatively poorer economic and social indicators, the persistence in the relative backwardness of the CEE countries might be seen as an indirect proof of the weakness of a developmental strategy based solely on the market enhancing capacities of state bureaucracies.[13]

To summarise, the Europeanisation of the economies of the CEE countries in the first decade of transformation was primarily about state making and less about non-state institution building. As is discussed in the next part, those countries that have a functioning market economy in the region have a market preserving state and a regulative state. While some of the countries of the region have states that, according to surveys, are weaker then states in Sub-Saharan Africa, others have considerably higher market preserving and regulative capacities.[14] One of the lessons of the last decade of reforms has been that neither privatisation, nor the introduction of all the regulations of the developed world, as happened in many of the countries of the region, will create a market economy if the state is too weak to resist the pressure of redistributive groups. Such state capacities might be strengthened if power is less centralised within the state and if the 'non-hierarchical elements of the state' are correspondingly stronger.

MARKET MAKING AND STATE MAKING: DIVERGENCE AMONG THE CEE COUNTRIES

Diversity in economic development is not a new feature of economic change in Eastern Europe. Even before the political regime change in 1989, countries in the region had widely diverged in their patterns of industrialisation, and, as a consequence, in their patterns of industrial distortions. They have also differed in terms of their structure and patterns of foreign trade. Some were closer to autarchic patterns of economic development; others had gradually opened up their economies to the world market. They had different levels and forms of economic imbalances, and had experiences with different types of economic reforms. While the share of the private sector was generally low, in some of the countries the share of the so-called 'second economy' was higher. While in most of these countries the role played by market institutions was also limited, in some countries in the region it was possible to find an extensive use of such institutions. What was common to all the countries of the region was the unstoppable deterioration of their positions in the world market throughout the 1980s and the slowing down of their economic development.

This divergence in economic development remained a constant feature of the region even after the political regime change. In the 1990s, however, it has appeared in a much more dramatic and historically unprecedented form. In some of the countries of the region, after a relatively shorter period of transformational recession, economic recovery began early, and by the second half of the decade these countries were approaching the level of economic development they held in 1989 as measured by GDP.[15] In these countries, economic restructuring has been considerable, and most are now on the path to what can be called sustainable economic growth. The number of such countries is still very small, however. The majority of the citizens in the region still live in countries where after the loss of 40–60 per cent of GDP, it is only the inequalities that have grown, and their economies continue to stagnate or decay.[16]

Washington vs. Brussels

Economic reformers throughout the region were pushed and pulled in two diverging directions at the beginning of the economic transformation. On the one hand, the recipes coming from across the Atlantic and forming part of what was called the Washington consensus, have stressed the importance of de-statisation and de-regulation in the process of market making. While it has never been formulated in the framework of an encompassing blueprint, the message coming from Brussels was at least as clear: market making is about the re-making of the state, about re-regulation of relations among economic actors, and about the re-institutionalisation of the economy. The proponents of the Washington consensus measured progress in economic reforms in terms of the level of freedom from the state. The criteria of success formulated by the EU, on the other hand, besides the level of liberation, consisted of measures such as progress in the regulation and development of state capacities, including administrative and developmental planning capacities. According to the experts of the international financial institutions in Washington, market making was primarily about making economic activity a private business. The Eurocrats visiting the region, however, have left no doubt about their seeing the market as one of the state-made social institutions, and as a specific structure of state-made rights and obligations continually policed and monitored by the regulatory state. The more concrete prescriptions based on the Washington consensus were formulated as measures liberating economic activity from the state: liberalisation of prices, liberalisation of trade and privatisation. These measures were supposed to 'get prices right', thus allowing the price mechanism to effect co-ordination among economic actors undisturbed by the state, and so leading economic development towards the radiant future.

While measures of economic liberalisation also formed part of the policy proposals coming from Brussels, the EU prescriptions were mainly about 'getting institutions right' as a condition of getting prices right, and also as a condition of being considered for accession to the EU. 'Getting institutions right' was mainly about strengthening state capacities to create and preserve the market order, to police and monitor competition, and to enable non-state actors to improve their market positions by creating and monitoring diverse non-state institutions of economic governance. As of the second half of the 1990s, this also includes increasing developmental planning capacities at the various levels of the state apparatus.

In the first few years of economic reforms, it was basically the Washington consensus that shaped policies in the region. Extensive regulation of the economy began only in the middle of the decade and the building up of regulative state capacities also began long after the introduction of liberalising measures in most of the CEE countries. Within the region, however, progress in this field is highly uneven, and, as will be seen below, it is still divergence that is the major defining characteristics of the situation.

The most important lessons of the first decade of reforms from this viewpoint could be summarised as follows. First, liberalisation of prices and trade brought about beneficial economic effects in those countries where states had the capacity to re-regulate relations among economic actors and prevent their misuse in asymmetries in economic power.[17] Second, privatisation has improved the functioning of the economy in those countries where states had a strong capacity to uphold property rights, to maintain the rule of law, to create a predictable policy environment, and to regulate relations among economic actors.[18] Third, liberalisation and privatisation have led to economic restructuring and economic growth in those countries that had states with a strong capacity to uphold rights and preserve competition, but only those countries that had states with robust defences against state capture had market preserving and regulative capacities.[19] Finally, the introduction of even the most extensive regulations did not improve the quality of the markets if the legal effectiveness of the state was low; the use of legal transplants and even the introduction of extensive legal reforms were not sufficient in countries with states that had a weak capacity to maintain the rule of law and to enforce their own laws.[20]

TABLE 1
REGIONAL AVERAGES OF THE CREDIBILITY INDICATOR AND ITS COMPONENTS

Region		Components of the credibility indicator				
	Credibility indicator	Predict-ability	Political stability	Violence	Reliability of judiciary	Lack of corruption
All countries	3.23	3.21	3.25	2.80	3.04	3.86
High-income industrial countries	4.14	3.85	4.27	3.64	3.98	5.04
South and Southeast Asia	3.69	3.55	3.56	3.28	3.94	4.12
Middle East and North Africa	3.28	3.36	2.86	3.57	2.61	4.01
Central and Eastern Europe	3.22	2.93	3.51	2.72	3.14	3.82
Latin America and the Caribbean	3.12	3.17	3.60	2.43	2.63	3.79
Sub-Sahara Africa	2.91	3.06	2.57	2.59	2.76	3.55
Commonwealth of Independent States	2.69	2.87	2.91	2.16	2.35	3.16

Source: Aymo Brunetti, Gregory Kisunko and Beatrice Weder, 'Credibility of Rules and Economic Growth: Evidence from a Worldwide Survey of the Private Sector', *The World Bank Economic Review* 12/3 (1998), pp.353–84.

Table 1 offers measures for the regional averages of the credibility indicator and its components. These measure the perception by private firms of the extent of credible state commitment to preserve the market order. Based on this survey, we can speak about progress in market making if states are in place with the capacity to build up among economic actors a stable expectation that their property rights are safe, that they can count on the state to enforce their contracts in case of disputes, and that they do not have to fear losing their gains as the result of sudden changes in policies by unpredictable or corrupt governments. As can be seen from the table, the expectations of private economic actors about state capacity to enforce contracts or produce predictable policies without being corrupted are actually lower in the former Soviet Republics than even in the Sub-Sahara African countries or in Latin America. On the other hand, the subjective evaluation of state capacities to preserve the market order are significantly higher in the Central and Eastern European countries.

Networks and State Capture

In 1989, the year when the political and economic changes began in the region, the neighbouring EU member countries had states with robust capacities to preserve market order, enforce competition and regulate relations among economic actors led by some commonly acceptable notion of public good. More specifically, these states had a well-developed capacity to uphold economic rights, enforce obligations, maintain predictable policy environments for economic actors, and prevent the misuse of asymmetries in economic and informational power. These state capacities were sustained by intra-state mechanisms that reduced the dangers of arbitrary policies and hence also reduced the risks of a general regulatory capture by powerful economic groups. Most of the Central and East European nations did not have such states at that time.

The rapid devolution of the economic power of states in micro-decisions to private actors in many of these countries did not result in the emergence of market order, competition and the re-emergence of economic development. Instead, in the countries of the region where the states and democratic institutions were weak, market reforms resulted in the economies that were dominated by predatory groups and of states that were dominated by the same groups. Contrary to the expectations of the reformers, the post-privatisation property regimes in the region were not based on forms in which management and ownership were separated and in which corporate governance was conducted by banks or through transactions on the stock exchange. Rather, the dominant role in the new property regimes, at least in the first half of the decade, was played by different forms of under-regulated cross-ownership of firms and financial institutions, with, in several cases, state agencies co-owning these firms and banks.[21]

The formation of these networks was closely linked to the enormous growth in the uncertainties caused by rapid liberalisation, and, in many countries, to the insecurity of property rights. The evolution of the balance of power between these networks and the state was the major factor determining the path of economic development in these countries throughout the 1990s. The relative powers of the financial-industrial groups and states were largely shaped by the level of economic distortions inherited from the past regimes, the speed of the liberalising policies, and the characteristics of the states themselves.[22] In countries where the inherited economic distortions were high, market reforms meant a dramatic redistribution of economic opportunities and powers for a large number of firms and regions that lacked the capacity to adjust to the exigencies of the market. The more rapid the liberalising measures, the more firms were pushed to form networks – first, in order to survive, and later for 'going for the state' as a strategy of survival.[23] Countries that inherited economies with highly distorted economic structures, that introduced liberalisation too rapidly, and that had newly formed states in which power was strongly centralised, represented the worse cases. In these countries, mainly the post-Soviet republics, states lacked the capacity to resist these networks and hence were easy prey.[24] In the Central European countries, on the other hand, the inherited levels of economic distortions were much lower, the speed of reforms was slower than in the post-Soviet republics, and states had stronger capacities to resist capture. It was in these countries that the regulative state could emerge by the second half of the 1990s.[25]

State Capacity

To date, there are three elements of state functions that remain in short supply in the region. The first is the state's capacity to uphold the general rights of economic actors and to create a predictable policy environment for them. According to the World Bank survey summarised in Table 1, such state capacities are at their weakest in the world within the countries of the former Soviet Union, being weaker even than in the countries of Sub-Sahara Africa or Latin America. In the Central European countries the capacity of states to uphold rights and maintain a predictable policy environment is stronger, yet still weaker than what can be found in the most advanced capitalist societies.[26] The second type of state capacity in short supply is the capacity to prevent the use of state institutions by powerful private groups to redistribute wealth and opportunities to themselves. According to a recently published survey, in many of the Eastern European countries economic actors can reasonably expect that competitors can literally purchase policies and regulations at the different branches and levels of government.[27] Perception of such state capture by private groups is low only in a smaller group of post-communist countries. Finally, the third type is the capacity to regulate relations among economic actors in a balanced way and prevent the misuse of asymmetries in economic and information power within the market. Again, according to recent surveys, most of the states of the region could not introduce extensive and effective regulations enforcing competition and/or market orientation even in such decisive areas as the financial markets.[28]

These are exactly those state characteristics that shape the overall capacity of states to constitute and preserve the market order, and to enforce competition and market orientation. In the absence of these capacities in several of the countries of the region, economic actors are hesitant to invest in the formal sector of the economy and prefer to enter into only very elementary forms of economic transactions, such as barter. In several of these countries predatory groups dominate 'markets' and states are captured by those very same groups.[29] Problems of social and economic development in these countries are different than in those that have more or less functioning market economies. While the question the latter countries face is how to correct the economic and social problems of otherwise functioning market orders, in the former countries economic and social problems are related to the non-existence of functioning markets, or more precisely, to the corruption of states and markets by self-seeking groups.

Decision Making

The capacity of states in democratic countries to constitute functioning markets is largely the result of the way decision making about social and economic issues is structured within the state. While in countries with corrupted markets and captured states decision making is excessively centralised and limitations on executive powers are weak, in the leading reform countries state power is more decentralised.[30] In the latter countries, when state executives make their policies they have to take into account diverse representations of the public good – represented by coalition partners, parties in different houses of the legislature, different levels and branches of the government, autonomous state agencies, and the organisations of civil society and economic society. In such a state, the horizontal accountability of executives by other autonomous state agencies reduces the risk of misusing state power and the encroachment on the rights of non-state actors. Independent judiciaries with the powers of judicial supervision, and rules that make any change to basic rights an arduous task, prevent executives from taking arbitrary decisions and hence force them, and the non-state actors, to honour the law. The existence of autonomous state agencies that can force incumbents to respect specific rules in the use of public resources, and of state agencies that represent specific rights or the rights of specific minority groups, further extend the accountability of executives. It is through the institution of distributed authority and the permanent pressure on executives to take diverse representations of public good into account that the likelihood of state capture is reduced. On the other hand, the state is up for grabs in countries where power is concentrated and where mechanisms that would tie the hands of executives and prevent them from arbitrarily intervening in the economy are lacking.[31]

After nearly a decade of struggle to liberate economic activity from the state, many of the countries in the region now face the problem of how to liberate a state that has been captured by economic groups. If they want to create a functioning market order, they will need a state that is capable of regulating the highly uneven distribution of economic power in a balanced way. But, in order to re-balance their economies, they first need states liberated from the hold of powerful economic groups. The task of (re)making states with the capacity to constitute and preserve market order still lies ahead in many of the countries of the region.

Functioning Regulative States

Based on these various features, it is possible to conclude that Poland, Hungary, the Czech Republic, Slovenia and Estonia have well functioning regulative states, with Lithuania, Latvia, Bulgaria, Slovakia and Romania lagging behind. The task of market making and, correspondingly, state making, still lies ahead in the remaining 14 countries in the region, including nearly all the former Soviet Republics as well as some of the South Eastern European countries. This rank order basically corresponds to the 'success' indicators used in comparative transition studies and to the EU reports on accession countries.[32] The countries belonging to the first group undertook a considerable restructuring of their economies, their economic growth started in the second half of the 1990s, and some are now among the fastest growing economies in Europe.

The emergence of a functioning market-preserving and regulative state in these countries was largely the result of domestic political and economic processes, although the EU also played a considerable role in helping to consolidate and upgrade their regulative and administrative capacities. In addition, the promise of participation in the EU social and economic cohesion programmes played a considerable role in renewing and re-making the developmental planning capacities of these states. The EU role in this field was partly direct, by setting mandatory goals in the form of the *acquis* and by giving financial and technical help for the implementation of these requirements. The EU also played a considerable indirect role by placing these countries in a regulative competition framework through the more or less forced opening up of their economies. That said, the Europeanisation of states in these countries is still highly uneven, and state building has affected mainly central governments that are hesitant to share their powers with other branches and levels of government. Moreover, the autonomy of the newly created regulatory agencies is questionable in several of these countries (for example, the Czech Securities Exchange Commission, or the Hungarian Banking and Capital Market Supervisory Authority), while the cohesion and autonomy of the state bureaucracies in some of these countries is weakened by the remaining elements of the 'spoils system', and by the possibility that the staff or the organisation of the state bureaucracy could be changed according to political criteria. Finally, local development is under the control of central governments in most of these countries and hence financial and political autonomy at the local levels is weak.[33]

DIVERGING CONVERGENCE?

The economic developmental problems of those CEE countries with a more or less functioning market economy differ almost on a country-by-country basis within the region. Nevertheless, they all face the challenge of 'inventing' institutions of economic development that could increase the competitiveness of their economies, make development socially more inclusive, and support the process of their catch-up growth. While the specific countries within the current EU belong to different 'sub-types' of capitalism, nearly all of the institutions that are cited as providing them with a competitive advantage are weak or absent even within the leading reform countries of Central Europe.[34] The often cited institutions of 'co-operation for competitiveness' of the continental European forms of capitalism, including co-operative industrial relations and established long-term relations among banks, firms, regional and local governments, labour and business associations, are basically lacking in the region. And while a considerable role has been played by the old and the newly invented forms of developmental associations of diverse non-state actors in transnational market making within the EU, in the CEE countries it was the regulative state that was basically the prime mover of economic development during the first decade of reforms.

Industrial Relations

Both trade unions and business associations are weak and fragmented in most of the CEE countries. Although institutions of tripartite concentration are present, they are under-utilised in most of these countries. Nevertheless, during the early 1990s, several national-level tripartite pacts did help to encourage governments to initiate large scale reforms. Once these were introduced in most of the countries of the region, governments turned to labour-exclusive policies, further weakening organised labour and, in some of these countries, also organised domestic business.[35] The number of firm-level collective agreements is low, there are very few sector-level collective agreements, and the coverage of labour through collective agreements, ranging between 20 and 50 per cent, is much below the EU level. The growing competitive pressure on governments, sectors and firms in many of the continental EU countries led to the re-making of collaborative institutions at firm and sector level, and in many countries the movement to EMU led to the rebirth of social pacts at the national level. In the Central European countries, by contrast, managers and state bureaucrats dominate economic restructuring without any significant concertation. While the Copenhagen criteria include elements of strengthened social dialogue at various levels, these prescriptions form the 'soft' part of the *acquis* and are not enforced by the EU.

One cannot expect any automatic convergence in industrial relations once the first group of CEE countries is inside the transnational market making regime. The organisation and the fragmentation of labour and business differs from one country to another within the region, and change in this field will depend on the existing conditions and the strategies of the non-state (trans)national organisations in both parts of Europe. In some of the CEE countries, the desire to join the EMU and meet its economic criteria might well encourage political elites to considerably upgrade the system of industrial relations – as was the case in Ireland or Italy in the 1990s. In other countries, the persistent fragmentation of labour and business might induce national governments to weaken labour further and push the system of industrial relations more in the direction of the Anglo-Saxon model of 'disorganised capitalism'. Finally, the inclusion of labour and business representatives in the national, sectoral and regional development planning processes – another unenforced chapter in the 'official guidelines of Europeanisation' – might alter the balance of forces between governments and organised economic actors.[36]

Developmental Planning

One of the unique features of Europeanisation at the level of market making has been the introduction of developmental planning in those CEE countries that are busy leaving behind their dysfunctional planned economies. To be sure, this 'European' developmental planning differs dramatically in its principles from the central planning of the state socialist regimes. Labelled as the 'dictatorship over needs', the later provided the central party state with exclusive and uncontrolled prerogatives to define the goals of economic development. Linked intimately to the European new left's 'Third Way' ideology, the recent European developmental planning embodies diametrically opposing principles. These include the empowerment of diverse social and economic actors to participate in the framework of local and national partnerships together with the organs of the state in designing and implementing developmental programmes under the conditions of extended and multi-level accountability.[37]

The social and economic cohesion policy of the EU that funds national, regional and sectoral developmental programmes might considerably alter relations between central governments, local and regional self-governments, and various organised social actors. At the moment, in most of the CEE countries, the economic and political autonomy of local and regional actors is weak, and restructuring is moving in many countries towards decentralised administrative self-empowerment of the state. Except in Poland, and as a result of recent changes, in the Czech Republic, political decentralisation that would increase regional autonomy is almost absent, the political organisation of local self-governments is fragmented, and the regional organisation of labour and business is weak. Weak local financial autonomy, as well as the centralisation and centralised redistribution of locally generated incomes, further weaken the potential developmental role of localities.

The CEE countries first joining the EU might gain access to EU development funds in the range of 1.5 to 2.5 per cent of their GDP, an amount that equals or in some countries even surpasses the present volume of FDI they recently receive. The terms of conditionality regarding access to these funds might considerably alter the developmental possibilities of non-state actors in these countries. They might further strengthen the prerogatives of central governments, or they might empower local, regional and national-level non-state actors. As things stand right now, in the 'first planning period', between 2004 and 2007, the EU Commission might decide to go for the funding of a single National Development Plan in each country only, changing its previous practice of funding a centralised sectoral and several decentralised regional programmes. But although this change in policies might prove convenient for the Commission, it might also directly effect the development of relationships between central governments and other social and economic actors. Central governments in the accession countries have been doing their best to preserve their prerogatives and the change in the policies of the EU could give them further encouragement. The institution of development planning was introduced in the late 1980s as a mechanism to empower non-state actors to frame markets from below in a more inclusive way, and as a prime mover in decentralised democratic experimentation. Ironically, it could well turn out that the same institution in the CEE countries will instead become the mechanism by which central states become (re)empowered.

In conclusion, the constellation of strong states, weak non-state actors and forms of social and economic governance has played a considerable role in shaping the social and economic characteristics of market making in the region in the first decade of Europeanisation. This study was not intended to speculate about the probable social and economic consequences of joining the next stage of transnational market making under the conditions of the general weakness of forms of social and economic governance that could frame markets in a more inclusive way. The persistent weakness of the organisations of non-state actors and forms of governance, together with the expected rapid transfer of the accumulated powers of domestic governments to supranational levels, might have dramatic consequences from the viewpoint of the citisens of these countries. Adjustment to the new conditions will almost certainly prove path dependent, and will be shaped by the already existing conditions within these countries. But it will also be largely influenced by the characteristics of EU policies vis-à-vis these countries.

NOTES

1. See, for example, B. Greskovits and D. Bohle, 'Development Pathways on Europe's Periphery: Poland and Hungary Compared' (ms, Central European University, Budapest, 2000).
2. These are, the Czech Republic, Estonia, Hungary, Poland and Slovenia (European Commission, *Regular Report From the Commission on Progress Towards Accession*, 2000).

3. On the issue of the integration of CEE countries to the EU economy see the insightful analysis of Laszlo Csaba, 'Az Union keleti politikája és a kibövités', *Europai Szemle* 12/1 (2001), pp.95–103.
4. Laszlo Bruszt, 'Heterarchies and Developmental Traps', in K.K. Hinrichs and H. Wiesenthal (eds.), *Kontingenz und Krise, Institutionenpolitik in Kapitalistischen und Postsozialistischen Gesellschaften* (Frankfurt, New York: Campus Verlag 2000); B. Greskovits, 'Hungary's Post-Communist Development in Comparative Perspective', in Werner Baer and Joseph L. Love (eds.), *Liberalization and its Consequences. A Comparative Perspective on Latin America and Eastern Europe* (Cheltenham: Edward Elgar 2000).
5. Laszlo Bruszt, 'Market Making as State Making: Constitutions and Economic Development in Post-Communist Eastern Europe', *Constitutional Political Economy* (forthcoming).
6. On the social and economic impact of such co-operative institutions see A. Hicks and L. Kenworthy, 'Cooperation and Political Economic Performance in Affluent Democratic Capitalism', *American Journal of Sociology* 103/6 (1998), pp.1631–72.
7. See among others Marino Regini, 'Between Deregulation and Social Pacts: The Responses of European Economies to Globalization', *Politics and Society* 28/1 (2000), pp.5–33; Michael J. Gorges, *Euro-Corporatism? Interest Intermediation in the European Community* (Lanham, MD: University Press of America 1996); Michael F. Kluth, *The Political Economy of Social Europe: Understanding Labour Market Integration in the European Union* (London: Palgrave 1998); Michel Freyssenet *et al.* (eds.), *One Best Way? Trajectories and Industrial Models of the World's Automobile Producers* (Oxford: Oxford University Press 1998); Giuseppe Fajertag and Philippe Pochet (eds.), *Social Pacts in Europe – New Dynamics* (Brussels: OSE – European Trade Union Institute 2000); Robert Boyer *et al.* (eds.), *Between Imitation and Innovation: The Transfer and Hybridization of Productive Models in the International Automobile Industry* (Oxford: Oxford University Press 1999); Kathleen Thelen and Ikuo Kume, 'The Effects of Globalization on Labor Revisited: Lessons from Germany and Japan', *Politics and Society* 27/4 (1999), pp.477–505; Philippe Pochet (ed.), *Monetary Union and Collective Bargaining in Europe* (Brussels: Peter Lang 1999).
8. See Greskovits and Bohle, 'Development Pathways'; David Stark and Laszlo Bruszt, *Post-Socialist Pathways: Transforming Politics and Property in Eastern Europe* (New York: Cambridge University Press 1998).
9. Martin Rhodes, 'Capital Unbound? The Transformation of European Corporate Governance', *Journal of European Public Policy* 5/3 (1998), pp.406–27.
10. On the ongoing fight to redefine the 'European model' see, for example, Jon Erik Dolvik, 'Redrawing Boundaries of Solidarity? The ETUC, Social Dialogue and the Europeanisation of Trade Unions in the 1990s', in Emilio Gabaglio and Reiner Hoffman (eds.), *The ETUC in the Mirror of Industrial Relations Research* (Brussels: European Trade Union Institute 1998), pp.295–347. For a different perspective, see Wolfgang Streeck, 'European Social Policy after Maastricht: The Social Dialogue and Subsidiarity', *Economic and Industrial Democracy* 15/2 (1994); and Wolfgang Streeck, 'The Internationalization of Industrial Relations in Europe, Prospects and Problems', *Politics and Society* 20/4 (1997), pp.429–51.
11. Elena Iankova, 'Converging with Europe? Central and Eastern Europe's Return to Capitalism' (Cornell University, Institute for European Studies Working Paper 99/1, 1999).
12. Greskovits and Bohle, 'Development Pathways'.
13. Portugal joined the EU in 1986 with a per capita GNP that was 27 per cent of the EU average, much lower then the contemporary figures for the leading reform countries of CEE. See 'More Members for the EU? A Report on EU Enlargement', Helsinki: EVA Center for Finish Business and Policy Studies, 1997, cited by 'Converging with Europe?'.
14. Aymo Brunetti, Gregory Kisunko and Beatrice Weder, 'Credibility of Rules and Economic Growth: Evidence from a Worldwide Survey of the Private Sector', *The World Bank Economic Review* 12/3 (1998), pp.353–84.
15. The concept of 'transformational recession' stems from Janos Kornai, 'Transformational Recession: The Main Causes', *Journal of Comparative Economics* 19/1 (1994), pp.36–63). For reliable data on post-communist divergence, see the *Transition Reports* of the European Bank for Reconstruction and Development (EBRD) from 1997, 1999 and 2000 (London, EBRD).
16. For an excellent overview of economic conditions in the region see the EBRD *Transition*

Report 1998.

17. J.E. Stiglitz, 'Whither Reform?' World Bank Annual Bank Conference on Development Economics, Washington, DC, 1999; Bruszt, 'Heterarchies'; J. Hellman, 'Winners Take All: The Politics of Partial Reforms in Postcommunist Transitions', *World Politics* 50/2 (1998), pp.203–34.
18. K. Pistor, Martina Raiser and Stanislaw Gelfer, 'Law and Finance in Transition Economies', *Economics of Transition* 8/2 (2000), pp.325–68; Andrei Schleifer and Robert Vishny, *The Grabbing Hand: Government Pathologies and Their Cures* (Cambridge: Harvard University Press 1998); Stiglitz, 'Whither Reform?'
19. Bruszt, 'Market Making'; Hellman, 'Winners Take All'; Stiglitz, 'Whither Reform?'; D. Weimer (ed.), *The Political Economy of Property Rights: Institutional Change and Credibility in the Reform of Centrally Planned Economies* (New York: Cambridge University Press 1997).
20. Pistor *et al.*, 'Law and Finance'.
21. J. Johnson, 'Russia's Emerging Financial Industrial Groups', *Post-Soviet Affairs* 13/4 (1971), pp.333–65; Y. Kuznetsov, 'Learning in Networks', in J.M. Nelson, C. Tilly and L. Walker (eds.), *The Post-Communist Political Economies* (Washington DC: National Academy Press 1997), pp.156–77; G. McDermott, *The Communist Aftermath: Industrial Networks and the Politics of Institution Building in the Czech Republic* (Cambridge: Massachusetts Institute of Technology 1998); Stark and Bruszt, *Post-Socialist Pathways.*
22. On the role of the legacies of the past, economic distortions and state characteristics see Bruszt, 'Heterarchies'; Greskovits and Bohle, 'Development Pathways'; Greskovits, 'Hungary's Post-Communist Development'; V. Popov, 'Output Change During Transition: The Role of Initial Conditions and Economic Policy', *Voprosy Ekonomiky* 7 (1998), pp.1021–47 (in Russian); V. Popov, 'Internationalization of the Russian Economy: What Went Wrong', *Emergo: Journal of Transforming Economies and Societies* 5/2 (1999), pp.53–85.
23. Bruszt, 'Heterarchies'.
24. Ibid.; Hellman, 'Winners Take All'; J. Hellman and G. Kaufmann, 'How Profitable is Buying State Officials in Transition Economies?', *Transition* 11/2 (2000), pp.8–11
25. On the differences in the speed of reforms see Greskovits and Bohle, 'Development Pathways'.
26. Brunetti *et al.*, 'Credibility of Rules'.
27. Hellman and Kaufmann, 'How Profitable'.
28. For an extensive survey on the divergence in the level of effectiveness and extensiveness of state regulations of financial markets in the region see the EBRD *Transition Report 1999.*
29. Hellman, 'Winners Take All'; Stiglitz, 'Whither Reform?'; Bruszt, 'Heterarchies'; L. Polishchuk, 'Misssed Markets: Implications for Economic Behavior and Institutional Change', in Nelson *et al.* (eds.), *Transforming Post-Communist Political Economies*; D. Woodruff, *Money Unmade: Barter and the Fate of Russian Capitalism* (Ithaca: Cornell University Press 1999).
30. Bruszt, 'Market Making'; Hellman, 'Winners Take All'; Stark and Bruszt, *Post-Socialist Pathways*; EBRD *Transition Report 2000.*
31. Bruszt, 'Market Making'.
32. See, for example, EBRD *Transition Report 2000.*
33. An example from Hungary from an EU expert dealing with regional developmental issues: 'According to some estimations more than half of the Hungarian municipalities would not be able to apply for the Structural Funds under the present system because they do not possess sufficient financial resources. This means that a large part of the Hungarian territory and population would be excluded from direct contributions from the European Union to improve their economic and social situation': see Luis Madeureira Pires, 'Study on the Present Institutional Structure of Regional Development in Hungary and its preparation for the EU Structural Funds' (Budapest: Phare 2001).
34. On the literature on comparative capitalism in general, see Stark and Bruszt, *Post-Socialist Pathways*; on capitalist divergence within the EU see Rhodes, 'Capital Unbound'. See also J. Hollingsworth, Philippe C. Schmitter and Wolfgang Streeck (eds.), *Governing Capitalist*

Economies (Oxford: Oxford University Press 1994); Philippe C. Schmitter, 'Sectors in Modern Capitalism: Modes of Governance and Variations in Performance', in Renato Brunetta and Carlo Dell'Aringa (eds.), *Labour Relations and Economic Performance* (London: Macmillan 1990); and Wolfgang Streeck and Philippe C. Schmitter (eds.), *Private Interest Government: Beyond Market and State* (London: Sage 1985).

35. A. Tóth, 'Attempts to Reform a Workers' Movement without Mass Participation', in Jeremy Waddington and Reiner Hoffmann (eds.), *Trade Unions in Europe Facing Challenges and Searching for Solutions* (Brussels: European Trade Union Institute 2000); A. Tóth, 'Diverging Convergence: Organised Labour as a Factor in the Hybridisation of Production and the Consequences for Convergence of Subsystems of National Industrial Relations Systems' (ms, Budapest, Institute of Political Sciences, 2001); A. Tóth and R. Langewische, 'Introduction: Challenges of Transformation and Preparations for EU Accession', *Transfer* 6/3 (2000), pp.370–85.
36. In Hungary, for example, a 1999 Act excluded representatives of both labour and business from participation in developmental planning at all levels.
37. For an insightful analysis of the origins of EU developmental planning see Liesbet Hooghe, 'EU Cohesion Policy and Competing Models of European Capitalism', *Journal of Common Market Studies* 36/4 (1998), pp.457–77.

Health not Wealth: Enlarging the EMU

DANIEL GROS

The aim of this brief contribution is to provide a basis for a focused discussion about the economic perspectives of the candidate countries and how they would fit into the EU (and EMU). At present the starting point for most discussions about enlargement is that the candidate countries from Central and Eastern Europe (CEE) are much poorer than the EU average and that their institutional framework is also somewhat weaker. Therefore, it is often argued, the candidates should not rush into EMU until they have converged. The relevant convergence, so the argument goes, is 'real' convergence, not merely the convergence to the Maastricht criteria (often referred to as 'nominal' convergence). 'Real' convergence is never well defined, but is usually taken to mean convergence in per capita income. The main thesis of this study is that this position is wrong. Health (potential growth) rather than wealth (income) is the decisive criterion. The key question is thus whether Euro area membership fosters growth and thus helps to achieve convergence in income.

A finding that Euro area membership accelerates convergence to the EU-15 income level does not imply that there will be no problems. On the contrary, quick convergence in income levels implies for some time divergence (or at least sustained differences) in growth rates. This type of divergence should be manageable, as it poses only the problems of success.

A brief contribution to the debate like the present one cannot cover all aspect of the story. It concentrates on two specific aspects: section two discusses to what extent this enlargement is 'specific' in terms of its size, the economic structures of the applicants and their past as socialist economies. Section three then provides an attempt to estimate the economic benefits of EU and Euro area membership. The conclusions then summarise and point out an unavoidable convergence–divergence issue.

SIZE AND SPECIFICITY OF THE COMING ENLARGEMENT

It is often argued that this coming enlargement is unprecedented in terms of the increase in population and other measures. However, this is not the case if one considers the size of the countries that joined during previous enlargements, relative to the size of the EC they then joined (see Table 1). In fact, this enlargement is thus significant in terms of population because all ten Central and Eastern European candidate countries (CEE-10) would increase the population of the EU by over one-quarter (the increase is equivalent to the increase in the German population due to unification). However, by most economic measures the weight of candidate countries is negligible, even if one assumes that their economies will grow rapidly.

Table 2 shows that in terms of GDP, evaluated at current exchange rates, the ten accession countries combined would be about one-fifteenth (six per cent) of the Euro area. This corresponds roughly to the weight of Netherlands alone. Most of this, more than two-thirds, is accounted for by the Luxembourg group (Czech Republic, Hungary, Estonia, Slovenia, Poland). In terms of monetary indicators the story is not much different. Given that the candidate countries have rather small financial sectors their combined monetary supply amounts to generally slightly more than eight per cent of the corresponding Euro area aggregate. This implies immediately that even serious problems with the banking sectors in the CEE-10 could never materially affect monetary conditions in Euroland. Moreover, in the financial area most of the weight within the CEE-10 is accounted for by the relatively more advanced Luxembourg group of applicants.

TABLE 1
SIZE OF THE COMING ENLARGEMENT COMPARED WITH PREVIOUS ENLARGEMENTS

	Population	GDP in euro	Trade
UK+Denmark+Ireland as % of EC-6	33.5	27.9	13.1
Spain +Portugal as % of EC-10	17.5	8.3	4.7
CEE-10* as % of EU-15	28.0	4.1	10.9
Turkey as % of EU-15	17.0	2.4	7.0
Turkey as % of EU-25	13.2	2.3	6.0

Notes: * Czech Republic, Estonia, Hungary, Poland, Slovenia, Latvia, Lithuania, Slovakia, Bulgaria, Romania.
Source: Own calculations of European Union and European Bank for Reconstruction and Development (EBRD) data.

TABLE 2
ACCESSION COUNTRIES: INDICATORS OF RELATIVE SIZE (1998 DATA)

				Money			Deposits	
	Population in mln. annual	GDP at current exchange rates	GDP in PPS (% of euro area)	M0: Cash (% of euro area total)	M1 (% of euro area average/	M2 (% of euro-area GDPl)	Demand deposits (% of euro GDP)	Time savings, (% of euro area total)
Czech Republic	10.3	0.9	2.1	1.75	0.82	1.13	0.69	1.38
Estonia	1.5	0.1	0.2	0.12	0.06	0.04	0.05	0.03
Hungary	10.1	0.7	1.7	1.24	0.55	0.90	0.08	0.83
Poland	38.7	2.4	4.7	3.11	1.35	1.90	0.96	2.36
Slovenia	2.0	0.3	0.5	0.21	0.11	0.27	0.09	0.39
Latvia	2.4	0.1	0.2	0.22	0.07	0.05	0.04	0.03
Lithuania	3.7	0.2	0.4	0.25	0.09	0.06	0.06	0.04
Slovakia	5.4	0.3	0.8	0.57	0.27	0.40	0.22	0.50
CEE-8 (sum)	**74.1**	**5.0**	**10.6**	**7.47**	**3.32**	**4.75**	**2.19**	**5.56**
CEE-3 [Hu, Cz, Pol] (sum)	**59.1**	**4.0**	**8.5**	**6.10**	**2.72**	**3.93**	**1.73**	**4.57**
Bulgaria	8.3	0.2	0.6	0.38	0.11	0.11	0.05	0.11
Romania	22.5	0.6	2.1	0.38	0.16	0.31	0.09	0.25
Turkey	63.5	2.5	7.0	1.18	0.51	1.95	0.35	1.6
1990/91 data								
Portugal	9.9	1.3	2.2	1.94	2.20	2.51	2.5	3.9
Spain	38.9	9.8	11.0	21.31	11.64	8.53	9.4	14.0
Italy	56.8	21.0	21.4	27.20		17.68	29.2	9.6
Greece	10.2	1.7	2.3	2.91	1.29	1.77	0.8	2.2
Club Med (sum)	**116.0**	**34.0**	**37.0**	**53.36**	**15.30**	**30.49**	**41.9**	**29.7**

Source: ECB, Monthly Report, February 2000, IMF, International Finance Statistics, April 1999. The data on money and deposits for the Club-Med countries is for 1998.

SPECIFICITY OF THIS ENLARGEMENT

The Candidates are much Poorer and 'Different'

It is widely known that the candidates are much poorer. The most widely used indicator of living standard is GDP per capita at purchasing power standards. On this account the Luxembourg group is on average at about 50 per cent of the EU-15 average. This is somewhat lower than the values for Portugal and Greece at the beginning of the 1990s (several years after their accession to the then EC and eight years before their participation in the Euro area).

In terms of broad indicators of economic structures it is difficult to find strong systematic differences between the candidates and the poorer member countries. The share of agriculture in GDP is already rather low in the Luxembourg group, around five per cent, and in most of the Helsinki group countries (Latvia, Lithuania, Slovakia, Bulgaria, Romania) as well.

The share of industry in GDP is also not notably different from some current member countries. The fundamental reason why it is so difficult to make any firm judgement about systematic differences in economic structure is that there are large differences even among the present EU members. For example, in terms of the share of industry in GDP the range is large even only among the so-called 'Club Med'[1] countries. In both Portugal and Italy the share of industry is rather high, at around 30 per cent of GDP. This cannot be considered a sign of high (or low) level of development since Italy's GDP per capita is slightly above the EU average and Portugal's is the poorest member country. By contrast, industry is relatively much less important in Spain and Greece, providing only around 15 per cent of GDP. As all these four countries are already successful members of the Euro area there is apparently a very large range of economic structures that is compatible with membership in EMU. On the basis of the limited data that is available it appears that the candidates do not fall outside this range.

In terms of employment the differences in economic structures would appear to be larger, particularly with respect to Romania, Bulgaria and Poland, where a huge part of the labour force is officially employed in agriculture. However, while this will undoubtedly create social problems in these countries and problems for the Common Agricultural Policy, it is less relevant for the issue of EMU membership since value added in this sector is such a small part of GDP.

Moreover, one cannot avoid questioning the reliability of the data and of the definitions used for identifying farmers, particularly concerning Poland and Romania. In the former communist countries many that are classified as farmers exercise this activity only on a part time basis and it appears that their average age is close to 60, so that their numbers will anyway be shrinking rapidly over the next few years. A comparison with the Club Med is again instructive. The average here is actually the same as for the Luxembourg group as most Club Med countries share the characteristics of many applicants that relative productivity is particularly low in agriculture (the share in GDP is only a fraction of the share in employment). The 1991 data for Portugal shown in Table 3 are actually almost the same as the 1998 data for Poland, both for industry and agriculture. Thus the concerns regarding the large shares of employment in agriculture for the candidates are likely to be overstated.

The Candidates are still in Transition

Is this enlargement different because the CEE-10 are 'transition' countries, that is, countries that do not yet have an established institutional

TABLE 3
ACCESSION COUNTRIES: STRUCTURAL INDICATORS (1998)

	Per capita GDP in euro (% of euro area per capita GDP)	Per capita GDP in PPS (% of euro area per capita GDP)	Share of industry in GDP (%)	Share of agriculture in GDP (%)	Employment in agriculture (% of total civilian employment)	Employment in industry (% of total civilian employment)	Degree of openness (exports plus imports, as % of GDP)	Exports to EU (as % of total exports)
Czech Republic	24	60	32	4	6.0	32.0	61	62
Hungary	21	48	25	5	8.0	28.0	46	71
Poland	18	36	24	4	19.0	25.0	26	64
Estonia	16	36	18	6	9.0	26.0	85	79
Slovenia	44	68	28	3	12.0	34.0	54	63
Latvia	12	27	21	4	19.0	21.0	53	86
Lithuania	13	31	21	9	21.0	21.0	69	43
Slovakia	17	46	27	4	8.0	30.0		56
CEE-8 (average)	**21**	**44**	**25**	**5**	**13.0**	**27.0**	**56**	**65**
CEE-3 [Hu, Cz, Pol] (average)	**21**	**48**	**27**	**5**	**11.0**	**28.0**	**43**	**66**
Bulgaria	7	23	22	19	26.0	26.0	46	58
Romania	8	27	32	16	40.0	25.0	30	70
Turkey	14	40	22	16	42.3	16.8	26	59
1991 data								
Portugal	37.1	61.0	31	5	18	34	34	80
Spain	68.8	76.5	17	4	11	33	18	65
Italy	101.1	101.9	31	4	9	32	19	53
Greece	43.3	59.4	15	14	21	24	22	62
Club Med (average)	**63.0**	**75.0**	**24**	**7**	**15**	**31**	**23**	**65**

Source: ECB Monthly Report, February 2000; European Commission, 1999 Regular Reports, Statistical Annex of European Economy and 'The Agricultural Situation in the EU 1994 Report'. The data on employment for Estonia is for 1997. For Greece the data is for 1993 (except for the share of agriculture in GDP which is for 1992).

infrastructure for a market economy? We would agree that the institutional infrastructure in the accession candidates is weaker than in most present EU members. However, it seems that this weakness is just a consequence of low level of income (per capita).

Gros and Suhrcke find that the more advanced candidate countries in Central Europe have institutional frameworks that are judged by foreign investors, and in surveys, as being 'normal' for their level of development (or even slightly better than one would expect).[2] There is little reason to believe that progress will not continue as the overall catch-up process continues. Gros and Suhrcke also show that the more advanced candidates have actually financial sectors that are appropriate *for their level of development*. In this area it appears that the transition is over. This does not mean that there cannot be problems in this area. The problems that erupted in the Czech banking sector over the last years serve as a reminder that serious corporate governance problems might persist even in systems that were regarded as rather strong. But a number of EU countries faced rather similar problems not so long ago. Moreover, given the rapid pace of bank privatisation and take-overs by institutions from the EU (although this is sometimes still politically controversial), most of these problems should be overcome soon. At any rate the screening process should uncover any remaining institutional deficiencies. This will guarantee that at the time of accession the candidate country should have an institutional framework that is compatible with the smooth functioning of the EU.

BENEFITS OF ENLARGEMENT

The public discussion in the EU-15 about the budgetary cost of enlargement sometimes obscures the fact that enlargement should bring economic benefits. Among the candidates, EU membership is often just taken as an economic imperative and detailed calculations of the economic benefits are not undertaken. However, if one wants to gauge the long term perspectives of Central and Eastern Europe one has to have an idea of their likely size. How large will they be? This question is difficult to answer because everything depends on the alternative. For example, if one were to assume that the Czech Republic could become a sort of Switzerland if it did not join the EU one would conclude that membership does not bring this country any appreciable economic benefits. For its neighbour, the Slovak Republic, one might assume instead that the country would go back into the orbit of Russia and stop its reforms if it did not have the alternative of becoming a member of the EU. These are admittedly extreme examples, but they are useful to highlight the general problem underlying all attempts at measuring the welfare benefits of enlargement.

A further reason why it is difficult to quantify the economic effects of enlargement is that it affects all aspects of the economy. One cannot therefore just look at the impact of a number of separate markets and sum the results. This is why Baldwin *et al.* use a so-called 'computable general equilibrium' model taking into account the interactions between trade, labour markets and investment via the capital markets to mention only the most important elements of this type of model.[3] They assume in a first 'conservative scenario' that the main effect of EU membership is to reduce the cost of trading between the ten associated states and the EU by ten per cent and to eliminate trade barriers for agricultural products.[4] The first element is the key to their results. The ten per cent reduction in trading costs reduces total costs by 2.5 per cent since in their model the starting level of the cost of trading across borders is 25 per cent of the transaction value. With membership this is supposed to go down to 22.5 per cent. They find that under this scenario real income in the candidate states would increase by about 1.5 per cent and by only 0.2 per cent in the EU. The small impact on the EU is understandable if one takes into account that exports to the associated states account for about two per cent of the GDP of the EU-15. However, one would expect the impact on the CEE countries to be much larger because their trade with the EU-15 accounts for up to 25 per cent of their GDP.[5] Moreover, the ten per cent reduction in trading costs is completely arbitrary. Such an ad hoc assumption is actually not necessary, since, as we will show below, it is straightforward to use existing detailed estimates.

A gain of 1.5 per cent for the candidate states seems thus very conservative, given the estimates that have been made of the benefits from integration within the present group of member states. Enlargement implies essentially an extension of the internal market and monetary union.[6] The benefits of these two integration projects for the present membership have been estimated and could be used as a guide. Recent estimates of the transactions cost savings from the introduction of the Euro are in the neighbourhood of one per cent of GDP.[7] It is more difficult to estimate the gain from participation in the internal market. Emerson found that this should yield welfare benefits of between 2.5 and 4.5 per cent of EU GDP.[8] Could one use this estimate for the candidates as well? Several arguments would indicate that the benefits for the CEE countries should be at the higher end of this range, or even larger. The key consideration is that all the CEE countries are very small economies, which should thus benefit more from the additional competition fostered by the internal market than the larger and more diversified EU economies. Moreover, integration and market opening in the EU has proceeded well beyond the sectors considered in the initial '1992' programme.

Even if one does not take into account these elements, any estimate of the welfare gains for the CEE is bound to be higher than that for the EC-15 since intra-EU-trade accounts for about 15 per cent of EU GDP, whereas trade with the EU accounts on average for well over 20 per cent of the GDP of the CEE countries. The benefits for the new members should thus be at least one-third higher – 4.4–6.0 per cent of GDP for participation in the internal market and 1.3 per cent for using the common currency. Table 4

TABLE 4
MEASURABLE BENEFITS TO THE CEE-10 FROM EU MEMBERSHIP (AS % OF GDP)

Common currency	1.0 – 1.3
Internal market	4.4 – 6.0
Total	5.4 – 7.3

Source: Own calculations based on estimates for the EU-15 of the gains from a common currency and an internal market.

provides the details for these back-of-the-envelope calculations, which lead to the result that EU membership should yield a measurable benefit of between 5.4 and 7.3 per cent of GDP for the CEE countries.[9]

These measurable gains are already sizeable, but much larger gains can be obtained if one assumes that membership transforms conditions under which the associated countries have access to the world capital market. At present interest rates in the associated countries are much above those in the EU, even for countries that have strong reputation for price stability like the Czech Republic, or a currency board, like Estonia. For other countries, such as Poland, the domestic real interest rate is even higher.

Where does this risk premium come from? Baldwin *et al.* argue that the risk premium that one currently observes on interest rates in the associated states is not due to monetary factors, but to uncertainty about the future of reforms.[10] The crucial assumption is then that only membership can dissipate the doubts in the minds of investors and reduce this risk. Countries that are not allowed to become members would not be able to assure investors about the durability of their reform programmes. The size of the reduction in the risk premium that would come with enlargement is difficult to pinpoint. Baldwin *et al.* use Portugal as an example and argue that accession to the EU would imply a reduction in the risk premium of about 15 per cent (that is, the real interest rate would drop from, for example, 9.0 to 7.65 per cent). The result under this scenario is that real income in the associated states might increase by 30 per cent! This at first sight astonishing result is actually not too surprising given that the models of capital accumulation used by economists imply that the long term capital stock is extremely sensitive to changes in the real interest rate.[11]

What should one think about these very large potential gains from membership arising from a reduction in the risk premium? A first point to note is that this approach assumes that investors will only upgrade the new members and not downgrade the existing ones. While this is possible, one could also argue that the new equilibrium of political forces within the enlarged Union will make economically sound policies less likely. The loss to the EU from a slight increase in its risk-premium could easily exceed the gains of new members on account of a lower risk premium for them. Moreover, the quantification of the gain in the risk premium is totally arbitrary. The assumed alternative (continuing uncertainty about reforms) is not likely for those countries that will actually be able to join first. The countries that will not be able to join because they cannot implement the *acquis* would actually be those with the highest risk premium and thus those that would benefit most from becoming members. For those that have the choice, a reduction in the risk premium might thus not be the first source of advantages from membership.

However, these illustrative calculations of the potential gains from membership are useful because they highlight one important aspect. There are certain gains from joining the internal market and EMU that can be quantified. These gains should be in the neighbourhood of five per cent of GDP for the associated states that are very open economies. But the potentially more important gains are not quantifiable, and these come from joining an area that embodies through the internal market rules the principles of open competition in the largest market of the world and that guarantees sound macroeconomic policies within the context of EMU. This framework for sound policies should favour growth through a lot of channels and might ultimately raise income by even more than 30 per cent. But one has to admit that this is not a judgement that can be proven with scientific methods.

Another useful lesson from these estimates is that the welfare gains for the EU are also real, although much smaller in terms of the EU-15 GDP. Expansion to the east would increase trading opportunities for the EU-15. The CEE countries account for less than five per cent of the EU GDP and about 10–15 per cent of the EU's external trade. As the gain from the internal market is about 4–5 per cent of EU GDP, the gain to present EU members from the inclusion of the ten CEE countries in the internal market and the Euro zone should thus be about 0.4–0.5 per cent of GDP, or about 25 billion Euro per annum. This alone would be more than the total budgetary cost. Moreover the gains for the EU can only grow over time as the economies of the associated states grow along with their trade. Their share in the overall external trade of the EU has already doubled since 1990 and on current trends it could well double again by 2005/6. At that point the estimated benefit would be twice as large as it appears from today's point of view. However, the budgetary costs would not increase proportionally. By the time the formal decision on enlargement has to be taken it is thus likely that the economic benefits of enlargement to the EU-15 will even more clearly outweigh the costs than they already do today.

CONCLUSIONS

The main findings of this study are that the structure of the economies of most of the candidates (the CEE-8 – that is, the CEE-10 less Bulgaria and Romania) are not so different from those of the current EU-15 members that they would not fit into the EU, or the Euro area. Their legal and institutional frameworks are generally of lower quality than the EU average, but they are also clearly better than one would expect given their low income level. Moreover, the candidates are likely to benefit considerably from EU and EMU membership. This suggests that the long term economic prospects of the candidates are rather good. They start from a low level of income, but they are likely to have healthy, growing economies, which might be better able to absorb shocks than the more established ones of the richer EU member countries.

The position taken by many policy makers today is rather similar to the prevailing opinion during the early 1990s when it was generally assumed that only the strong core countries would be able to enter EMU and withstand the rigours of price stability (and that the poor countries had to be bribed by the Cohesion Fund). Reality turned out to be different. The 'peripheral' countries are more dynamic than the core. A similar outcome should result from enlargement. Indeed, a number of studies by investment banks, international financial institutions and independent economists suggest that the combination of low income (and wages), market access and a stable institutional framework for a market economy should lead to growth rates of around 4–5 per cent over the next decade. This is considerably more than the 2–3 per cent growth usually expected for the (core) EU countries. While this would not lead to a quick catch-up, it suggests that the new members are unlikely to have problems within an enlarged Euro area. A two speed EMU might thus emerge, but it will be quite different from what many expect, as the old 'core' economies would be relatively stagnant compared to the CEE countries. There might thus be permanent conflict between the core, whose performance would call for low interest rates, and the CEE countries, whose higher growth (and higher inflation rates due to the Balassa-Samuelson effect) would call for higher interest rates. But fortunately this conflict is unlikely to cause big problems because the weight of the CEE in the Euroland economy is minor, and because experience has shown that most countries are quite content to accept a combination of low interest rates, moderate inflation and, above all, strong growth. Hence the CEE countries are unlikely to press strongly for higher interest rates. But these considerations point to one source of tension that is unavoidable: convergence in income levels requires for some time divergence in growth rates.

NOTES

1. Portugal does not have a coast on the Mediterranean Sea, but it is nevertheless usually counted as an honorary member of Club Med.
2. Daniel Gros and Marc Suhrcke, 'Ten Years After: What is Special about Transition Countries?' (Centre for European Policy Studies, CEPS Working Document No. 143, May 2000).
3. Richard E. Baldwin, Joseph François and Richard Portes, 'The Costs and Benefits of Eastern Enlargement: The Impact on the EU and Central Europe', *Economic Policy* 24 (April 1007), pp.127–76.
4. Membership will also force the Central and Eastern European countries to reduce their tariffs on imports from the rest of the world. But since these imports are small compared to their imports from the EU this effect is not important for the size of the welfare benefits.
5. The share of exports to the EU countries as a percentage of total exports in most of the candidate countries is well above 60 per cent, the average for CEEC-8 reaching 65 per cent.
6. Since agriculture accounts for only a minor fraction (6–10 per cent) of GDP, the gains from freeing trade in this sector cannot be large in relation to GDP.
7. See also Chapter 7 in Daniel Gros and Niels Thygesen, *European Monetary Integration* (London: Addison Wesley Longman 1998).
8. Michael Emerson, *Redrawing the Map of Europe* (London: Macmillan 1998).
9. Four to five times the amount found by Baldwin *et al.*, 'The Costs and Benefits'. Moreover, a large part of the gains in real income found by these authors do not correspond to welfare gains since they result from increased capital accumulation, which does not come for free (like the transactions costs savings from a common currency) but requires households to postpone consumption.
10. Baldwin *et al.*, 'The Costs and Benefits'.
11. For details, see Daniel Gros and A. Steinherr, *Winds of Change, Economic Transition in Central and Eastern Europe* (London/Cambridge, MA: Longman and MIT Press 2001), Chapter 11.

The Welfare State in Transition Economies and Accession to the EU

HANS-JÜRGEN WAGENER

Eastern enlargement of the European Union will create a new, south-eastern, periphery of the Union, a periphery which is partly situated close to the economic core. It has been shown that distance from the core, be it Brussels or Düsseldorf, is a factor strongly influencing economic convergence as it happened in Western Europe after World War II.[1] Under normal conditions, countries like Czechoslovakia, Slovenia and, of course, Eastern Germany should be on a productivity level comparable to Western Germany, Austria and Italy, with countries like Poland and Hungary on a level perhaps comparable to Spain. Such was the situation immediately before and after the war.[2] However, conditions in Eastern Europe were not normal – the region came under the hegemony of the Soviet Union and it was forced to adopt the Soviet political and economic system. So it did not take part in the impetuous convergence process that has characterised the economic development of Western Europe for the last 40 years. The present productivity level is at best 50 per cent of what it could have been. Eastern Europe moved away from Europe and Eastern Central Europe from the core of it. Peripherisation is the result of 40 years of communism.

After the collapse of Soviet hegemony and of the Soviet-type system, the countries of Eastern Central Europe (ECE) immediately declared their intent to 'return to Europe', which means above all catching up with the post-war political and economic development. A central feature of the European economic and political system is the welfare state. Despite a great diversity in its institutional arrangements, there is a common commitment and there are shared values which allow us to speak of a European welfare state that can clearly be distinguished from the Anglo-American and Japanese social cultures. With the abolition of the market and private striving for profit as driving forces of the economic system, the Soviet-type economy made social policy pointless – there was no longer an autonomous economic sphere whose working and results were to be regulated, complemented or changed by political power. Hence, the communist welfare state, if there is such a thing (for let it be clear, a high share of education and health services in final demand and an income distribution in favour of the non-active or poorer parts of the population do not in themselves make a welfare state) must be something completely different from the European welfare state. This is true even if social justice, one of the shared values within the latter, was also one of the catch-words of communism.

Return to Europe poses a double task for those who endeavour to make the journey: the transformation of the political and economic system and the catching up of productivity levels. Neither is independent of the other. For, as the theory of conditional convergence suggests,[3] convergence clubs are defined by their systemic properties. What is not undisputed, of course, is whether the European welfare state belongs to these essential properties. So it may be assumed that on their way back to Europe the countries of ECE have more degrees of freedom in this respect than in others where there is theoretical consensus and a well defined *acquis communautaire*.

Seen from the side of the incumbent members of the European Union, the return to Europe of the ECE countries is treated as eastern enlargement of the Union, the most comprehensive enlargement project since 1973 when the United Kingdom, Ireland and Denmark joined the Europe of the Six. At that time basic conditions for accession had been formulated which, for the present case of eastern enlargement, have since been restated at the Copenhagen summit. Next to the general conditions of democratic rule of law and a functioning market order, it is the *acquis communautaire* which erects the highest barrier to entrance to the Union. The Copenhagen conditions also mentioned competitiveness: the accession candidates should be able to withstand competition from the Union and the Union should not suffer unduly from competition from the acceding countries.

It is generally thought that these conditions pose little problem in the context of social security. While the Economic and Monetary Union (EMU) is a highly developed part of the *acquis* (not in all its elements obligatory as membership of the Euro-bloc shows), the European Union is not yet a social union and will not be so for the foreseeable future. Convergence of social conditions will be the outcome of economic convergence; it cannot be its precondition. Hence, candidate countries are free to choose welfare regimes which they think appropriate for their stage of development and their social culture. Some advisers recommend – and some critics fear – that ECE countries should orient themselves towards American flexibility and low key welfare provisions, thus becoming model cases of growth and efficiency, in one view, or Trojan horses in the race to the bottom of welfare, in the other.

Even if the social *acquis* is not very comprehensive, however, it is far from being an empty set. It can be ascertained on four levels. First, the level of the single market with health and safety prescriptions; second, the level of the social protocol which has been incorporated in the Treaty of Amsterdam with, for example, working time and equal opportunity regulations; third, the level of social dialogue, such as the rules demanding social partnership; and, fourth, the level of what is called the 'soft *acquis*', that is, some kind of European social culture that cannot be made binding for any candidate country, but which it is expected to share.

It is obvious that some of the elements of the social *acquis* imply costly investments on the side of the less developed candidate countries. On the other side, competition from low wage and low social cost labour is a point of concern in some incumbent member states.

The remainder of this study will attempt to assess the measures taken to transform the social security system in the post-communist countries of ECE. The guiding question should be whether by enlarging the European Union in this direction, the *acquis* in its broader meaning, not as a body of legal regulations, but as an economic and social culture, comes under a threat. In the next section a brief survey of the starting conditions, the communist welfare state, is given. Transformation of the social security system can be divided into two phases which will be discussed in the third and fourth sections. This is followed by some considerations concerning harmonisation conditions of access, and then a brief conclusion.

THE SOCIALIST WELFARE STATE

It has become common to begin any reflection on the post-socialist welfare state with Kornai's dictum that the Hungarian and, implicitly, the socialist welfare state in general, was born 'prematurely', that is, the countries of Eastern Europe introduced lavish welfare measures without the necessary economic basis or a correspondingly high level of GNP.[4] This statement is in contrast to the received pre-1989 opinion that the socialist welfare state, as far as size and scope are concerned, was very much in line with Western developments, thus confirming the then popular convergence hypothesis.[5] Such inter-system comparisons suffer from several shortcomings: GNP comparisons are on a very shaky basis because of price and quality problems, and the organisation of the welfare state is so different that quantitative evaluation is almost impossible. A second remark with respect to Kornai's dictum refers to the fact that development is not the only determinant of welfare state size. Ideology, or shared opinions and values, is a second factor which has the effect that, also within the West, continental ideas about social security differ from Anglo-American ones, and ECE, already before the communist takeover, shared the continental tradition. But even on the European continent we find different levels of welfare provision. The latecomers to social security, Sweden and The Netherlands, for example, have much more comprehensive systems than, say, Germany and Austria. Also in the East commitment to social security and equality differed in the pre-communist as well as in the communist period, with Czechoslovakia caring more for both than did Poland, for example.

Be that as it may, if not lavish – there was nothing lavish under communism, not even the fringe benefits of its ruling class – the socialist welfare state was comprehensive and sizeable. However, it was a worker's privilege rather than a citizen's right. In daily life, of course, the difference was minimal, since almost everybody was a worker. Those who were not, but were working people, got incorporated into the socialist welfare state rather late and under special conditions: *kolkhozniki* in the Soviet Union, private farmers in Poland, private small scale entrepreneurs in the GDR. The close link between social security provisions and the worker status derives from the first and foremost property of the socialist welfare state – full employment. The full employment guarantee was made possible by the specific role of the firm in the socialist system, this being primarily a social unit rather than an economic one. Without any competitive pressure and with a state guarantee of existence, the state-owned enterprise could provide any wished-for employment and take over many of the tasks of the social security system. Since, as a rule, these firms were big, they also had a regional function and could adopt local administrative tasks which otherwise would rest with the local communal or provincial administration. A second social security short-cut was the practice of price subsidies which, incidentally, makes the calculation of the size of the socialist welfare state so cumbersome. By fixing only symbolic prices for the necessities of daily life, such as food, clothing, housing and public transport, the socialist welfare state was convinced to have solved the problem of poverty and hence did not need any carefully designed targeted measures.

Technically, the formerly independent social insurance systems – in ECE more or less closely following the Bismarckian model – were incorporated in the state budget and state administration. The firms were paying the workers' contributions into the budget and they, or more precisely the enterprise organisation of the trade union, were administering the claims of their workers. Pensions were rather small, thus inducing an additional labour supply, and they had the special problem of hidden inflation: the older a pension claim, the smaller its real value. Health care was directly provided by the state – a statistically comprehensive provision that suffered from low quality and under-financing, leading to the widespread practice of side-payments by the clients in order to get proper and timely treatment. Education was the pride of communism. In short, economics and politics and, in this case, economic policy and social policy were not separated. The workers stood under the protective guarantee of a paternalistic state, and were free of any responsibility.

Obviously, this system could not continue once the transformation from socialist planning to capitalist markets had come on the agenda. Nevertheless it is common knowledge that the transformation of the social security system was not among the priority objectives of reform policy and could be treated as second order phenomenon.[6] This needs a brief explanation. Indeed, the transformation programmes preferentially aimed at stabilisation, liberalisation, privatisation and, when the objective 'institution building' was made concrete, it was the introduction of a functioning banking system and capital markets that got pride of place. Implicitly it was thought that the new economic regime had inherited an operating social security system from the old regime which it could then deal with when the priority objectives had been settled. Typically, Leszek Balcerowicz's account of the Polish transformation process does not include the terms social security and welfare in its index, nor do the topics show up in the text.[7] In the early 1990s they were not important, although, especially in Poland, they were soon to become so. Indeed, stabilisation, liberalisation and privatisation thoroughly changed the inherited social security system. For with these policies was brought about the separation of economy and polity, thus assigning a completely new and purely economic role to the firm.

Liberalisation had two effects. It separated the firm from the state and transformed it into an independent economic unit with (more or less) hard budget constraints. In order to survive in the market, firms, even if they still were state-owned, had to cut all costs which were not necessary with respect to commercial production. Overstaffing was reduced immediately and unnecessary social provisions were relinquished. Transition to the new system may have been eased by some budget subsidies or soft bank credits, especially for big old firms. But stabilisation puts limits to such softening measures, since they inevitably have inflationary consequences. As a result, unemployment was unavoidable and unemployment benefits became an immediate necessity. At the same time, the decline of formal sector employment reduced the revenues of the social security system. This decline was not uniform all over the region. While in the Czech Republic the lowest level (1989 = 100) was reached at 89.7, in Hungary the corresponding figure was 69.8.[8] It is easy to imagine that the strain on the welfare state was much more serious in Hungary than in the Czech Republic. Further, certain social services, up to then provided by the firm, either got out-sourced or disappeared altogether. Effective privatisation reinforced this tendency.

The second effect of liberalisation was the freeing of prices which, together with stabilisation, also meant the discontinuation of price subsidies for life's necessities. Where nominal wages or transfer payments were inflexible, real incomes must have dropped, occasionally under the poverty line. At the same time, the pension, health and education systems could be continued for the time being in a more or less unreformed way, transferring only the administrative tasks from the firm to the state which did not have the appropriate administration to start with. Social policy, above all the pension system, has been used in the first phase of transformation to cushion or to compensate for the immediate social consequences of the transition crisis.[9] The crisis being an unexpected phenomenon, governments may have worked under the assumption that the rather rapidly increasing costs of such measures to the social security system would be of a transitory nature. Only when and where it turned out that this is not the case did fiscal problems move social policy to centre-stage. In short, unemployment benefits, social compensation and the technical administration of welfare benefits were of first-phase transformation concern, while the basic models failed to get on the agenda before the second phase.

TRANSFORMATION OF THE WELFARE STATE

Transformation of the welfare state has an important preliminary stage: transformation of the state. This is by no means a trivial affair. The old communist state crumbled throughout the region, and yet the transformation of the political, economic and social systems could only be accomplished under the guidance of a strong state. The solution to this conundrum lay at the roots of transformation success. Successful transformers, after the inevitable transitional crisis, resumed economic growth and accomplished in-depth structural changes. These countries have comparatively well established democracies and effective governments and are typically to be found in Eastern Central Europe. Less successful transformers did not overcome the initial crisis and slid into a protracted depression. In these countries state governance is weak, is very often captured by particular interests, and is unable to perform its normal functions. Such cases are typically to be found in the former Soviet Union (FSU), with Russia and the Ukraine being the most spectacular cases. As a result, these countries are situated in a kind of limbo: the state is weak and poor and cannot live up to the expectations of the population. Compensatory social policy as a response to the transition crisis is out of the question. The firms, albeit privatised, are not fully restructured and operate in what has been called a 'virtual economy'.[10] Workers are staying with their old firm even if they do not get paid, since certain welfare provisions, such as housing, are still on offer. For the rest, the citizens have to look after themselves, which effectively means that large strata fall into poverty.

It is therefore typical for the FSU countries that poverty has increased significantly during the 1990s, while in ECE this has happened only moderately: the incidence of poverty increased between the periods 1987–88 and 1993–95 in Hungary from one to seven per cent of the population, in Poland from six to ten per cent, in Estonia from one to 34 per cent, in Romania six to 48 per cent, and in Russia two to 39 per cent.[11] The inequality measures show similar developments.[12] This is not the place to speculate about why state transformation succeeded in ECE rather than in the FSU. Many factors may have played a role, among which geographical, historical and institutional proximity to the European Union, or the West in general, figure prominently.[13] The expectation of membership in the EU in due time served as a transformation anchor for the political and economic systems, as well as for the social security system.

With respect to many institutional aspects the anticipation of access to the Union predetermined the choices of the transformation countries in ECE. This was not the case with respect to the welfare system, however. That said, econometric research has shown that a dummy variable 'Europe' is positively correlated with the share of government expenditure in GNP,[14] reflecting what is perhaps a particular European welfare culture. Indeed, there is a general commitment in the EU to social security, even though the 'responsibility for organizing and financing of social protection systems is in the hands of Member States'.[15] This statement refers to the great variety of welfare systems within the Union and their deep political-historical entrenchment, a feature which makes even marginal reforms a very difficult and often impossible endeavour. For the transformation countries, however, it implies that they may choose between different models of welfare systems, and liberal reform advisers are warning against restricting the choice only to European models, thus disregarding the East Asian experiences. In this view, high government expenditure, and high welfare expenditure in particular, is considered a threat to economic growth.[16] When social expenditure is disentangled from capital expenditure and government consumption, on the other hand, only the latter can be connected with negative growth effects, while both former categories are seen to improve growth prospects.[17] Nor does the growth record of the successful transformation countries in ECE, which have somewhat developed 'European' welfare systems, corroborate this hypothesis.

Following Esping-Andersen,[18] it has become customary to identify three worlds of capitalist welfare systems, distinguished from one another according to the commodification of labour, the matrix of social equity (stratification vs. equalisation), and the public–private welfare mix. The first of these is the liberal model, which tries to avoid poverty by a minimal safety net and leaves the rest to private responsibility and initiative – the most prominent example being the US, with a share of public social security and health expenditures of 14.6 per cent of GDP in 1990. The second is the conservative-corporatist model which adheres to the contribution-related benefit criterion of mandatory insurance-type regimes and subsidiarity between family, firm and the state – Germany's Rhenanian model being a typical example, with public social security and health measures accounting for 23.5 per cent of GDP in 1990. The third model is the Scandinavian or social democratic welfare state model, which guarantees social citizenship rights and adheres to the redistributive ability-to-pay criterion – Sweden is the best known example, with 33.1 per cent of Swedish GDP being devoted to public social security and health expenditures in 1990.[19] As always with ideal-type distinctions, borderlines between systems are more fuzzy in reality. But the difference sizes of the examples certainly testifies to significant differences.

It was generally expected that the transformation countries in ECE, or at least those of their political parties with leftist inclinations, would be attracted by the Scandinavian model of the welfare state. On the other hand, liberal reformers and some of their Western advisers were enchanted by Margaret Thatcher's anti-welfare state rhetoric, or at least by that of her favourite social philosopher Friedrich von Hayek. Indeed, Vaclav Klaus' dictum of a market economy without adjectives, and in particular without the adjective 'social', became notorious. Not surprisingly, it was found that neither the one nor the other preference could be found within the political practice of the transformation countries. The liberal rhetoric has not led to uncompromising liberal models, even in the Czech Republic, despite some claims to the contrary,[20] with the difference between rhetoric and reality being dubbed the 'Klaus-paradox' and being adequately explained as a political compromise by Müller.[21] Nor did the enlightened left in ECE – the orthodox communist left in Russia and Czechoslovakia insisted on the old socialist model – propagate the social democratic welfare state model. It seemed too close to the old model, it was unsustainable in the economic situation of the transition countries, it did not conform to the market system which was the primary objective of transformation, and it seemed to be in a crisis in its own countries of origin.[22] So what was then the guiding line? As Cook *et al.* put it: 'Add Beveridge-style minimums to a fundamentally social insurance-based welfare system, and you have the social market model pushed by the left in contemporary post communist Europe.'[23] With a somewhat stronger emphasis upon the state welfare system, such was also the result of the first transformation phase. It is a clear result of path dependency: the Bismarckian social insurance model was predominant in the region before the communist takeover, and the state welfare system is characteristic of the communist system, as we have seen.

The first step in welfare system transformation was a partial return to the pre-war regime: a re-institution of the Bismarckian social insurance which formally, but not materially, had survived in some countries under the communist regime. Such reforms were distributed over the whole ten year period of the 1990s: Hungary and Czechoslovakia, for instance, reintroduced health insurance funds at the beginning of the decade; in Poland a similar reform became effective as of 1 January 1999. The Bismarckian model is less redistribution and more contribution-related, while the public still expected a broad protection against risks, an expectation which was honoured by writing basic social rights into the new constitutions. This was a major achievement compared to the communist regime: linking the welfare state with the rule of law and thus giving the constitutional courts a say in social policy. Of course, the adapted system came quite close to the continental conservative-corporatist model, and it may be questioned whether the choice was made deliberately to accommodate the median voter,[24] or whether it was the rather *ad hoc* and often contradictory result of some fiscal specialists' efforts to keep the social security system going under the new conditions.[25]

Most countries formally succeeded in separating the social security funds from the state budget proper, albeit not necessarily with their own legal status and self-administration, and separating the pension funds from health care insurance. Yet the weak level of contributions due to unemployment, shadow activities and non-compliance could not make up for the increased expenditures and hence constituted a considerable burden to the state budget. Subsidies had to cover the deficit. If the communist welfare state was not living beyond its means, the post-communist welfare state certainly was. In Poland, the most extreme case, the share of social expenditure in GDP increased from 17 per cent in 1989 to 32 per cent in 1995. Less dramatic increases happened in the Czech Republic, Hungary and Slovenia.[26] These increases are mainly due to unemployment and pension benefits. The share of the latter in GDP increased over this same period in Poland from 6.6. to 14.6 per cent, in the Czech Republic from 8.3 to 9.1 per cent, and in Hungary from 9.1 to 10.6 per cent.[27] The reasons for such a short term rise were of course not demographic, but policy-related. The shares of health and education increased between 1990 and 1993 in Hungary and the Czech Republic and then diminished in the former and stabilised in the latter. In Poland it remained more or less constant on a somewhat lower level.[28] According to another estimate, the share of health care expenditure in GNP went up by almost three percentage points in the Czech Republic after 1992, while in Hungary it decreased by 2.5 percentage points.[29] In both these countries this share was significantly higher than in Poland where the old tax-financed and state-run health care system remained in force till the end of 1998. Needless to say, the situation in FSU countries, notably Russia, the Ukraine and Moldova, was completely different.

It would be wrong to state that the health and education systems remained more or less unaltered in the sense that they remained generally poor. The Czech Republic, Hungary, Slovenia, and recently Poland, introduced mandatory health insurance systems and started to decentralise and partly privatise provision of health services which, however, is still predominantly a state or communal affair. But the quality of services, here as in education, depends on capital and labour. The former is urgently needed for thorough re-equipping, the latter was notoriously underpaid under the old system. Given the fact that the share of health care expenditure in GNP is slightly above eight per cent in Hungary and the Czech Republic,[30] and hence on a Western level, the problem appears to be less one of additional means than of a fundamental restructuring of the sector. In Poland the system seems to be under-financed, as stated. Again, we notice a huge difference in the health status of the population between the FSU, where the state literally collapsed, and ECE, where the situation did not improve significantly but was more or less stabilised.[31] One reaction to this state of affairs is a creeping privatisation and commercialisation of health services: the more deficient the services, the sooner the general public, or that stratum that can afford it, is willing to finance private treatment. This happens from Poland to Bulgaria and, naturally, in Russia. The mounting costs of the pension schemes in ECE are due to different reasons, among which hidden unemployment, indexing (to rising prices, not to falling real wages), and policy pressures are prominent. The differences within the region are considerable. So the relative income position of pensioners during the period 1987–88 and 1992–93 improved in Poland and Slovenia, remained more or less unchanged in Hungary, Slovakia and Romania, and deteriorated in the Baltic states, Bulgaria and the Czech Republic.[32] The problem of ageing could have no impact in so short a period, but will, of course, make itself felt in the future. In short, there are several motives, mainly fiscal and systemic, not to go on muddling through, but to enter the second phase of transformation by reforming the welfare state, and by starting with the pension system.

SECOND PHASE REFORMS OF THE PENSION SYSTEM

Fiscal and systemic problems with the welfare state, especially in the context of an ageing society, are not unique to ECE. Similar questions are also confronted in the present EU member states and elsewhere. The naive outside observer could presume that, given the stage of development and of political and social culture of the Union, the member states have found solutions that are superior to the inherited Anglo-American, continental or Scandinavian models, and that could be imitated by the young democratic market economies in the East. Nothing could be further from the truth. The inherited welfare state systems of the West exhibit a remarkable tenacity, due on the one hand to the fact that they result from a long and fierce social struggle in the past, and on the other to the fact that the present political systems which have to agree to reforms are highly complex and delicately equilibrated matrices of interests – less friendly critics speak of Euro-sclerosis – with the effect that changes happen, as a rule, in the margin, and that radical system transformations are rather difficult to achieve. As noted above, the Union itself has very little competence and leverage to develop and impose own ideas about social security, and the Treaty of Amsterdam (art. 136 and 137) makes it very clear that national preferences are to be observed and that each member has a right of veto in this field.

The situation is quite different in the so-called emerging markets, to which the transition countries belong. In addition, there is an international institution with outspoken ideas about the welfare system and with considerable leverage to make itself heard in these countries – the World

Bank. The characteristics of the pension system favoured in the environment of the World Bank[33] follow from the so-called Washington consensus,[34] which is based upon fiscal stabilisation, regulative liberalisation and organisational privatisation – the very objectives of transformation in ECE. It should be mentioned that the Washington consensus does not contain recommendations with respect to social security, either because there was no consensus in this area or because it was then considered of secondary importance. Nevertheless, fiscal stabilisation, regulative liberalisation and organisational privatisation clearly provide the theoretical basis of World Bank institutional policy recommendations. For the pension system this implies a three-pillar model[35] with a minimal poverty-targeted first pillar on a pay-as-you-go (PAYG) basis, a mandatory private insurance second pillar on a fully funded (FF) basis, and a voluntary private insurance third pillar. The difference with the prevailing European systems is to be seen in the shift from the first to the second pillar – privatisation and an individual contribution-related scheme where the arrangement can be personal or occupational. Upon closer inspection we see that the stress is lying on privatisation. For, if not perfectly, the venerable Bismarckian model (which seems never to have been fully understood by the Washington advisers who confound it with the Beveridgian welfare state) was individual contribution-related and was fully funded. However two spells of high inflation in twentieth century Germany have diluted the funds (and shown the dangers of such a system if it is not backed up by the state) in such a way that it could not be practised even while still formally in force (up to 1957).

The objective of the World Bank model is not only old age income security, but enhanced economic growth.[36] It is assumed that funded systems will produce a higher savings rate than PAYG schemes and that funds accumulated in private insurance companies will play a more active role in the capital market than funds accumulated in a public pension system. From this follow the logic and the dilemma of the model: emerging markets need capital for growth, but their capital markets, and their financial stability in general, are poorly developed and very sensitive. However, the idea of combining old age security and increased capital accumulation must be attractive in the transition countries that are eager to catch up with the European Union.

A radical implementation of this 'new pension orthodoxy',[37] as happened 1981 in Pinochet's Chile, would imply almost a return to the pre-welfare state world with individual responsibility and poor laws, were it not for the mandatory character of the private insurance. It would not correspond with, at least in Europe, the evolved idea that it is exactly in the context of long term welfare protection that individual decision making and the market need some subsidiary state support, or with the European social security culture that includes a strong element of solidarity. Nor can there be any guarantee that a system relying almost exclusively upon the capital market would be able to provide the hoped for long term income security. On the other hand, a reconsideration of the public–private mix is deemed necessary in many countries and 'three-pillar' models are discussed and adopted all over the world. It was particularly Argentina which succeeded in 1994 in transforming its state-dominated pension system by a democratic decision making process into a complementary public–private system.

This is not the place to analyse the merits and demerits of PAYG and FF systems, however, or their possible combinations, or their introduction or reform. Suffice it to say that the EU Commission is also recommending an 'appropriate balance between funded and PAYG (pay-as-you-go) systems'.[38] The Commission is motivated here by its concern both for macro-stability within the EMU and for more employment-friendly flexibility in the labour market. Both these motives must play a decisive role in Eastern European pension reform considerations.

The first phase pension system reforms in ECE had achieved a certain formal, although not financial, separation of pension schemes from the state budget (with the exception of the Czech Republic, where the pension system was in surplus and was happily used by the state budget), the (re-) introduction of employee contributions, some kind of indexation arrangements, and some basic parameter changes (for example, replacement rates). The second phase pension system reforms can be grouped in three clusters:[39] first, parametric changes of the existing PAYG system; second, notionally defined contribution schemes; and, third, notionally mandatory fully funded schemes.

Parametric changes of a PAYG system can imply very different things. In most parts of Western Europe it has meant, up to now, a tinkering with replacement rates, the pension formula, or the retirement age. All this is also done in ECE. But when the change implies a switch from a Beveridge-type tax-financed general fixed pension to a Bismarck-type contribution-financed and contribution-related pension, we may speak of a more radical change. The problems of such a transition are financial, for the first scheme was strongly redistributive, while the latter is meant to be less so. However, if the flat rate pension was close to the subsistence minimum, which as a rule it was in the whole region, a contribution-related differentiation of retirement benefits requires additional funds.

Notionally defined contribution (NDC) schemes are, in fact, a radical paradigm shift within the public pensions system that in this way loses much of its PAYG character. The basic idea is rather simple: each employee has his or her own capital account with the public social security system where the contributions, be it employers' or employees' or other contributions, are registered. But these individual capital accounts are notional: no real funded accumulation takes place. At the end of the working career, the accumulated notional capital together with the statistical life expectancy define the actuarially fair pension benefits. The system has several advantages: it is contribution-related, its claims can be carried across state borders by employees, and the risk of demographic change is not carried by the paying, but by the receiving generation (in the present context of ageing populations, many people consider this an advantage). This innovation was developed by Swedish pension specialists and pioneered with the help of Swedish advisers in Latvia in 1996, before it also became a core element of the Swedish pension system reform passed by parliament in 1998.[40] The new Swedish system may be called a four-pillar system with a tax-financed (and means-tested) minimum pension, a public tier along the lines of the NDC principle, a mandatory private FF tier and voluntary private provisions. Although this model may gain paradigmatic character in the future, its introduction was greatly helped by special Swedish circumstances that do not prevail everywhere. By considering the introduction of a mandatory private FF tier, the present German government is also heading for a four-pillar system: poverty relief by social assistance is a communal responsibility, the core institution is a public PAYG insurance scheme that is meant to be supplemented by a mandatory private FF tier, and the system is rounded off by voluntary private provisions.

The introduction of mandatory fully funded schemes in Eastern Europe is a very special case of institutional transfer. Unlike many other instances where the *acquis communautaire* has shaped the paradigm for transformation targets, the transfer occurs in this case from Latin America to Eastern Europe – with the help of intermediation and support from the World Bank. As noted, there is in fact no *acquis communautaire* with respect to pension schemes in the EU, and the current member states are themselves confronted with the need to reform their old age provisions for demographic, fiscal and market-related reasons. Moreover, contrary to received wisdom in political science,[41] it turns out that by comparison to the established democracies in Western Europe, the new democracies in Latin America and Eastern Europe encounter less resistance from entrenched interests when determining and implementing radical reforms. The Danish population, for example, which enjoys the most comprehensive tax-financed public pension scheme, inevitably lives under the impression that they have a lot to lose through any reform, and hence will resist it. Resistance to reform is moderate in ECE, however,[42] and does not impede some radical changes which may still be associated with the general expectation that in a 'period of extraordinary politics'[43] there may be a lot to be gained by transformation.

The most radical reform in transition countries has been introduced, following the Chilean precedent, in Kazakhstan in 1998. The whole CIS region is full of problems of its own, not least that of serious payment arrears and, consequently, widespread poverty among the aged. Such problems are not solved by radical privatisation. Of more interest are the Hungarian and Polish reforms which implemented truly 'multi-pillar models' combining a PAYG tier with a mandatory fully funded insurance. The Hungarian reform came into force in 1998. In fact, it yields a four-pillar system which, as we see, seems to become the rule in Europe. It supplements the dominant and still to be reformed public PAYG system with a mandatory private insurance tier. At the low end there is a means tested minimum pension, and at the high end a voluntary 'third' pillar. The difference between mandatory private pension funds and voluntary insurance contracts can be seen, here as elsewhere, in the scope of prudent regulation. Of course, the whole financial sector of banks and insurance companies is carefully regulated and supervised by the state in well functioning market economies. Legislating mandatory private pension funds gives the state a special responsibility to guarantee solvability and liquidity which it will fulfil by additional prudent regulation. Here we can establish one of the core features of welfare state privatisation: the state partly retreats from own provisions transferring the production of services to competing private enterprises which are, however, carefully regulated and controlled to protect their clients. The risks of the market and of market failure (bankruptcy, adverse selection, moral hazard, the latter two playing an even more important role in health insurance) cannot be borne by the individual citizen. Elements of redistributive solidarity which are implicitly present in welfare state arrangements will only in exceptional cases be taken over by the private providers. They will have to be made explicit and organised in targeted state measures.

In Poland the new system came into force in 1999. The first public tier itself underwent a thorough reform: its organisation – the ZUS which also covers disability, sickness and accident risks – was separated from the state and got its own legal status, it is financed by employers' and employees' contributions, and it pays benefits according to the notional defined contribution principle. It is supplemented by a minimum pension, which may be seen as a pillar of its own in order to avoid poverty among the aged. The second pillar is a mandatory fully funded tier managed by strictly regulated private pension funds. It is financed only by employees' contributions and, naturally, disburses contribution-defined benefits. The third pillar, as everywhere, is composed of voluntary individual old age provisions. Contrary to the Argentine model, membership of the second tier is not optional in Poland (except for the transitory period and people of intermediate age). In the final state, each employee will pay contributions into, and obtain benefits from, both sources. According to present legislation, the first public PAYG tier is dominant. Indeed, resemblance to the Swedish reform cannot be ignored and Swedish advisers were active in the country.

The transition to a new pension system is a lengthy and costly affair, since notional as well as real funds have to be accumulated and benefits must be paid in the meantime. So it is not to be expected that the state budget will encounter any appreciable relief of the welfare state expenses in the short run. In addition, transitory arrangements, the details of which we have omitted in this brief overview, will be and, in the countries that have taken the reform steps, already are rather complicated, and are difficult to grasp for the general public. Secondly, these reforms put a heavy burden on the administration: administering those transitory arrangements, administering NDC accounts and implementing prudent regulation require experienced personnel and expensive equipment. Thirdly, private pension funds will flourish only in an environment of strong and stable capital markets. It remains to be seen how Hungary and Poland, and their followers Bulgaria, Latvia, Croatia and Macedonia, will get along with these problems. It is not purely hypothetical to fear that Kornai's dictum of a premature welfare state comes true in the end in the form of a premature radical welfare state reform.

WELFARE STATE ACCESSION PROBLEMS?

Since the Union has not developed a voluminous *acquis* in the field of social protection, the starting hypothesis regarding accession will be that there are few problems in this respect for the ECE countries. Following from the patterns identified in the previous section, it can be argued that any type of pension scheme ought to be acceptable for the EU in view of the differences between the new Swedish, the Danish, the German or the British systems.

Of course, the Commission must be concerned about the free movement of capital, labour and services within the single market. And here the diversity of pension systems, as well as health care systems, forms a major impediment to labour mobility. The lack of harmonised regulations for state-organised PAYG pension schemes and of public as well as private health care provisions clearly makes it unattractive for labour to move freely between member states. A second concern of the Commission is fiscal stability, and with it the stability of EMU. Intergenerational solidarity in PAYG systems draws a cheque on the future which may become expensive when demographic parameters are changing – as is currently the case in most European countries. The temptation must be great for governments to postpone part of the additional burden to a more distant future by issuing bonds. In that case member states with smaller such liabilities, like the UK, will have to share in the consequences of increasing capital costs.[44] But all these are general problems, and have little specific relevance to the new candidate members.

As we have seen, the fiscal crisis has induced several of the transformation countries in ECE to engage in radical welfare state reforms, and in this regard they are already ahead of many incumbent member states that currently complain about the heavy burden of ageing and rising health care costs. Solutions have to be national and may follow different welfare state paradigms. However, it is intriguing to consider that particular radically reformed welfare state regimes will gain a certain weight after Eastern enlargement within the Union, influencing the institutional policy choice of those late-coming reformers. As far as third-pillar private social insurance systems are concerned, which in the form of occupational welfare provisions play an important role in many Western countries, the Union endeavours to become more active in reaching a single market in the field of services.[45] But here also national sovereignty is quickly involved. The points of concern are prudential rules for supplementary pension schemes, co-ordination of tax systems and the influence on social partners to negotiate schemes that do not inhibit labour mobility. Occupational schemes play a minor role in ECE, partly due to the traditional overall state responsibility for social security and partly due to the low degree of organisation of social partners after the switch to the market order.

There could be seen to be an accession problem, and in some member countries it is seen as a veritable menace, in that all the membership candidates are poorer, in the majority of cases considerably poorer, than the least developed country of the EU-15. The expected consequence is migration from the poor to the rich countries. Insofar as such migration is wage-induced, there is little wrong with it from an economic point of view. However, if migration is induced by differences in welfare provisions, things become more difficult. Differences that are linked to labour contribution and income, as in contribution-related private insurance schemes, again pose little problem from an economic point of view, although the possibility of moral hazard in health care insurance cannot be excluded. As soon as welfare systems with strong redistributive elements are involved, however, it depends very much of the concrete arrangement whether the resulting migration implies an inefficient allocation of labour or not. Reforms introducing NDC and FF schemes go into the right direction, but the existing systems also can cope with the problem.

Two popular catch cries in this context are 'welfare state tourism' and 'social dumping'. Both are suggestive, but they are also essentially wrong in their implications. The freedom of labour mobility relates to the employed and not to the unemployed. The employed, however, will gain with their labour contribution claims that are not only paid out as a take-home wage, but also in the form of social security benefits. These claims are backed up by the workers' productivity, which is higher in capital-intensive highly developed countries than in labour-intensive less developed countries. The term social dumping implies a deliberately low social security standard in order to gain a competitive edge. As long as the labour market is not completely rigid, lower non-wage labour costs will be compensated by higher wage labour costs. The distribution of firm labour costs between the two may be a parameter of economic policy; total labour cost is not. Interestingly, the reproach of social dumping is always directed towards low labour cost countries, not high wage countries like the US or Japan, which have significantly less developed welfare states than Europe. They are rather used as paragons of 'reasonable' welfare state regimes by liberal critics of the European paradigm. Within the EU there is a particular practice that may be subsumed under social dumping, namely importing workers from low wage member states (which, under normal conditions, as just stated, must be due to lower productivity and not to lower social security contributions) and paying them partly or fully in their home countries. Trade unions consider this as unfair competition, and following the accession of extremely low wage countries, such practices may become an even more serious problem. At the same time, however, it is clear that the harmonisation of social security payments would not solve this problem.

We come to the conclusion that the diversity of social security arrangements within the Union may have negative effects upon the mobility of labour. This state of affairs will not be significantly deteriorated when new members from ECE join the club. The enormous difference in total per capita welfare between the Union average, and even the least developed incumbent member states, on the one hand, and the accession candidates, on the other, poses serious problems and strains on their neighbouring countries and on the Union budget. Nevertheless, it seems unwarranted to suggest that 'the European Union therefore faces a challenging task to harmonise its differing social security systems before it expands eastward'.[46] If taken seriously, this would postpone the enlargement for an indefinite period.

CONCLUSIONS

Capitalism is said to be all about efficiency, communism all about distribution. If this were true, transformation would be about getting from the welfare state to the nightwatchman state. And observers of the social consequences of transformation were justified in ascribing to the transition from one evil to another the undeniable deterioration of the social situation in Eastern Europe. Yet things are somewhat more complicated. The liberal policies of stabilisation, liberalisation and privatisation that are indispensable in order to introduce a market order do not need to imply the neo-liberal spectre of a wholesale abolition of the welfare state. No such thing happened in the region. What has happened in part of the region was state collapse. And therefore one has to differentiate carefully between ECE and the FSU. All the horror stories about transformation-induced alcoholism, falling life expectancy, deteriorating health status and appalling income inequalities are true for the CIS region, and in particular Russia, the Ukraine and Moldova, but much less so for ECE. The Balkans and the Baltic states have been hit more by such evils than the four Visegrad countries and Slovenia (and also Croatia). That is, those countries where transformation was carried out swiftly and with determination witnessed the strongest economic upturn and suffered least from the social consequences. And it is only these countries that will be able to fulfil the accession conditions of the EU.

Taken literally, the communist welfare state is a *contradictio in terminis* since there was no autonomous economic system whose way of functioning and results would have to be altered, complemented or supported by the use of political power. Under communism political power is all-pervasive – Lenin's primacy of politics. The re-introduction of the market fundamentally changed the role of the firm and this implied a concomitant change of the social security system. The latter change, in fact, did not keep pace with the former, and thus caused the immediate deterioration of the social situation. The first phase of welfare state reform can therefore be described as a kind of muddling through that sought to avoid the worst and to adapt the institutions that were inherited from the past to the immediate requirements of transformation. In many cases this kind of muddling through ran into fiscal problems and induced the second phase of welfare state reform.

Health care and education pose even more intricate problems than old age, invalidity and unemployment income security. Not only is there the necessity to reorganise the financial provisions of these systems and reconsider the public–private mix, but, being sectors of production, their achievements also depend on capital equipment and labour resources. The latter have been inherited in ample quantity from the old system, making restructuring a necessity. The legacies with respect to the former are rather poor. Hence improvement of both sectors will be achieved only over a longer and costly investment period. Expenses for health care and education in the ten accession candidates in ECE as a share of GNP are only about ten per cent lower than in the EU-15 on average,[47] which, given the fact that GNP (at purchasing power parities) is on average only 40 per cent of the EU average, implies of course a considerably lower absolute level, albeit one that is partly compensated by the lower labour costs.

Only when the new economic order was more or less established did some countries enter a second phase of welfare state transformation in which more consistent models were developed. The political economy of this process is interesting in itself.[48] The willingness to reform, stronger for instance in Poland and Hungary than in the Czech Republic, can be explained by a welfare state crisis and, above all, by a fiscal crisis, thus reducing the possible influence of different shared ideas about social security. Political legacies from the communist and the pre-communist period constrain the extent of reform and determine its direction. Having been part of the European welfare state tradition, in particular its Central European variant, these countries were not prepared to take over the World Bank model without alteration. The public–private mix of the new pension models in ECE and, as we have seen, also in Sweden (Germany has a similar reform in the making) differs significantly from the World Bank advice in whose three-pillar model the brunt of social security costs is borne by the private second pillar, with the public first pillar providing only for poor relief. The new European four-pillar model uses the mandatory fully funded private pillar as a complement to, rather than as a substitute for public social security. So, in the end, it will be the state, as legislator, regulator and organiser, that remains responsible for the quality and legitimacy of welfare state transformation: as Orenstein notes, 'state capacity is probably the single greatest determinant of the ability to create and manage a welfare state'.[49] In sum, it is good governance that is the single greatest problem facing the transformation countries in Eastern Europe.

NOTES

This study benefited from the discussion at the first session of the Reflection Group on Diversity and Unity in the Enlarged European Union. Helpful comments by Dr Katharina Müller and Dr Frank Bönker are also gratefully acknowledged.

1. By Stanley Fischer, Ratna Sahay and Carlos A. Végh, 'How Far Is Eastern Europe from Brussels?' *IMF Working Paper* (Washington: IMF 1998).
2. Hans-Jürgen Wagener, 'Rückkehr nach Europa', *FIT Discussion Papers* No.16/99 (Frankfurt (Oder): Frankfurt Institute for Transformation Studies 1999).
3. Robert J. Barro and Xavier Sala-i-Martin, 'Convergence', *Journal of Political Economy* 100 (1992), pp.223–51.
4. János Kornai, *Highways and Byways. Studies on Reform and Post-Communist Transition* (Cambridge, MA: MIT Press 1995), p.131.
5. Frederic L. Pryor, *Public Expenditures in Communist and Capitalist Nations* (London: Allen & Unwin 1968); Francis G. Castles, 'Whatever Happened to the Communist Welfare State?' *Studies in Comparative Communism* 19 (1986), pp.213–26. See also Ulrike Götting, *Transformation der Wohlfahrtsstaaten in Mittel- und Osteuropa. Eine Zwischenbilanz* (Opladen: Leske+Budrich 1998), pp.77–80.
6. Dena Ringold, 'Social Policy in Postcommunist Europe: Legacies and Transition', in L.J. Cook, M.A. Orenstein and M. Rueschemeyer (eds.), *Left Parties and Social Policy in Postcommunist Europe* (Boulder, CO: Westview 1999), pp.11–46; Hans-Jürgen Wagener, 'Social Security – A Second Phase Transformation Phenomenon?' in Katharina Müller, Andreas Ryll and Hans-Jürgen Wagener (eds.), *Transformation of Social Security: Pensions in Central-Eastern Europe* (Heidelberg: Physica 1999), pp.13–30.
7. Leszek Balcerowicz, *Socialism, Capitalism, Transformation* (Budapest: CEU Press 1995).
8. UN-ECE, *Economic Survey of Europe* 1 (Geneva: United Nations 2000), p.228.
9. Claus Offe, 'The Politics of Social Policy in East European Transitions: Antecedents, Agents, and Agenda of Reform', *Social Research* 60 (1993), pp.649–84.
10. Clifford G. Gaddy and Barry W. Ickes, 'Russia's Virtual Economy', *Foreign Affairs* 77/5 (1998), pp.53–67.
11. Branko Milanovic, *Income, Inequality and Poverty during the Transition from Planned to Market Economy* (Washington: The World Bank 1998), p.77; the figures may be disputed, the trend is unquestionable.
12. Ibid., p.41.
13. See Hans-Jürgen Wagener, 'Warum hat Russland den Zug verpasst?' *Leviathan: Zeitschrift für Sozialwissenschaft* 29 (2001), pp.110–40.
14. Luca Barbone and Hana Polackova, 'Public Finances and Economic Transition', *Moct-Most* 6/3 (1996), pp.35–61; Barbara Fakin and Alain de Crombrugghe, 'Fiscal Adjustments in Transition Economies: Social Transfers and Efficiency of Public Spending', *Policy Research Working Paper* No.1803 (Washington, DC: World Bank 1997).
15. Commission for the European Communities, *A Concerted Strategy for Modernising Social Protection*, COM 99/347 (Brussels, 1999).
16. Jeffrey D. Sachs, 'Reforms in Eastern Europe and the Former Soviet Union in Light of the East Asian Experience', *Working Paper* No.5404 (Cambridge, MA: NBER 1996).

17. William Easterly and Sergio Rebelo, 'Fiscal Policy and Economic Growth', *Journal of Monetary Economics* 32 (1993), pp.417–58.
18. Gosta Esping-Andersen, *The Three Worlds of Welfare Capitalism* (Cambridge: Polity Press 1990).
19. Gosta Esping-Andersen, 'After the Golden Age? Welfare State Dilemmas in a Global Economy', in Gosta Esping-Andersen (ed.), *Welfare States in Transition. National Adaptations in Global Economies* (London: Sage Publications 1996), p.11.
20. Götting, *Transformation der Wohlfahrtsstaaten in Mittel- und Osteuropa*, p.170.
21. Katharina Müller, *The Political Economy of Pension Reform in Central Eastern Europe* (Cheltenham: Edward Elgar 1999), pp.137–9.
22. Such, at least, were some of the objections in the region (see Götting, *Transformation der Wohlfahrtsstaaten in Mittel- und Osteuropa*, pp.84–8; Péter Gedeon, 'Social Policy in Transition', *Eastern European Politics and Societies* 9 (1995), pp.433–58; Linda J. Cook, Mitchell A. Orenstein and Marilyn Rueschemeyer, 'Conclusions', in Linda J. Cook, Mitchell A. Orenstein and Marilyn Rueschemeyer (eds.), *Left Parties and Social Policy in Postcommunist Europe* (Boulder, CO: Westview 1999), pp.235–47.
23. Cook *et al.*, 'Conclusions', p.343.
24. Ibid., p.343.
25. Ringold, 'Social Policy'.
26. Ibid., p.30.
27. See Mechtild Schrooten, Timothy M. Smeeding and Gert G. Wagner, 'Distributional and Fiscal Consequences of Social Security Reforms in Central-Eastern Europe', in Katharina Müller, Andreas Ryll and Hans-Jürgen Wagener (eds.), *Transformation of Social Security: Pensions in Central-Eastern Europe* (Heidelberg: Physica 1999), p.282.
28. European Bank for Reconstruction and Development, *Transition Report 1999. Ten Years of Transition* (London: EBRD 1999); most other transformation countries do not have relevant data.
29. Peter Mihályi and Ryszard Petru, 'Health Care in the Czech Republic, Hungary and Poland – the Medium-term Fiscal Aspects', *CASE-CEU Working Papers Series* No.28 (Warsaw: CASE 1999), p.28.
30. Ibid.
31. Ellen Goldstein *et al.*, *Trends in Health Status, Services, and Finance: The Transition in Central and Eastern Europe*, 2 Vols. (World Bank Technical Papers 341 and 348, Washington, DC: The World Bank 1996).
32. See Götting, *Transformation der Wohlfahrtsstaaten in Mittel- und Osteuropa*, p.178.
33. World Bank, *Averting the Old Age Crisis. Policies to Protect the Old and Promote Growth* (Washington, DC/Oxford: Oxford University Press 1994).
34. John Williamson (ed.), *Latin American Adjustment. How much has happened?* (Washington, DC: Institute for International Economics 1990).
35. See Müller, *Political Economy*, p.27.
36. See its subtitle 'Policies to Protect the Old and Promote Growth', World Bank, *Averting the Old Age Crisis.*
37. Müller, *Political Economy*, p.29. The term originally derives from Rubén Lo Vuolo, 'Reformas previsionales en América Latina: el caso argentino', *Comercio Exterior* 46/9 (1996), pp.692–702.
38. Commission of the European Communities, *A Concerted Strategy*, p.13.
39. See Katharina Müller, From the State to the Market? Pension Reform Paths in CEE and the Former Soviet Union, *The Vienna Institute Monthly Report* 6 (2000), pp.20–29.
40. Up to now, this is the only far-reaching reform within EU member states.
41. Frank Bönker, *The Political Economy of Fiscal Reform in Eastern Europe: A Comparative Analysis of Hungary, Poland and the Czech Republic* (Cheltenham: Edward Elgar forthcoming 2002).
42. See Béla Greskovits, *The Political Economy of Protest and Patience. East European and Latin American Transformations Compared* (Budapest: Central European University Press 1998), according to whom this may be accounted for precisely by the existing welfare state.
43. Balcerowicz, *Socialism.*

44. Cathryn Ross, 'Comment on Schneider', in Irwin Collier *et al.* (eds.), *Welfare States in Transition. East and West* (Basingstoke: Macmillan 1999), pp.158–63.
45. Commission of the European Communities, *Towards a Single Market for Supplementary Pensions,* COM(99) 134 (Brussels, 1999).
46. Ondrej Schneider, 'Enlargment of the European Union and the Harmonization of Public Pension Systems', in Irwin Collier *et al.* (eds.), *Welfare States in Transition. East and West* (Basingstoke: Macmillan 1999), p.142.
47. European Bank for Reconstruction and Development, *Transition Report 1999.*
48. See Müller, *Political Economy*.
49. Mitchell A. Orenstein, 'Postcommunist Welfare State Transformation and its Place in the Theoretical Literature' (conference paper, Brown University, 1999), p.10.

Approaching the EU and Reaching the US? Rival Narratives on Transforming Welfare Regimes in East-Central Europe

JÁNOS MÁTYÁS KOVÁCS

A SOCIAL BORDER?

According to a recent journalistic truism, the Iron Curtain that was dismantled in 1989 as a political and ideological frontier has since re-emerged as an economic and social border. *Schengenland* protects itself from its Eastern neighbours with the help of import quotas and visa obligation, police build-up along the border, and a blend of diplomatic arrogance and precaution. The truism is based on the identification of the new 'police frontier' with a social border, or, more precisely, with a welfare cascade that ranges from the former Iron Curtain to Siberia. In the light of this assumption, the Iron Curtain remained a border beyond which social exclusion, human deprivation, poverty and criminality prevail. Probably, East-Central Europe (ECE) can still be salvaged, but the farther you move to the east, the more severe social crisis you find. Because this contradicts established European values, and – perhaps more importantly – because of the need to protect Western markets after *Osterweiterung*, one of the elementary requirements of entrance to the European Union for the ex-communist countries is a quick and steady increase in wages and social performance levels.

As frustrating as it may be for Eastern Europeans, it is impossible to question this truism about the rich and poor halves of Europe in the field of general social statistics. Of course, one could doubt its inherent geographical determinism (is Georgia socially more backward than Albania?) or point out those fields of social policy (for example, family allowances), in which the shrinking 'communist welfare state' still provides more generous services than many of its advanced Western counterparts. Also, a thorough comparison of the general social policy performance of, for example, the Czech Republic and Hungary today with that of Greece or Portugal at the time of their accession to the European Community may reveal striking differences in development in favour of the ex-communist countries.

This study, however, intends to cast doubts on the social border thesis from another perspective. The proponents of that thesis usually confuse performance indicators with regime characteristics and attribute poor performance to a particular welfare regime. This regime is frequently portrayed as a hybrid consisting of the relics of communist social policy and of a neophyte imitation of the US model of welfare. According to the implicit assumption, almost an axiom, Eastern Europe has taken resolute steps towards 'Americanising' its welfare regimes. The related accusation is, however, explicit: the ex-communist countries are committing a grave mistake by abandoning the 'European tradition' in social policy and *thereby* preserving the Western frontier of the former Eastern Bloc as a border between more and less humane societies. They are combining the worst of two possible worlds, welfare provided by incompetent and corrupt state bureaucrats with social myopia of the free market.

This study tries to show that, first, new poverty, social exclusion and so on in Eastern Europe is, to a large degree, a result of post-1989 economic recession. 'Neo-liberal' arguments are frequently used by local policy makers to make a virtue out of the necessity of introducing austerity measures in the economy. At any rate, in most countries of the region any 'Americanisation' of the welfare regimes has remained a rhetorical exercise rather than a powerful economic strategy.

Second, the considerable drop in general social performance may well represent a kind of 'back to normalcy' process whereby the levels of welfare provision have been adjusted to the actual economic capacity of the new democracies during the first years of the transformation. Nevertheless, path dependency is strong, and, surpassing the stage of austerity, the ex-communist welfare states tend to recover in many fields, and even radically liberal/communitarian reforms end up with compromise and stalemate in the social sector.

Third, as a consequence, while the fact of a social border cannot be disputed in real terms (though the gap between East and West is being reduced by the economic upswing in East-Central Europe), it would be difficult to identify that border as a demarcation line which also separates two essentially different types of welfare regime. Although occasionally Eastern European social reformers may make bolder experiments than their West European colleagues in marketising/privatising certain welfare schemes, these experiments are far from being irresistible under the pressure of the social legacies of communism, the daily challenges of the transformation, new statism/conservatism and the requirements of European integration; and similar reforms have been initiated (also with mixed results) by a few West European welfare states as well. Hence, a clear separation of regime types would be impossible even if they proved to be homogeneous on both sides of the former Iron Curtain. Given their heterogeneity in the West as well as in the East, the 'border of models' may run, in a certain field of welfare and at a certain moment, between Great Britain *and* Hungary on the one side and Germany *and* the Czech Republic on the other.

In crossing the real borders between the former blocs in Europe in any direction, the traveller becomes a prisoner of new differential stereotypes of welfare such as 'solidaristic versus socially irresponsible', 'organised versus chaotic', and so on, which complement the old one of 'rich versus poor'. These are based, in a way justifiably, on visible and tangible indicators of welfare such as the number of abandoned children, street beggars and tuberculosis patients, or the measure of air pollution, the size of average old age pension or the frequency of work accidents. However, if social policy analysts indulge in the preservation and multiplication of these indicators, they run the risk of elevating their differences onto a symbolic (almost mythical) level. To be sure, drawing symbolic borders which separate 'us' and 'them', the 'same' and the 'other' in a strict moral hierarchy can easily become a self-fulfilling prophecy – a prophecy that may inhibit social innovation by exerting enormous pressure on the 'unlucky' Eastern half of the continent to imitate the 'lucky' Western one, even if the latter represents only one of the successful development types in global context and even if its success has recently been questioned both from inside and outside.

If catching up with Europe is confined to sheer imitation, Eastern Europe may remain unlucky. By the time it copies any of the current welfare regimes of Western Europe, these regimes will probably not have been able to produce the same performance levels as they do today. While the European Union adjusts to the global competition of tomorrow, the accession countries may adapt their own social systems to those of the Union of yesterday and today and, as a result, may lag behind the world again. Therefore, the newcomers have to undertake the almost impossible task of satisfying today's conditions of entrance while preparing for those of tomorrow. Given the long building process and, later, the considerable inertia of welfare institutions, Eastern European social reformers have no choice other than trying to have the entrance examiners of the Union accept such welfare policies in the ex-communist states that those same examiners probably would not put forward in their own countries.

DISTURBING QUESTIONS

The term 'premature welfare state of communism', coined by János Kornai some time ago, is widely discussed in East-Central Europe today. Dedicated followers of free-market orthodoxy and nostalgic communists are making efforts to interpret the metaphor of the premature infant according to their own preferences. While the former opt for active euthanasia – they would like to accelerate the death of the struggling infant – the latter would like to keep the incubator going even if the infant has already died. Between the two extremes represented by a few radicals there is an overwhelming majority of social scientists and policy makers with diverse convictions who would be happy to find a viable combination of the two approaches.

Indeed, can the communist welfare regimes be transformed without falling into the trap of conserving the statist, inefficient and pseudo-egalitarian character of the old system of social policy; seeking new forms of welfare collectivism along the national-conservative/populist 'Third Roads' between capitalism and communism; triggering popular discontent by dismantling the old welfare regimes too rapidly, in a haphazard way; and targeting an end-state which has become unsustainable in the Western world during the past two decades?

These disturbing questions become annoying if one considers that the transformation of the communist social institutions and policies is taking place in fragile new democracies, in a period that was introduced by an unprecedented economic recession, amid repeated privatisation and marketisation drives, and in economies which have recently and vehemently opened up to global competition and are challenged by the vision of a near-term enlargement of the European Union. One can no longer disregard the related question: 'to what extent are the emerging welfare regimes in East-Central Europe not only sustainable but also compatible with the European model(s)?'

In answering this question, one can hardly apply the convenient method of fixing, in one way or another, the European standards of social policy and then examine to what degree the newcomers have approached it. The emerging welfare regimes in East-Central Europe are far from being identical and there has always been a variety of social policy models in Western Europe. In addition, the ECE experts do not find stable institutional arrangements in the West to copy but rather another reform process, the 'domestication' of the classical welfare state(s). True, the general trends are not dissimilar: partial retrenchment, decentralisation, marketisation and privatisation of public welfare services as well as an upsurge of the voluntary sector, that is, decreasing state involvement, are the main characteristic features of regulating welfare on both sides of the former Iron Curtain, although some countries such as Sweden and the Netherlands are, at the same time, extending new entitlements. Nevertheless, to tell if the two changing systems are likely ever to be harmonised is terribly difficult. Who would be willing to predict today whether in ten or 15 years from now the post-communist welfare regimes will be compatible with the European standards of that time?

Theoretically, if one excludes the unlikely case of spontaneous perfect harmonisation, where East-Central Europe catches up with Western Europe without overtaking it in any respect, there may be two kinds of incompatibility. Despite any similarity of the two reform processes, either the Western or the Eastern part of Europe will happen to become in the long run less statist and more private (and/or 'voluntary') than the other in terms of the welfare mix. To put it simply, either the EU or the ex-communist social regimes become more 'North American' (if the latter does not change in the meantime).

Currently, there is a growing consensus in the West about social trajectories in the ECE region. Unfortunately, this consensus has been forged under the influence of spectacular media images of societal polarisation in Eastern Europe as a whole (for example, Russian new-rich women in fur coats shopping in Paris versus children dying in a demolished AIDS clinic in Romania). Not only journalists but also many Western scholars assert that ex-communist countries are in a rush to jump over, first, the Scandinavian model of social protection, and then the Bismarckian, the Beveridge-style and the South European welfare systems, in order to arrive in the world of US-type social regimes. If this is true, one should be prepared for the ironic situation, in which certain countries of the region will prove to be EU-incompatible in the future not because they are still too communist-bound but because they are excessively pro-capitalist.

For a long time, the conventional wisdom was that East-Central Europe should be allowed to join the European Union only after a protracted phase of adaptation because, among other reasons, its social performance was poor in absolute terms. If the pro-capitalist – many observers will say, neo-liberal – experiments succeed, while similar West European reforms slow down or get stuck (*horribile dictu*, if Europe creates a 'social fortress'), will these experiments not also constitute an obstacle?

THE DIALOGUE OF THE DEAF

For the purposes of this study the literature was addressed with a general interest in current economic and political thought in Eastern Europe and in particular with a desire to investigate the re-emergence of the 'social question' in the ECE region.[1] In exploring the social policy discipline in the region, one finds oneself in a battlefield in which political mines lurk everywhere and where antagonists frequently use a highly combative, ideological language against each other, which camouflages the empirical facts of the underlying social processes and the research techniques applied to understand these facts.

By and large, the cast consists of liberal-minded economists on the one side and sociologists with social democratic leanings on the other. The roots of their conflict reach back to the period of reforms under late communism, during which they drifted into a 'state versus market' debate of a rather scholastic nature. At that time, the pro-market economists (market socialists, as they were called) asked the social policy experts to prove that their interventionist, social-protectionist claims (a reaction, by the way, to the falling welfare performance of the planned economy) were different from those made by the communist hard-liners. The sociologists felt offended by this accusation and responded to it by simultaneously alluding to the '*laissez faire* fundamentalism' of market socialists and refuting state dirigism. It may well be that the conflict started the other way round and sometimes intersected the disciplinary frontiers. However, one thing was certain. The unfolding controversy reminded the observer of a dialogue of the deaf, in which mutual recrimination concerning the social indifference of economists versus the economic ignorance of sociologists frequently replaced reasonable arguments.

The conflict between the two groups, which had partly been repressed by their internal solidarity against the communists, erupted in 1989, causing huge waves of emotion all over the region. It should have originally revolved around day-to-day problems of crisis management (such as what kind of welfare services/expenditures could or should be reshaped, curtailed or deleted to reduce the overall budget deficit in the short run). Instead, it was elevated onto the level of social philosophy. Here 'state' and 'market' were confronted again: the sociologists stressed how expensive the market is in terms of social costs and played down government failures while the economists argued the other way round instead of comparing the social costs and social benefits of both institutions in a detailed analysis.

On the eve of the Eastern European revolutions, most of the social policy experts hoped that in the future there would be enough room for a kind of 'sound interventionism'.[2] They would no longer have to face incompetent, arrogant and pitiless state bureaucracies; the welfare programmes could be reconstructed to become more just and efficient at the same time; and certain welfare schemes would be managed by the civil society on a non-profit basis rather than marketised and privatised, and streamlined rather than abolished. The '*communist* welfare state' should be dismantled, they believed, but the welfare state must be preserved or – more exactly – created anew following Scandinavian rather than any other Western European patterns, not to mention North America.

Now imagine this group of welfare reformers who in 1989 found themselves confronted with a great number of economists in their countries who wanted to launch strict stabilisation programmes, which were complemented by ambitious plans for marketisation and privatisation. Moreover, these economists were supported by an influential choir of foreign advisors, Western policy makers and leaders of international economic organisations. Occasionally, they applied a rather low-quality neo-liberal rhetoric to justify austerity. This mix of restrictive vigour, deregulation drives and neo-liberal rhetoric prevailing in the first years of the post-communist transformation came as a real culture shock for the welfare reformers of East-Central Europe. As a first reaction they fell back on routine language and continued demonising the former economic reformers (now transformers) as 'Chicago Boys', 'Wild-East Thatcherites', and so on, who represent the same kind of social indifference as before – but now as agents of an 'international neo-liberal conspiracy'. 'This is Latin America. You are responsible!', pointed the social policy expert at the economic transformer. 'Do you long for the *ancien régime*?', so went the response, and the dialogue of the deaf continued.

DID ANYTHING HAPPEN? TWO AND A HALF NARRATIVES

Today, the antagonists are probably less strained and determined. Economic recession was followed by a rapid recovery, in particular in Hungary and Poland. Many of the major steps towards welfare transformation ended with a compromise or were postponed. The welfare sectors display considerable inertia and neither the rhetoric nor the actual programmes of the post-communist governments vary greatly. 'New social democracy' in the West also offers the warriors a sufficient dose of relativism and pragmatism to bury their hatchets.

As regards the scientific environment of social transformation, hundreds of new research projects are under way; the involvement of Western scholars of a variety of persuasions has resulted in more sophisticated techniques of survey and analysis; East–West studies are complemented by East–East comparisons; normative fervour is counterbalanced by detached explanation; interdisciplinary research is ascendant and rival tendencies appear *within* the individual disciplines. Consequently, 12 years after the revolution, one may hope that the bilateral conflict described above will be moderated by cross-cutting the cleavage with the help of new insights, which mediate between the dominant discourses or transcend them for good.

Nevertheless, before the bright future materialises, it would not be too bad to know what has 'really' happened in the welfare sectors of East-Central Europe in the course of the past decade. Given the still rather passionate moods in social science throughout the region and the lack of comprehensive and comparative works,[3] it is extremely difficult to reconstruct the most recent history of welfare in the ECE states. Let us first see how the insiders interpret the course of this history. We focus on three (more exactly, two and a half) competing narratives of welfare development: for the sake of brevity, they are named the 'leaping in the dark', the 'marking time' and the 'muddling through' stories. The two stories that originate in the conflict between economic and social reformers are retold first. Then the main lines of a third, experimental 'half-narrative' will be drawn. Finally, the 'what has happened' question relating to the problem of EU compatibility is briefly discussed.

Needless to say, the narratives are my constructions and they are probably more sharply specified than many of the authors would like to see. If not stated otherwise, what comes below is *their* text in a stylised form, though some of the references include authors who share only one or two conclusions of the given narrative. Three countries of East-Central Europe – the Czech Republic, Hungary and Poland – are chosen as backgrounds to the stories. The examples pertain to quite a few important fields of social welfare with the clear exception of education. The narratives are reconstructed around two main topics: the general performance and the institutional design (mix) of the welfare regimes.

'Leaping in the Dark'

According to this first narrative, since 1989 a fundamental – and appalling – change has taken place in the region concerning both the performance and the institutional character of the welfare systems.[4] Following some years of stagnation, public provisions have been drastically reduced by (a) narrowing the scope and the period of eligibility entitlements – sick pay, unemployment benefits, family allowances, pensions, and so on – that is, by partly abandoning universalism for targeted transfer payments; (b) fixing the statutory minimum wages or pensions too low and linking certain benefits to it; (c) lowering the quality standards of the services; (d) introducing the principle of private insurance – health care, old-age pensions; or (e) inflating away the real value of the government transfers – pensions, family allowances, and so on. With the privatisation of state enterprises a vast number of health clinics, kindergartens, apartments and holiday homes – a considerable share of public welfare provision – disappeared almost overnight.[5] The remaining social services became more expensive through curbing or termination of the government subsidies, introduction of co-payment schemes (day care, medicine, hospital treatment, and so on) and taxation of certain transfers. Also, public expenditure on welfare has not grown through decentralisation:[6] although the local administration units get relatively more funds now than before, the sum total of local and central expenditures on social services was not increased.

What is emerging is a new (more exactly, old) paradigm, a kind of a 'liberal' or 'residual welfare state', as Gosta Esping-Andersen or Richard Titmuss described it.[7] Communism left behind a 'service heavy, transfer light' welfare system,[8] which is being transformed into one that provides significantly fewer services while not increasing the government transfers proportionally (or indeed also decreasing them). After World War II, the communists in East-Central Europe had inherited Bismarckian-style social arrangements; while expanding and deepening them, they reinforced the statist-hierarchical components of these arrangements. When communism collapsed, the baby was thrown out with the bath water: instead of democratising[9] and partly liberalising public welfare in moving toward the Scandinavian models or at least toward *Soziale Marktwirtschaft*, that is, instead of keeping the 'Western' features of the social system and throwing away 'Eastern'-type pseudo-paternalism, the essentials of state-financed and state-provided welfare were made questionable.[10] This is retrenchment,[11] nothing else. Yet the state cannot be replaced in some of its social policy functions (organising redistribution on the national level, granting social rights, and so on) and the welfare sectors, if left alone, suffer from a series of market failures. The state is not to be venerated but used carefully.

Following 1989, most economic transformers named welfare the main culprit of the alleged public overspending. Obviously, expenditures also could have been cut back in other chapters of the state budget. Nevertheless, the post-communist governments exploited austerity to 'educate' the citizens[12] – for short-term savings (such as consumption of medicines) and long-term calculating behaviour (such as private pensions) – by forcing them to accept the amorphous and overlapping principles of individual responsibility, self-reliance and self-insurance. Originally, the cutbacks were said to be provisional but they were built into the new welfare mix. The education strategy was skilfully based on the fact that communism had immensely discredited the ideals of equality and solidarity as well as of state intervention in general. The local educators and their Western advisors were even more zealous and met less resistance in the ECE countries than in the West, and their references to austerity and economic rationality often disguised the vested interests of certain lobbies, sheer ideological commitment and/or lack of expertise. Moreover, because the subject of individual responsibility was loosely defined, the principle of self-reliance offered the new governments a legitimate opportunity to shift part of the social burdens (child care) onto the families. Here neo-liberal arguments prepared the soil for conservative solutions which forced women to leave the workplace and return home.

Undoubtedly, the 'communist welfare state' had safeguarded the principles of universal coverage and free services only on paper.[13] Yet, if the transformers violate them every day, then nothing can stop the transition countries in their decline. Health service is the worst example throughout the region. Although social security contributions have not been reduced, a bed in hospital is very expensive. But in order to be operated on in time, one still needs to bribe the doctor in order to jump the queue, as under the old regime. It is also necessary to bring along toilet paper, food and medicine to the hospital, not to mention a well-trained relative to replace the nurse. In optimal care, the Soros Foundation will have equipped the hospital with high-tech machinery, there will be only a few well-to-do people (including foreigners) in the queue and, following surgery, the patient will not get a bad cold lying near a broken window.

Besides abandoning universalism and the principle of free services, there was another important symbolic gesture. The doctrine of statutory social rights (such as the right to work) was practically renounced by avoiding any definition of the object, the extent and the institutional setting of public welfare responsibility, in the new constitutions of the region. The authors of these basic laws did their best to formulate the state's responsibility for social protection of the citizens in a way to exclude future accountability.[14] Under communism, these rights were not enforceable because democracy was suspended; today, paradoxically, it is democratic parliaments that hinder their concretisation.

The social spheres that were evacuated by the state have not been refilled by private (non-profit or for-profit) initiative. The mushrooming of non-governmental welfare organisations in East-Central Europe must not mislead the observer. They are either low capacity/quality substitutes for public services or they favour the rich; they serve tax evasion purposes and expropriate public money or charge exorbitant prices or – most likely – die fast. Private health insurance and pension schemes, the two major 'innovations' of the new, mandatorily mixed welfare regimes in the region, are probably less efficient than the system of publicly financed and state-managed social security and certainly more unjust and risky. The privately funded schemes privilege the already privileged. In the case of the pension system, for instance, the private/public combination favours those with middle and high incomes and secure jobs who have not yet retired.[15] In other words, the principle of individual responsibility prefers the strong to the weak. Thereby, even partial privatisation of financing health care and the pension system confuses most links of solidarity between generations and social strata and contributes to the growth of income inequalities and eventually to the disintegration of the fabric of the society. The emerging welfare mix is getting increasingly biased towards the middle class (the actual voters and taxpayers), particularly towards its upper echelons. This process is defended by means of the utopia of an unlimited downward expansion of the middle strata of society. At the same time, the rich are allowed/prompted to opt out from certain public welfare schemes, which removes their responsibility for the functioning of the social system as a whole.

Welfare policy degenerates into poor relief with social assistance and workfare becoming the main instruments of social protection. The 'truly needy', the 'deserving poor', must undergo humiliating and expensive means-testing procedures and may long for the non-existent charity offered by the new elite. Meanwhile, whole groups (disabled, homeless, long-term unemployed, elderly with low pensions, large families, ethnic minorities, chronically ill, inhabitants of declining regions, and so on) fall through the ever growing holes of the safety net. New forms of social exclusion and deprivation (such as mass unemployment, child poverty, malnutrition, prostitution) are generously tolerated by the state; deep poverty has become legitimate again; and excessive polarisation between an ever growing underclass and a thin layer of the new rich is even applauded. At any rate, the widespread use of the metaphor of 'social safety net'[16] reflects the cynical attitude of the transformers: one should not offer each citizen a protective rope or safety belt when performing acrobatic stunts in the circus of life; it is quite enough for the society to prepare for the case if some of them (those who tried to perform but could not) fall down; the others, the 'undeserving poor', may fall through the net.[17]

As a result of the general social decay, in East-Central Europe most socio-biological indicators ranging from life expectancy at birth to the frequency of old and new diseases deteriorate sharply. On average, people have fewer children, become sick more often and die younger, and, during their lifetimes, are poorer and enjoy less social safety. Owing to the neo-liberal course of the transformation, the region has lost hundreds of thousands of human lives.[18] A good part of them might have been saved if the transformers had shown courage in real invention instead of merely copying ambiguous social arrangements such as the Chilean pension schemes. For instance, the fresh start in 1989 would have provided an excellent opportunity for the new social policy makers to introduce a basic income regulation in the ECE countries to prevent the escalation of poverty.[19] However, they preferred the revitalisation of old stigmas to enacting new citizenship rights for the needy.

What about the new challenges for the declining ECE social systems, which go beyond the standard tasks of transition to capitalism? The 'communist welfare states' were able to cope with the social consequences of global competition and communication (migration, drug trafficking and international crime in general) insofar as they managed to close their borders with police forces and non-convertible currencies. The close-down, of course, led to huge welfare losses in other fields. However, today the welfare policy makers of the region do not even make attempts at taking the new challenges seriously. They tend to delegate the new social troubles to the sphere of responsibility of the young and weak non-governmental organisation (NGO) sector. Moreover, instead of designing major public assistance programmes for migrants and launching long-term prevention and rehabilitation initiatives for drug addicts, they build new fences at certain frontiers and increase punishment norms.[20]

With some decentralisation of public welfare administration and the development of Janus-faced NGOs, social citizenship under post-communism has reached its pinnacle in terms of democratic rights. Irrespective of their political colours and the will of their voters, governments in East-Central Europe tend to implement an aggressively neo-liberal course of economic transformation. As a consequence, the only institutions which remained to represent the welfare interests of the citizens are the trade unions. However, they have never had strong (or – in the case of Poland – they lost much of their) popular support, could not manage to stabilise their relations with the new social-liberal parties, and are incessantly blackmailed by the threat of unemployment and exposed to the malevolence of the legislators. Hence the citizenry, fragmented as it is, has to assist passively in the fundamental deterioration of its own welfare situation. Meanwhile, as substantiated by a series of opinion polls and deeper sociological surveys, the same citizenry would prefer Swedish-type (publicly guaranteed) safety to (privately owned) freedom if they were asked by their own parliamentary representatives.[21]

What has happened is indeed a leap in the dark – both figuratively and literally. The region has jumped into uncertainty and exposed itself to the 'dark forces' of global capitalism, monetarist dictatorship or international economic organisations.[22] Although the proponents of this 'Great Leap Backward' are firmly convinced that, in jumping over Europe, North America will be the ideal final destination, in the end they will inevitably arrive not in the northern but in the southern part of that continent. The welfare regime of the US without the strength of its economy and the community ethos of its citizens leads nowhere else. In any event, in leaving behind communism and hoping to join a 'social Europe', creating a whole new civilisation that combines safety with freedom, to anyone with a social conscience it would be almost as frustrating as the Latin America option to be reconciled with the philosophy of the US-type quasi-welfare state.

Finally, those in East-Central Europe who insist on the concept of the minimum state in welfare transformation run the risk that a coalition of nationalists and unreconstructed communists expropriate the idea of social protection. Thus, in trying to minimise 'welfare waste', the neo-liberal transformers may generate the largest social costs by actually jeopardising the new democracies.[23]

'Marking Time'

The next story is based on a deep frustration contrasting the disillusionment of the previous narrators. According to this response to the 'what has happened' question, the really appalling development is that there is no development: East-Central Europe has not yet been able to leave behind the 'communist welfare state'. The region is still marking time at the start line. It is far from heading towards Latin America but may eventually arrive there if it continues to insist on the utopia of providing welfare irrespective of the actual economic conditions of the post-communist transformation. It is not the alleged 'neo-liberal haughtiness' of economists but a sort of socio-political myopia that may cause social decay and political turmoil.

Let us suppose for a moment that a permanent and general decay of welfare has really occurred in the ECE countries both in terms of the performance and the style of the social system. Even if this assumption were correct, one ought to ask oneself, say the narrators of this story, whether the allegedly comprehensive deterioration is:

1. A clear consequence of liberal transformative policies or has much deeper roots stretching into the *ancien régime*. If the latter is true, one is dealing with an optical illusion: at least part of the decay did not happen after 1989, but only became visible in the new democracies (poverty, unemployment, and so on). It may also be that in certain fields the transformation has even slowed down the deterioration of social performance in the region that had begun under communism. And, conversely, what decay is currently visible (due to the lobbying power of certain groups such as pensioners or medical doctors) is not necessarily the greatest hardship.[24]
2. Characteristic of all ex-communist countries or primarily of the non-Central European ones.[25] If the latter is true, one ought to examine those circumstances (differences between pre-communist welfare traditions, the levels of communist welfare provision, and – above all – the strategies of post-communist economic and political transformation) that explain the relative softness of the 'social crisis' in the ECE region. 'Neo-liberal radicalism' may have contributed not only to the dismantling of old welfare arrangements but – through stabilising the economy and restarting growth – also to the recovery of social transfers and services.[26]
3. Really the creation of 'neo-liberal zealots', 'obsessed monetarists', and suchlike, or simply that of ordinary economists who do have 'social conscience' but can count as well. If the latter is true, their aim was not to suppress welfare spending for good but to adjust it realistically and temporarily to the overall performance of the economy, in other words, to cut back social expenditures now in order to raise them later on. Austerity was not a pretext for orchestrating a neo-liberal conspiracy, so why should Latin-Americanisation prove inevitable? True, adjustment is also tantamount to restructuring and streamlining but no one has claimed that East-Central Europe must jump over the West European models of the welfare state.
4. An accomplished fact that has been corroborated by reliable statistical analysis based on comparative longitudinal surveys made in the respective countries, or a strong working hypothesis, which builds on fragmented statistics, expert estimates and a speculative blend of street-level observation, intuition, anecdotal evidence, opinion poll results and

political discourse analysis. If the latter is true, one cannot tell whether or not the gloomy predictions will actually materialise. Moreover, these predictions may justify themselves: if politicians accept them in fear of social unrest and push up welfare expenditure, they may eventually destabilise the economy resulting in actual welfare cuts.

5. Would be resolutely blocked by the citizens via more public spending or – provided they are aware of the real costs of social expenditures *they* have to cover in the form of taxes and social security contributions – the same citizens would opt for a 'lower tax – higher private insurance' alternative. If the latter is true and the citizens could be liberated from the prison of fiscal illusions[27] concerning 'free' social services and helped to recognise that the taxes are redistributed in a way that has not in fact been negotiated with them, then it will be difficult for many social policy experts to refer incessantly to *the* people who yearn for a much greater protection by the state even if this results in some loss of their liberties. In any event, sociological surveys conducted in the region repeatedly show that the people are more inclined to individualist than collectivist values.[28]

Like their antagonists, those who tell the 'marking time' story have deep-seated (and not completely unfounded) reservations about the other. In contrast to the accusation of 'social negligence', they discover in the minds of their adversaries a large dose of nostalgia with regard to the actual welfare achievements of communism. Apparently, they say, the others have forgotten that the 'communist welfare state' was not only authoritarian and hypocritical but also monolithic and wasteful. In other words, it not only escaped democratic control and broke its own promises but also banned pluralism, that is, competition within the welfare sectors, and used resources lavishly.

This inherent inefficiency of the Soviet-type welfare state had to a large degree contributed to the economic decomposition of the communist system. So why carry along that burden to post-communism?[29] Why paralyse state budgets for many years to come? Why make false promises any longer? Why expect the premature infant to be as strong as those who have had the privilege of a full term to prepare for life? There is a *quid pro quo*, and the trade-offs cannot be disregarded.[30] Welfare expenditure competes with other sorts of public spending and originates in taxation. Hence, any restructuring in favour of welfare in the state budget or any rise in social spending may retard economic growth, generate unemployment, force the citizens to enter the underground economy (in which, by the way, they are unprotected), and so on – thereby reducing, in the last analysis, the tax base of future social provisions. In this way, we can easily hurt those whom we wanted to help initially. Why would a fiscal crisis be better than a social one?[31] Why not accept short-term hardships in order to avoid medium-term social chaos? In any case, at a certain point one has to deactivate the time bombs left behind by communism: during its last phases, welfare entitlements were simultaneously extended and compromised by falling standards of provision; this gap generated high expectations, and currently the citizens demand the new governments to comply with the obligations made by the old ones.

Furthermore, in East-Central Europe public welfare spending traditionally implies the empowerment of extremely costly, unprofessional and corrupted state and corporatist bureaucracies. Health care is perhaps the best example not only for horror stories about service delivery but also for invulnerable vested interests of such bureaucracies (empty hospital beds, idle personnel, repeated diagnoses).[32] Privatisation of the welfare sectors (or their pluralisation) is not dictated by ideological fanaticism. As in the case of other public sector activities, the state administration inherited from communism must not be entrusted to carry out major welfare programmes until it goes through the purgatory of market competition. Paradoxically, the welfare state should be rolled back in order to create efficient and clean public welfare again. Until then, it remains risky to offer the state administration taxpayers' money because it tends to expropriate and waste part of it and alter the rules of use according to the changing exigencies of the political game.

Yet, if one casts a glance at comparative data, it comes as a surprise that (a) in the course of the deep recession in the first half of the 1990s, the ECE countries managed to increase public social expenditures relative to GDP; (b) they have introduced a couple of new welfare provisions (unemployment, child care) and did not abolish any from among the major social transfers and services of the former regime; (c) while reducing social spending in certain fields (price subsidies, social housing), they succeeded in maintaining spending (in health care) or even raising it (in pensions, social assistance); (d) thus, what happened during the second half of the 1990s was closer to a stagnation than to a dramatic fall of the share of welfare expenditures; (e) in the course of the past 12 years, East-Central Europe has undoubtedly descended from the level of Scandinavian welfare states in terms of the ratio of social spending to the GDP but has not yet reached the level of the less advanced OECD countries, not to mention that of the comparable middle-income countries in Asia and Latin-America (in which – due mainly to differences between the pension systems – the ratio is at least twice as low as in the ECE region[33]). Hence, what else is this than marking time in the transformation of welfare regimes? There is much, less circumstantial, evidence to support this thesis, say the narrators.

However, first a word of caution is needed.[34] In the beginning, welfare spending might rise because certain kinds of public expenditure that had been put under different headings under communism (for example. enterprise level social services) became parts of the social budget (local welfare provision). Further, it may well be that in absolute terms social provisions dropped with the GDP (though, by and large, the 1989 levels have been reached or surpassed by now), and probably more people compete for almost the same pool of public transfers and services than before. Hence, the average standards of public welfare provision fell in certain fields (unemployment benefit, social assistance) – a reason indeed for anxiety. Nonetheless, even these falling standards are too high in relation to the economic potential of the ECE states. More importantly, the large drop in price subsidies of basic goods at the very outset of the transformation was offset by a surprising increase in public pensions and a less surprising rise of expenditure on social assistance. (Medicine, rents, utilities, and so on have remained heavily subsidised until recently.)

Public spending on pensions, currently the largest item of social expenditure, grew primarily because the chances for claiming early retirement and qualifying for disability pensions have not been significantly constrained (compare lax regulations, fraud and the aim of curtailing unemployment), and the new governments were eager to buy off the pensioners as voters[35] with lucrative indexation techniques, growing pension-to-wage ratios and a slow increase of the unusually low retirement age. Similarly, in terms of family allowances, the policy makers could not help yielding to the nationalist/pro-natalist pressures also inherent in the communist tradition and did not scale back the main transfers in this field. (If they nonetheless tried to trim the provisions – as with the austerity package in Hungary in 1995 – they first bumped into social rights defended by the constitution, then into voters' preferences.[36]) Also, enterprise-level social policy has not disappeared entirely: part of it was taken over by the new local authorities and private firms.

As regards social assistance, access to unemployment benefits has indeed been made more stringent, and the same applies to poor relief programmes. Nevertheless, despite the fact that certain segments of the population suffer in many ways from the restructuring of welfare spending, it would be too much to speak about overall impoverishment (let alone, pauperisation) in the ECE region.[37] Here poverty is rather shallow: the typical poor person is situated just under the poverty line, fluctuates between the 'poor' and the 'not yet poor' position, and, with the help of an upswing of the economy (and the trickle-down effect), he may leave the bottom of society rapidly before getting stuck in the underclass. The indicators of social polarisation in East-Central Europe are still well below those of the most egalitarian OECD countries.[38]

So much for (to put it euphemistically) the path-dependent performance of the new welfare arrangements. Now let us see whether time also stands still in the world of regime change. As far as universal free coverage is concerned, the targeting of provisions is not sharp and precise, means testing remained an exception to the rule and co-payment is still minimal as compared to the market price. If these techniques were introduced at all, they were loosened up soon afterward. Accordingly, the pension system, health care and family allowances (not to mention education) continued to be biased towards the well-to-do. The process of denationalising the welfare sectors has proved to be protracted, partial and uneven (health care in the Czech Republic, pension schemes in Hungary and Poland); private insurance, if it is not being rolled back, is under heavy state regulation; the share of non-public delivery and financing remained small and did not attain a critical mass within welfare activity as a whole.[39]

To sum up, welfare sectors in East-Central Europe belong to the few relics of the command economy with all its dominant features such as over-centralisation, waste, rationing, shortage, paternalism, rent seeking and corruption.[40] Private/civic initiative still plays a minor role and freedom of choice is severely constrained. Under the pretext of the solidarity principle, excessive redistribution takes place, which favours the middle strata at least as much as those in need. The whole social system is non-transparent, complicated, full of exemptions and irregular procedures. It relies on a simplistic tax-and-spend philosophy (it is still a giant pay-as-you-go system with limited savings), which continues to breed free-riding (tax evasion). This in turn results in repeated tax increases, the aim of which is to keep the welfare promises embodied in untouchable but unaffordably broad entitlements. Higher taxes lead to an upsurge of parasitism – a vicious circle that was already well known under late communism. As a consequence, self-reliant behaviour cannot break through the routines of dependency culture; learned helplessness and 'public protection from cradle to grave' type expectations prevail; and the premature welfare state goes on debilitating its clients. It distributes alms instead of offering chances to work.

Is this a residual welfare system? Those who constantly talk about the social costs of the transformation (and hardly mention its benefits) and who panic about Americanisation can sit back and relax: alarmism is needless. This is not yet a 'market economy without adjectives', to use the term of the former Czech prime minister, Václav Klaus. As regards the social sectors, ECE is flirting with a Third Road between communism and capitalism, which could be the road to the Third World.

'Muddling Through'

This half-narrative has virtually no past in the communist era and is less coherent than the first two. Although it borrows from both of them it places itself outside their lasting controversy. It would be misleading to believe that this narrative differs from the others only in terms of a detached, deliberately non-normative interpretation of welfare history in the ECE countries over the last decade. The narrators of this 'muddling through' story tend to scrutinise each and every small technical detail of the emerging welfare regimes pedantically. Thus, they have a good opportunity to contribute to an image of social transformation in East-Central Europe, which is perhaps less spectacular but more realistic than the other two. In essence, this pedantry rests on two pillars of evolutionary pragmatism.

1. Institutional inertia and the value of incremental change.[41] In contrast to the intense messages of the above narratives ('stop changing!', 'start changing!'), nothing dramatic has happened: neither too much nor too little. It is equally futile to fear and to expect revolutionary changes. What has taken place, however, is a great variety of 'small transformations' of key importance.[42] A whole series of new organisations have been created for the public management of welfare or for private/civic social provision both at the central and local levels. Their interaction may result in strong institutional relations safeguarded by the rule of law as well as by new individual strategies and public awareness. At the same time, old institutions, no matter if they are embodied in organisations (ministries for social affairs, trade unions, hospitals) or in policies, routines, values, and so on (propensity for centralisation, corruption, forced solidarity), may show immense resistance to reform. At any rate, gradualism would be desirable, even if it were not induced by institutional inertia, because of mounting uncertainty concerning the end-state of the transformation process: which model of the welfare states should East-Central Europe choose from the changing Western menu? Since welfare regimes are extremely complex institutions, experimentation is not an evil. One should be prepared for slow

progress with stop-go cycles in the course of the trial and error procedure or for sheer improvisation. Minor moves and symbolic/creeping changes can accelerate, add up and become irreversible; but they can also burn out prematurely.[43]

For instance, symbolic changes such as even a partial renunciation of sacrosanct principles of the old regime (for example, universalism, decommodification, all-encompassing solidarity) may prove to be a first push in the re-organisation of the dominant philosophy of welfare policy. If the rearrangements within the public welfare budget (such as between price subsidies and social assistance, or central and local social services) or the moderate structural shifts between public and private initiative point in the same direction, and if these partial changes are synergetic and attain a critical mass, they may become comprehensive and irreversible. In this case, one may start considering whether or not a new welfare model is coming into being. One need not launch a sweeping privatisation drive in health care or the pension system in order to ensure that the former monolithic regime cannot return in its classical form. With the establishment of private insurance companies, new interest networks emerge, legal procedures and individual routines (long-term saving) build up, the whole capital market is bound to be re-organised – in other words, institutional guarantees gain strength if positive feedback mechanisms work. To make this happen, one must not shy away from piecemeal engineering or crafting, provided that eventually they do not force an over-ambitious master plan on the society.

2. Hybrid solutions and the 'good state'. However, if the reform process does not happen to be self-generating for one reason or another, hybrid arrangements may appear on the welfare scene and stay there for a long time. Given the huge number of welfare subsystems in which reforms evolve with different pace, or even diametrically opposite changes take place,[44] hybridisation with a great variety of intermediary solutions is very likely. It may produce, in a quite spontaneous manner, fairly original (re)combinations of welfare regime types. It would be too simple to assume that the welfare mix is a three-person game between the state, the market and the third sector. There are many more actors involved depending on the social prehistory of the country and the actual diversity of configurations of public regulation, private initiative and voluntary activity. Also, these actors can compete or co-operate in financing as well as in delivering welfare provisions, and suchlike. Therefore, instead of continuing the secular debate on 'state versus market', the eternal confrontation, we had better examine how these institutions mingle and merge (or conflict) in various kinds of

existing partnerships, including also the non-profit sector. The internal proportions of these intricate combinations should be identified and fine-tuned if necessary. Meanwhile, one should not refrain from endorsing state-dominated welfare mixes, if the market fails and the government is capable of making smart and limited intervention in the given field of social policy.[45]

If we revisit the past decade of East-Central Europe from this perspective, we will see neither a landslide marketisation/privatisation process in the social sphere nor a relatively intact welfare state of communism. As a matter of fact, the state remained the main redistributor of welfare. However, private social spending began to rise, and in delivering welfare services, the state initiated 'joint ventures' (such as outsourcing) with NGOs and private firms. The first grand design type of institutional reforms in regulating pensions and health care are also co-operative projects of financing, in which public administration bargains with private and corporatist actors about mixed governance. Even the state was divided into two: since the early 1990s, central administrations have had to face largely independent local authorities and co-operate with them as smoothly as possible. Social spending ceased to be decided upon behind the scenes within the confines of the communist party-state: instead, currently in every country of East-Central Europe there is an open struggle, in and outside the parliament, for every penny of expenditure; a struggle ranging from negotiations between the political parties to forge nationwide social deals, through tripartite agreements, to wildcat strikes.[46]

As regards the emerging hybrids, public institutions of welfare often turn out to be superior to their non-governmental rivals in terms of efficiency or distributive justice or both. This is especially the case if the state gets a little help from the non-state organisations.[47] It is well known that exclusively state-run social security is usually not flexible and rich enough to satisfy the rapidly changing demand for protection, particularly for high-quality protection, whereas it obliges those who have these 'extra' claims to be solidaristic with the 'average' citizen. Private insurance may be a useful partner here. Yet in health care or in unemployment protection, for example, the insurance market, if left alone, would 'adversely select' and discriminate against exactly those (the poor, the sick, the unskilled) who badly need security. Also, moral hazard and third-party payment problems may arise, and information is far from perfect. In these fields, the state is indispensable not only as a regulator and legal supervisor but also as a financing agent and a mass provider. Even universal schemes can be just and redistribution may be considered as a kind of insurance. Moreover, state spending on welfare can work as a classical stabiliser of the business cycle and – like the Asian tigers – a large part of social expenditure can be regarded as investment in future growth.

These two sets of arguments are meant to support the final conclusion: East-Central European welfare regimes are muddling through to achieve some degree of normalcy measured by an average of Western standards. The destination is unclear, the transformers are uncertain, they are perhaps reactive rather than proactive but (potentially) important things are happening. Maybe they can only find second-best solutions. These are, however, much more viable and original than the allegedly first-best solutions implied by the first two narratives. Comprehensive social contracts have not yet been elaborated, but there are a number of smaller or larger social deals in the making. This type of muddling through reminds the observer of groping rather than a steadfast pursuit of clear objectives. Actually, it is sometimes simply muddling along.

Part of the argumentation of this story needs to be modifyied and some new pillars added to uphold the 'muddling-through' hypothesis. First, the neutral position *vis-à-vis* the government requires more subtle evidence in the context of post-communism. Today, in East-Central Europe, even a market which often fails may prove to be more efficient and fair in welfare policy than most intervention made by a corrupt, non-professional, corporatist state. Again, health care serves as an example of a horrendous government failure, probably with the exception of certain domains of primary health service.

Secondly, the advent of parliamentary democracy in the region *equally* contributed to status quo-oriented and transformative policies. Following an initial period of grace, the new governments could not afford (even if they had wanted) to disregard the preferences of large constituencies for maintaining the level and the institutional guarantees of social safety. The temptation to delay painful decisions about social transformation was great; the short run costs of postponement competed with changing financial pressures;[48] and the end result was a series of ad hoc compromises attacking *and* defending 'acquired rights' and 'moral claims to entitlements'. At the same time, democracy and the rule of law promoted the establishment of new welfare institutions from trade unions to private kindergartens, and the introduction of new social policies from openly acknowledging poverty to granting free choice of medical doctor to the patients. Thus, both a neo-liberal rush and a communist intransigence were relatively unlikely outcomes. This is to reinforce one of the pillars of the third story.

Unfortunately, however, it is easier to say that things are complicated than to state how complicated they really are. In fact, it is extremely hard to draw the balance of the contradictory developments primarily because it is almost impossible to measure 'invisible welfare' provided by the new liberties. Interestingly enough, the analysts used to stress those social advantages, which stem from the collapse of the economy of shortage, from the new property rights, and from the free entry to the market (end of queuing, consumer choice, entrepreneurial rights). After all, if one wants to counterbalance the pessimistic thesis of the vast psychological costs of the transformation (growing insecurity and loneliness, loss of human dignity in unemployment and poverty[49]), there is a long list of additional advantages to quote: free (or less limited) travel, choice of workplace, residence, welfare mix, savings behaviour, association; access to medicine made abroad, to alternative (natural) treatment, protection of personality rights as patients, the opening up of the welfare facilities of the nomenklatura, public discussion of future social strategies and so on. Is it more humane to keep someone idle in a loss-making public firm or make him unemployed, retrain and assist him in finding a new job? Which sort of anxiety hurts deeper: the fear of losing one's job for economic or political reasons? Ask someone who was saved by an emergency helicopter belonging to an international charitable organisation (a vehicle that had not been permitted to enter the airspace of the Warsaw Pact) whether his welfare did not increase thereby? These corollaries of new freedoms cannot be nonchalantly put under the heading of 'empty opportunities' that sometimes cannot be exploited even by the winners of the transformation.

Owing to its 'invisible' components, there must have been a considerable rise in welfare (which might also appear in tangible items like income and wealth) in the first stages of the transition, not to mention the medium and long-term social consequences of new liberties such as the improvement of health conditions or old-age security. Obviously, these improvements may be dwarfed by the deterioration of other components of welfare.[50]

Thirdly, incommensurability is only one chapter in a large catalogue of problems related to statistical accounting, particularly in those fields in which the fiercest debates take place (size and character of poverty, social polarisation).[51] One example, that of the shadow economy, goes beyond the problem of statistics.[52] Under and after communism, informal welfare activity in the extended family as well as reciprocal self-help relations between individuals and families and even semi-commercial transactions have included such diverse forms of in-kind or in-cash protection as day-care, care for the elderly, housing, health care. Part of these activities were traditional and motivated by poverty and backwardness (home-made welfare). The other part was induced by the planned economy with all its friction and rigidity (shortages and the possibility of free-riding by means of corruption). Meanwhile, shortages partly evaporated, you are tempted to bribe those who have access to scarce goods less frequently, and free-riding became increasingly embodied in tax evasion. Nevertheless, if we take the informal economy into account, we may arrive at 20 to 40 per cent of GDP overall welfare spending in Poland and Hungary today. Or we may not, depending on the still non-existent statistical results. Has this unknown share of informal welfare grown or diminished over the past decade? If we intend to say something reliable about the performance of the social systems in East-Central Europe, we ought to know the answer. Similarly, in describing the welfare regimes in the region, even a 15 per cent share of informal welfare is high enough to regard it as an important element of the welfare mix.[53] Thus far, however, informal welfare is not less invisible than the social consequences of democratisation. Yet the relative strength of the informal social safety net could probably help us understand why the widely expected social explosion did not occur even in the less fortunate Eastern European countries.

Fourthly, in contrast to the other two narratives, which do not pay much attention to the country types, this one, which is really interested in intricacies of the social systems, ought to produce a classification scheme within the region.[54] According to this, the region departed from the communist version of a Bismarckian conservative corporatist regime, which included some features of the social democratic regime type. During the last couple of years, many of these Swedish-style features have been replaced with those of a liberal welfare regime. Ironically, any reference is lacking in the literature to the 'Latin rim' countries with their 'rudimentary welfare states'.[55] No doubt, the reader may learn some interesting details about the corporatist role of Solidarity in social policy in Poland, the strength of social democratic tradition in the Czech Republic or the large weight of informal welfare in Hungary. Nonetheless, a much deeper comparative analysis cannot be spared if we are to consider a serious response to the '*quo vadis*' question in the not too distant future.[56]

CONCLUSION: NO FATAL ERRORS

If the third narrative is more or less correct, no fatal errors (in any direction) have yet been made in welfare policy. Paradoxically, this negative statement may improve the image of the EU candidate countries of the region in Brussels. The 'communist welfare state' is being transformed *but* its relatively tightly knit safety net (including traditional protecting ropes) has not disappeared. At the same time, transformation is not excessive, the institutional experiments do not go much beyond their counterparts in Western Europe. The welfare regimes in the ECE countries have been instrumental in cushioning the blows of marketisation and privatisation, not to speak of the worst economic recession of the twentieth century. If mass migration or social dumping is to be expected, it is not the social systems of the ECE accession countries that should be blamed primarily.[57] Unintentionally, these systems did a lot to keep the migrants at home and make the exported goods more expensive. If we look around in Eastern Europe as a whole, these are not negligible accomplishments.

As a Hungarian social policy expert, when asked about the chances of EU accession in his field, said: 'If they do not want to take us, they will have to find a smarter pretext than our proud misery.' And he went on:

> Ironically, in those fields of welfare in which Brussels is interested today, we are – willy-nilly – comparatively good, at least in formal terms and because the insiders cannot require much, due to the low level of social integration in the Union. Labour and social legislation, equal chances, social dialogue etc., are not too dangerous terrains. As far as safety and health at the workplace is concerned, we will be saved by the continuing decay of our greatest accident – and disease – producers, the large state-owned firms in coal mining, steel and chemical industries. During the past ten years, these firms have poured out hundred thousands of unemployed, impairing thereby the welfare reputation of the country. It is high time for us to see the sunny side of the collapse: fewer disabled persons, less pollution.

Currently, the region is preparing for accession in 2004. The local experts are pretty sure that the Union will not set new hurdles in the social sector either in terms of performance indicators or regime characteristics. This prognosis is based on two foundations: the historical fact that indeed former entrants did not have to achieve pre-defined levels, for example in poverty reduction or life expectancy on the one hand, and pre-defined proportions within their respective welfare mixes on the other; and the assumption that, because of the diversity of welfare state types and their performances within the EU, Brussels lacks any grounds for justifying the introduction of new requirements of convergence. Thus far, the entrance examinations have reinforced the prognosis.

Nonetheless, the message sent by the Union to the candidate countries is twofold (or inconsistent).[58] On the rhetorical level, Brussels has not ceased to emphasise that Europe represents a unique social philosophy and quality on the globe, while, on the pragmatic level, it has made it clear that the welfare status of the would-be members does *not* feature at the top of the list of enrolment criteria.[59] To be sure, this ambiguity mobilises routine coping strategies on the part of governments in ex-communist countries. Paying lip-service to a (foreign) dominant ideology while trying to do what they had anyway wanted/had to do (at home) – this is exactly what the governments in the region were trained for under Soviet rule. Their response is, therefore, pre-programmed: it is an amalgam of avoiding making spectacular mistakes on the surface and of pursuing autonomous policies as far as in-depth reforms (or the lack of these reforms) are concerned.

The ambiguity of the EU message reinforces these governments in their own belief that there are no grand questions of principle in European matters of welfare. Many of the most important facets of social life are soft and negotiable. You may be weaker in welfare policy if you are stricter in introducing the Schengen rules or more advanced in environment protection, not to speak of market liberalisation.

In any event, the current administrations in the ECE region do not seem to be prepared to launch welfare reforms which might make their Western European partners anxious. Recently, the Czech government has practically been paralysed by the semi-formal grand coalition. True, its predecessor also hesitated to restructure the pension schemes, kept unemployment at an artificially low level and compromised health care privatisation by neglecting to protect the project from potential market failures. In Poland, following a partial marketisation of the pension system in 1999, the neo-socialist government elected in 2001 will probably not venture to introduce another reform programme of high political risk, especially today, in a period in which the country's reputation in Brussels is decreasing. Finally, in Hungary, the marketisation of health care proceeds very slowly, while the already existing private pillar of the pension system has repeatedly been weakened by the national-conservative government.[60]

The propensity of East-Central European administrations to postpone social reforms, and in particular those that are not being forced by the negotiators from Brussels (or are openly disliked by them), may backfire in the future. Accelerating certain EU-consistent social transformations means neglecting certain – probably, more vital – regime changes in welfare. The lack of these changes, some of which would go beyond the current European models of social policy, can in turn slow down the economic growth generated by the accession itself. As a consequence, accession may yet result in a lasting persistence of the social border – but this time *within* Schengenland.

NOTES

1. This study is based on research related to the *SOCO* (Social Consequences of the Economic Transformation in East-Central Europe) programme at the *Vienna Institute for Human Sciences* (www.iwm.at). For earlier assessments, see Zsuzsa Ferge *et al.*, 'Societies in Transition. International Report on the Social Consequences of Transition', SOCO Survey, Institute for Human Sciences, Vienna, 1996; János Mátyás Kovács (ed.), *Social Costs of Economic Transformation in Central Europe*, special issue of the *International Review of Comparative Public Policy* 7 (1996). An earlier version of the paper was issued as a European University Institute Working Paper – RSC 2000/50, Florence.
2. János Mátyás Kovács, 'Frustration with Liberalism? "Sound" Interventionism in East European Economics', in Martin J. Bull and Mike Ingham (eds.), *Reform of the Socialist System in Central and Eastern Europe* (London: Macmillan 1998), pp.77–92.
3. With the exception of the SOCO Survey (see Ferge *et al.*, 'Societies in Transition'), Ulrike Götting, *Transformation der Wohlfahrtsstaaten in Mittel- und Osteuropa. Eine Zwischenbilanz* (Opladen: Leske und Budrich 1998), and Katharina Müller, *The Political Economy of Pension Reform in Central-Eastern Europe* (Cheltenham: Edward Elgar 1999), most of the studies are only partially comprehensive and/or comparative.
4. The potential literature that can be cited is enormous – including especially the work of Deacon, Ferge, Nelson and Standing. For examples see Bob Deacon, 'Developments in East-European Social Policy', in D.C. Jones (ed.), *New Perspectives of the Welfare State in Europe* (London and New York: Routledge 1993); Zsuzsa Ferge, 'Social Policy Reform in Post-Communist Countries: Various Reform Strategies', *Social Reform in East-Central Europe: New Trends in Transition. Prague Papers on Social Responses to Transformation* 3 (1995), pp.1–38; Zsuzsa Ferge, 'Freedom and Security', in Kovács (ed.), *Social Costs of Economic Transformation in Central Europe*, pp.19–43; Joan M. Nelson, 'The Politics of Pension and Health-Care Reforms in Hungary and Poland', in Janos Kornai *et al.* (eds.), *Reforming the State: Fiscal and Welfare Reform in Post-Socialist Countries* (Cambridge: Cambridge University Press 2001); Guy Standing, 'Social Protection in Central and Eastern Europe: A Tale of Slipping Anchors and Torn Safety Nets', in Gosta Esping-Andersen (ed.), *Welfare States in Transition. National Adaptations in Global Economies* (Thousand Oaks: Sage 1996).
5. Götting, *Transformation*, pp.240–47; Martin Rein, Andreas Wörgötter and Barry L. Friedman (eds.), *Social Benefits after Communism: The Role of Enterprises* (Cambridge: Cambridge University Press 1996).
6. Júlia Szalai, 'On the Border of State and Civil Society in Hungary: Some Aspects of Self-Governance in the Period of Transition', in Kovács (ed.), *Social Costs of Economic Transformation in Central Europe*, pp.215–33.
7. Gosta Esping-Andersen, *The Three Worlds of Welfare Capitalism* (Princeton, NJ: Princeton University Press 1990); Richard M. Titmuss, *Social Policy: An Introduction* (London: Macmillan 1974); Adalbert Evers and Thomas Olk, *Wohlfahrtspluralismus* (Opladen, 1995). See also the literature cited in note 4, as well as Jiri Vecerník, *Markets and People. The Czech Reform Experience in a Comparative Perspective* (Aldershot: Avebury 1996), pp.196–7.
8. Standing, 'Social Protection', p.227.
9. Jacek Kuron, 'Man muß träumen. Soziale Gerechtigkeit als soziale Bewegung', *Transit* 6 (1993), pp.6–24; John Myles and Robert J. Brym, 'Markets and Welfare State: What East and West Can Learn form Each Other', in Zsuzsa Ferge *et al.* (eds.), *Social Policy in a Changing Europe* (Frankfurt/Boulder: Campus/Westview 1992), pp.27–37.
10. Zsuzsa Ferge, 'Social Policy Regimes and Social Structure. Hypotheses about the Prospects of Social Policy in Central and Eastern Europe', in Ferge *et al.*, *Social Policy in a Changing Europe*, pp.201–22; Zsuzsa Ferge, 'The Changed Welfare Paradigm: The Individualisation of the Social', *Social Policy and Administration* 31/1 (1997), pp.20–44; Zsuzsa Ferge, 'And What if the State Fades Away: The Civilizing Process and the State', in P. Taylor-Gooby and S. Svallfors (eds.), *Attitudes Toward Welfare Policies in Comparative Perspective* (London: Blackwell 1998).
11. Paul Pierson, *Dismantling the Welfare State. Reagan, Thatcher, and the Politics of Retrenchment* (Cambridge: Cambridge University Press 1994); Paul Pierson (ed.), *The New Politics of the*

Welfare State (Oxford: Oxford University Press 2001); N. Ploug and J. Kvist, *Social Security in Europe: Development or Dismantlement?* (The Hague: Kluwer Law International 1996); Stefan Svallfors and Peter Taylor-Gooby (eds.), *The End of the Welfare State? Responses to State Retrenchment* (London: Routledge 1999).

12. Bob Deacon and Michelle Hulse, 'The Making of Post-communist Social Policy: The Role of International Agencies', *Journal of Social Policy* 26 (1997), pp.43–62; Zsuzsa Ferge, 'A Central European Perspective on the Social Quality of Europe', in Beck *et al.* (eds.), *The Social Quality of Europe*, pp.175–9; Zsuzsa Ferge, 'The Actors of the Hungarian Pension Reform', in János Mátyás Kovács (ed.), *Small Transformations: The Politics of Welfare Reform – East and West* (Vienna: IWM 2001); Standing, 'Social Protection', pp.230–31, 251.
13. Anthony B. Atkinson and John Micklewright, *The Economic Transformation in Eastern Europe and the Distribution of Income* (Cambridge: Cambridge University Press 1992).
14. Götting, *Transformation*, pp.261–2.
15. Ferge, 'The Actors of the Hungarian Pension Reform'; Müller, *The Political Economy*.
16. Balázs Krémer, 'Haute couture neccek és frivol szociális hálók' (Haute Couture and Frivolous Social Nets), *Café Babel* 2 (1998), pp.39–51; Standing, 'Social Protection'.
17. See the literature cited in note 4, as well as Vecerník, *Markets and People*, pp.92–119.
18. 'Children at Risk in Central and Eastern Europe: Perils and Promises', *Economies in Transition Studies, Regional Monitoring Report* No. 4, Florence, 1997; Andrea Giovanni Cornia, 'Ugly Facts and Fancy Theories: Children and Youth during the Transition', *Innocenti Occasional Papers, Economic Policy Series* No. 49 (Florence: UNICEF 1995); Andrea Giovanni Cornia and Renato Paniccia, 'The Demographic Impact of Sudden Impoverishment: Eastern Europe during the 1989–94 Transition', *Innocenti Occasional Papers, Economic Policy Series* No. 49 (Florence: UNICEF 1995); 'Poverty, Children and Policy: Responses for a Brighter Future', *Economies in Transition Studies, Regional Monitoring Report* No. 3 (Florence: UNICEF 1995).
19. Anthony B. Atkinson, 'Social Policy, Economic Organization and the Search for a Third Way', in Ferge *et al.*, *Social Policy in a Changing Europe*, pp.225–37.
20. Endre Sik (ed.), *From Improvisation to Awareness?* (Budapest: Institute of Political Sciences 1998).
21. See note 4, and Vecerník, *Markets and People*, pp.217–40.
22. Compare Deacon and Hulse, 'The Making of Post-communist Social Policy', and Scott Thomas, 'Social Policy in the Economics in Transition: The Role of the West', in E.B. Kapstein and M. Mandelbaum (eds.), *Sustaining the Transition: The Social Safety Net in Postcommunist Europe* (Brookings Institution Press 1997), pp.147–66.
23. Jon Elster, Claus Offe and Ulrich Preuss, *Constitutional Design in Post-Communist Societies. Rebuilding the Ship at Sea* (Cambridge: Cambridge University Press 1998); László Szamuely, 'The Social Costs of Transformation in Central and Eastern Europe', *Kopint-Datorg Discussion Papers* No. 44 (Budapest:, Institute for Market Research 1997); Claus Offe, 'The Politics of Social Policy in East European Transitions: Antecedents, Agents and Agenda of Reform, *Social Research* 60/4 (1993), pp.1–36; Zsuzsa Ferge, 'Social Policy Challenges and Dilemmas in Ex-Socialist Systems', in Joan M. Nelson *et al.* (eds.), *Transforming Post-Communist Political Economies* (Washington DC: National Academy Press 1997), pp.299–322.
24. Mark Kramer, 'Social Protection Policies and Safety Nets in East-Central Europe: Dilemmas of the Postcommunist Transformation', in Ethan B. Kapstein and Michael Mandelbaum (eds.), *Sustaining the Transition: The Social Safety Net in Postcommunist Europe* (Brookings Institution Press 1997), p.51.
25. Kramer, 'Social Protection', pp.48–9; Branko Milanovic, *Income, Inequality, and Poverty During the Transition* (Washington, DC: The World Bank 1997).
26. Leszek Balcerowicz, *Socialism, Capitalism, Transformation* (Budapest: Central European University Press 1995), pp.261–8.
27. László Csontos, János Kornai and István György Tóth, 'Tax Awareness and the Reform of the Welfare State. Hungarian Survey Results', *Economics of Transition* 6 (1998), pp.287–312.
28. János Kornai, 'Reform of the Welfare Sector in the Post-Communist Countries: A Normative Approach', in Nelson *et al.*, *Transforming Post-Communist Political Economies*, p.281.
29. János Kornai, 'Paying the Bill for Goulash Communism: Hungarian Development and Macro-Stabilization in a Political-Economy Perspective', *Discussion Paper* No.1748 (Cambridge:

Harvard Institute for Economic Research 1996); Lajos Bokros and Jean Jacques Dethier (eds.), *Public Finance Reform During the Transition: The Experience of Hungary* (Washington: World Bank 1998).

30. Kramer, 'Social Protection', pp.56–9, Kathie Krumm, Branko Milanovic and Michael Walton, 'Transfers and the Transition from Socialism: Key Tradeoffs', *Policy Research Working Paper* No. 1380 (Washington DC: World Bank 1994).
31. See note 29.
32. János Kornai, *Az egészségügy reformjáról* (On the Reform of Health Care) (Budapest: KJK 1998); Péter Mihályi, *Magyar egészségügy: diagnózis és terápia* (Hungarian Health Care: Diagnosis and Therapy) (Budapest: Springer Orvosi Kiadó 2000); Éva Orosz, *Concepts and Realities of Reform: An Account of the Transformation of the Hungarian Health-Care System* (manuscript, 2001).
33. Kornai 'Reform of the Welfare Sector in the Post-Communist Countries', pp.290–94; Kramer, 'Social Protection', pp.72–77.
34. Iván Csaba and András Semjén, 'Welfare Institutions and the Transition: In Search of Efficiency and Equity', *Discussion Paper* No. 47 (Institute of Economics, Hungarian Academy of Sciences 1997), pp.5–9; Götting, *Transformation*, pp.264–8.
35. Jeffrey Sachs, 'Postcommunist Parties and the Politics of Entitlements', *Transition* 6/3 (1995), pp.1–4; World Bank, *Averting the Old Age Crisis. Policies to Protect the Old and Promote Growth* (Policy Research Report, Oxford: Oxford University Press 1994).
36. András Sajó, 'How the Rule of Law Killed Hungarian Welfare Reform', *East European Constitutional Review* 5/1 (1996), pp.31–41.
37. See various World Bank reports, including *Understanding Poverty in Poland* (1995), *Hungary: Structural Reforms for Sustainable Growth* (1995), *Hungary: Poverty and Social Transfers* (1996), and *Making Transition Work for Everyone: Poverty and Inequality in Europe and Central Asia* (2000), all published by the World Bank, Washington DC.
38. E.g., Kramer, 'Social Protection', pp.97–102; Vecernik, *Markets and People*, pp.47–92.
39. Marek Góra and M. Rutkowski, 'New Old-Age Pension System in Poland', *Spectrum* 2 (2000), pp.11–14; Jerzy Hausner, 'Conditions for the Successful Reform of the Pension System in Poland', in Kovács (ed.), *Small Transformations*; Martin Potucek, *Crossroads of Czech Social Reform* (in Czech) (Prague: SLON 1999); Vecernik, *Markets and People*, pp.191–217.
40. Kornai, 'Reform of the Welfare Sector in the Post-Communist Countries', p.273; Andrzej Rychard, 'Beyond Gains and Losses: In Search of "Winning Losers"', *Social Research* 63 (1996), pp.465–87.
41. See, for example, Nicholas Barr (ed.), *Labor Markets and Social Policy in Central and Eastern Europe* (Oxford: Oxford University Press 1994); Joan M. Nelson, 'Social Costs, Social-Sector Reforms, and Politics in Post-Communist Transformations', in Nelson *et al.*, *Transforming Post-Communist Political Economies*, pp.245–7; István György Tóth, 'A jóléti rendszer az átmenet idöszakában' (The Welfare System in the Period of Transition), *Közgazdasági Szemle* 4 (1994), pp.313–41 and his *Gazdasági aktivitás vagy szociális támogatások?* (Economic Activity or Social Assistance?) (Budapest: Tárki 1998); Hans-Jürgen Wagener, 'The Welfare State in Transition Economies and Accession to the EU' (Working Papers of the Robert Schuman Centre, Florence, 2001) (also this volume).
42. Barr, *Labour Markets*.
43. Götting, *Transformation*, pp.268–274.
44. Ibid., pp.21–6.
45. Nicholas Barr, 'The Role of Government in a Market Economy', in Barr, *Labor Markets*, pp.29–50; Iván Csaba, 'Fiskális illúziók és redisztribúciós csalás' (Fiscal Illusions and Redistribution Fraud), *Századvég* (Spring, 1997), pp.110–13.
46. M. Cichon and L. Samuel (eds.), *Making Social Protection Work: The Challenge of Tripartism in Social Governance for Countries in Transition* (Budapest: ILO 1994).
47. Csaba, 'Fiskális'; Péter Pete, 'Infantilizmus vagy racionális alulinformáltság?' (Infantilism or Rational Ignorance?), *Századvég* (Spring 1997), pp.131–6; Peter Orszag and Joseph Stiglitz, 'Rethinking Pension Reform: Ten Myths about Social Security Systems', in R. Holzmann and J. Stiglitz (eds.), *New Ideas About Old Age Security* (Washington: The World Bank 2001).
48. Gosta Esping-Andersen (ed.), *Welfare State in Transition. National Adaptations in Global*

Economies (Thousand Oaks: Sage 1996); Péter Gedeon, 'Hungary: Social Policy in Transition', *East European Politics and Societies* 9 (1995), pp.433–58; Béla Greskovits, 'The Use of Compensation in Economic Adjustment Programs', *Acta Oeconomica* 45 (1993), pp.43–68; Janos Kornai, Stephan Haggard and Robert Kaufman (eds.), *Reforming the State: Fiscal and Welfare Reform in Post-Socialist Countries* (Cambridge: Cambridge University Press 2001).

49. Nelson, 'Social Costs', p.251; Sachs, 'Postcommunist Parties'.
50. János Mátyás Kovács, 'Boxing the Shadow? "Neoliberals" and Social Quality after Communism', in Wolfgang Beck, Laurent van der Maesen and Alan Walker (eds.), *The Social Quality of Europe* (Dordrecht: Kluwer 1997), pp.207–15.
51. Ferge *et al.*, 'Societies in Transition'; Kramer, 'Social Protection', pp.77–81; Barbara Boyle Torrey, Timothy M. Smeeding and Debra Bailey, 'Vulnerable Populations in Central Europe', in Nelson *et al.*, *Transforming Post-Communist Political Economies*, pp.351–70.
52. Götting, *Transformation*, pp.258–60, 273.
53. Cf. Jane Lewis. 'Voluntary and Informal Welfare', in R. Page and R. Silburn (eds.), *British Social Welfare in the Twentieth Century* (London: Macmillan 1999); János Kornai, 'Hidden in an Envelope: Gratitude Payments to Medical Doctors in Hungary', in Ralf Dahrendorf and Yehuda Elkana (eds.), *The Paradoxes of Unintended Consequences* (Budapest: CEU Press 2000).
54. Bob Deacon, 'East European Welfare: Past, Present and Future in Comparative Context', in Bob Deacon *et al.* (eds.), *The New Eastern Europe. Social Policy Past, Present and Future* (London: Sage), pp.1–30, and Götting, *Transformation* are exceptions to the rule.
55. Stephan Leibfried, 'Towards a European Welfare State? On Integrating Poverty Regimes into the European Community', in Ferge *et al.*, *Social Policy in a Changing Europe*, pp.253–4.
56. The most recent comparative project of the *SOCO* programme studies the evolution of welfare regimes in East-Central Europe during the past 12 years (see Don Kalb and Janos Matyas Kovács (eds.), *Institutional Reform in Social Policy. East-Central Europe in a European Context (1989–2001)* (Vienna: IWM 2001). While this study's main thrust is to reconstruct the main narratives of welfare policy, this latter volume presents the recent history of welfare institutions in the region.
57. Cf. Jens Alber and Guy Standing, 'Social Dumping, Catch-Up or Convergence?', *European Journal of Social Policy* 10/2 (2000), pp.99–119; Giuliano Amato and Judy Batt, 'Final Report of the Reflection Group on "Long-term Implications of EU Enlargement": The Nature of the New Border', Robert Schuman Centre, European University Institute, Florence, Forward Studies Unit, European Commission, Brussels, 2000; Kalb and Kovacs, *Institutional Reform*; Vladimir Rys, 'The Entry of Transition Countries of Central Europe in the European Union', *Czech Sociological Review* 8 (2000), pp.131–9; and Wagener, 'The Welfare State in Transition Economies'.
58. Cf. Claus Offe, *The Democratic Welfare State. A European Regime under the Strain of European Integration* (Vienna: Institute for Advanced Studies 2000); Georg Vobruba, *Integration + Erweiterung. Europa im Globalisierungsdilemma* (Wien: Passagen Verlag 2001).
59. The accession countries have repeatedly been made to understand that migration is *the* issue in the field of employment and social policy. It is superior to health policy, equal opportunities, or social dialogue when it comes to the final decision about co-optation. According to the present state of affairs (October 2001), Chapter 13 of the accession talks, which deals with the issues of employment and social policy, has been provisionally closed in the case of the ECE region. The Commission's decisions are constrained by the following – rather foggy – stipulations: 'While the funding and organisation of social protection systems remain the responsibility of individual Member States, the EU requires that these systems have the capacity to develop and operate sustainable and universally applicable social protection systems in line with the Treaty objectives. The systems of the candidate countries must also be capable of co-ordinating with those systems currently operating in the EU which are themselves developing in a very dynamic way and undergoing significant reform' (http://europa.eu.int/comm/enlargement/chap13/ index. htm).
60. Kalb and Kovacs, *Institutional Reform*; Góra and Rutkowski, 'New Old-Age Pension System in Poland'; Potucek, *Crossroads of Czech Social Reform*; Jiri Vecernik, 'Neither Fish, nor Fowl: The Hesitation (Balancing?) of Czech Social Policy' (mimeo, IWM 1999).

Abstracts

Introduction: Diversity and Adaptation in the Enlarged European Union, *by Jan Zielonka and Peter Mair*

It is now taken as given that the European Union will be a much more diversified entity following its planned eastward enlargement. But precisely how much diversity will there be, and what are its implications? These questions are addressed in this article, as well as in the broader collection of essays which it introduces. By introducing a broad range of empirical evidence, we seek to challenge many of the theoretical assumptions about the scope, form and meaning of diversity in the process of European integration, and especially in the context of the forthcoming eastward enlargement. In fact, the map of unity and diversity in the enlarged EU proves to be extremely complex, and does not simply correspond to the old East–West divide. We also suggest that much of this diversity should be seen as welcome rather than as threatening for the Union, and that the enlargement process constitutes an important factor generating adaptation and accommodation.

Eastward Enlargement of the European Union and the Identity of Europe, *by Dieter Fuchs and Hans-Dieter Klingemann*

The constitution of a European demos with a collective identity is one of the preconditions for adjusting the legitimacy problem of the European Union (EU). The analysis attempts to clarify empirically whether there is sufficient commonality regarding Europeans' political value orientations to substantiate a collective identity. Particularly in view of the European Union's eastward enlargement, the question arises whether widespread cultural heterogeneity in Europe allows the formation of a European demos at all. In Europe we can identify a West–East axis of political value orientations. Democratic attitudes decrease the further to the East while at the same time there is an increase in etatist orientations. Thresholds can be observed which distinguish Western European countries on the one hand and Central and Eastern European countries on the other. Within the group of Central and Eastern Europe a further distinction can be made between the three Slavic republics of the former Soviet Union and the rest of the countries. These findings support Huntington‘s theory of civilisations.

Culture and National Identity: 'The East' and European Integration, *by David D. Laitin*

Relying on data from language use, religion and exposure to popular culture, this contribution evaluates the extent to which there is a cultural divide separating member states of the EU from Eastern European applicant states. To address this issue, the study makes three claims. First, despite the vibrancy of national cultures within Europe, there is an emergent cultural configuration that unites the continent. Second, the applicant states are very much part of this European cultural zone. In fact, with the cultural characteristics of the original six members of the EC held up as the European model, the applicant states are closer on several dimensions than are the later entrants into the EC. Third, there are greater incentives for individuals in the applicant states to co-ordinate culturally with the European configuration than for individuals living in the heart of Europe. The conclusion therefore is that there is no evidence of a cultural divide that would justify holding back membership of Eastern European states into the EU.

Discomforts of Victory: Democracy, Liberal Values and Nationalism in Post-Communist Europe, *by Vladimir Tismaneanu*

This article tries to identify the main threats to post-communist liberal democracies, especially those perils related to the weakness of pluralist traditions, institutions, and values and the rise of movements and ideologies rooted in cultural and political malaise, ressentiment, and disaffection. Nine such perils are identified in the second half the article, including Leninist legacies, salvationist popular sentiments, the rhetoric of reactionary nostalgia, the fluidity of political formations, the crisis of values, authority, and accountability, and the tensions between individualistic and communitarian values. The concern here is with a diagnosis of the main vulnerabilities of Eastern Europe's post-communist states in order to evaluate prospects for further democratic consolidation and risks for the rise and affirmation of ethnocratic parties and movements. Understanding the post-communist political and cultural situation, including persistent isolationist, anti-globalisation, populist and nationalist trends, is of critical importance for interpreting the main directions these countries will pursue in their efforts to join the European Union institutions.

Making Institutions in Central and Eastern Europe, and the Impact of Europe, ***by Darina Malovà and Tim Haughton***

The end of communism in Central and Eastern Europe offered the region a unique opportunity for institutional redesign. Thanks to the variety of historical experiences, inherited structures, transition paths and deal sweeteners during the round-table talks, post-communist Europe initially witnessed much institutional diversity. Throughout the course of the past decade, however, there has been a notable convergence of institutional designs across the region. The process of convergence has been, in part, a response to domestic political concerns, but the demands of the European Union have also played a role. This article plots the course of institutional development in the region, outlining some of the major cases of institutional redesign and highlighting both the positive and negative impact of 'Europe' on the process.

Making Markets and Eastern Enlargement: Diverging Convergence? ***by Laszlo Bruszt***

This study deals with the extent and content of 'Europeanisation' in the Central and East European (CEE) countries at the level of market making. It argues that Europeanisation at the level of market making was about creating states with strong capacities to preserve and regulate markets and with increased and reconstructed administrative and planning capabilities. The most successful CEE countries with their strong states and weak social and economic actors converged towards a moving target, that is, towards EU countries in the process of supranational market making with dramatically different constellation of powers among key economic actors. The paper discusses the specifics of national level market making in the CEE countries, the factors of divergence within the region, and the 'diverging convergence' between the CEE and the EU countries.

Health not Wealth: Enlarging the EMU, ***by Daniel Gros***

Economic health not wealth should be the decisive criterion when considering the prospects of the Central and East European (CEE) candidates for EU membership and the capacity of the EU to enlarge. Viewed this way the outlook is promising. The CEE countries are still very poor, compared to most of the existing EU members, but they are also much more dynamic. Growth rates are generally expected to remain around 4–5 per cent in CEE for the foreseeable future, compared to about 2–3 per cent for the EU. This still implies that full catch-up in terms of GDP per capita will take decades, rather than years, but full catch-up is not the relevant criterion if one is concerned about enlargement. Experience in the EU has shown that problems are much more likely to arise from established rich member countries with stagnant economies (Belgium in the 1980s and Germany today) than poor, but more dynamic states (such as Portugal and Ireland today). The fact that most of the so-called 'periphery' is now growing more strongly than the 'core' confirms that EU integration benefits poorer countries even more.

The Welfare State in Transition Economies and Accession to the EU, *by Hans-Jürgen Wagener*

Welfare state reform in East-Central Europe can be divided into two phases: in the first phase, when liberalisation, stabilisation and privatisation were of primary importance, only minor or absolutely necessary reform steps were taken. This soon led many countries into fiscal problems that triggered the second phase of substantial pension and health system reforms. Having been already part of the European welfare state tradition in the pre-communist period, the countries of East-Central Europe were not prepared to take over the essentially private three pillar model of the World Bank. Instead the forerunners of reform, such as Hungary, Poland and Latvia, are developing, together with some incumbent EU members, a new European four pillar model with a specific public–private mix. Even if the social *acquis communautaire* is not very restrictive for the candidate states, they seem keen to join the European welfare state culture.

Approaching the EU and Reaching the US? Rival Narratives on Transforming Welfare Regimes in East-Central Europe, *by János Mátyás Kovács*

Post-communist welfare regimes are frequently portrayed as a hybrid consisting of the relics of communist social policy and a neophyte imitation of the US model of welfare. Both components of that hybrid are regarded as incompatible with the 'European social model'. At the same time, most welfare reformers in East-Central Europe try to avoid falling into the trap of first, conserving the statist, inefficient and pseudo-egalitarian character of the old system of social policy; second, seeking new forms of welfare collectivism along the national-conservative/populist 'third roads' between capitalism and communism; third, triggering popular discontent by dismantling the old welfare regimes too rapidly, or in a haphazard way; and fourth, targeting an end-state which has become unsustainable in the Western world during the past two decades. Meanwhile, the emerging welfare regimes in the region are far from being identical and the reformers do not find stable institutional arrangements in the West to copy. In an effort to make sense of this complex picture, the paper examines what has 'really' happened in the welfare sectors in the region during the past decade by presenting three dominant narratives of the social transformation: 'leaping in the dark', 'marking time' and 'muddling through'.

Notes on Contributors

Laszlo Bruszt is Associate Professor at the Department of Political Sciences of the Central European University, Budapest. His major interest is in political sociology and economic sociology, and his more recent work focuses on the interplay between state building, institutional development and economic change. He is co-author with David Stark of *Postsocialist Pathways: Transforming Politics and Property in Eastern Europe* (1998), a comparative study of the opportunities and dilemmas posed by the simultaneous extension of property rights and citizenship rights.

Dieter Fuchs is Professor of Political Science at the University of Stuttgart. His major research areas lie in the fields of comparative politics, the theory of democracy and political sociology. He is co-editor of *Citizens and the State* (1995), and he has recently contributed 'The Democratic Culture of Unified Germany', to Pippa Norris (ed.), *Critical Citizens* (1999) and 'Demos und Nation in der Europäischen Union', to Hans-Dieter Klingemann and Friedhelm Neidhardt (eds.), *Zur Zukunft der Demokratie* (2000).

Daniel Gros is Director of the Centre for European Policy Studies, the leading think-tank on European affairs. He has served on the staff of the IMF, as an advisor at the European Commission, and as visiting professor at the Catholic University of Leuven and the University of Frankfurt. He has advised the governments of Russia, Ukraine and other Central and Eastern European countries on trade and exchange rate matters and their relations with the EU, and he is currently advisor to the European Parliament. Among his co-authored books are *Winds of Change: Economic Transition in Central and Eastern Europe* (1995), *The Euro Capital Market* (1999), and *European Monetary Integration* (1999).

Tim Haughton is a doctoral student at the School of Slavonic and East European Studies, University College London. His doctorate thesis attempts to explain Slovakia's political trajectory since independence. He has written a number of articles on Slovak politics for a variety of publications including *Europe-Asia Studies* and *Slovak Foreign Policy Affairs*. He also writes regularly for the leading Slovak newspaper *Sme*.

Hans-Dieter Klingemann is Professor of Political Science at the Freie Universität Berlin and Director of the Research Unit on Institutions and Social Change at the Social Science Research Centre Berlin (WZB). His present research focus is on the quality of the democratic process and on the consolidation of democratic systems. His books include *Citizens and the State* (1995), *A New Handbook of Political Science* (1996), *Mapping Policy Preferences. Estimates for Parties, Electors, and Governments 1945–1998* (2001), and *Wahlen und Wähler. Analysen aus Anlass der Bundestagswahl 1998* (2001).

János Mátyás Kovács has worked as a Permanent Fellow at the Institute of Human Sciences in Vienna since 1991. In 1973 he became a member of the Institute of Economics, Hungarian Academy of Sciences, Budapest, and since 1984 he has been teaching the history of economic thought and political economy of the transformation at Eötvös Lóránd University, Budapest. His publications include *Reform and Transformation in Eastern Europe* (co-edited with Márton Tardos, 1992), *Transition to Capitalism? The Communist Legacy in Eastern Europe* (1994), and 'Rival Temptations – Passive Resistance. Cultural Globalization in Hungary', in Peter Berger and Samuel Huntington (eds.), *Many Globalizations* (2002).

David D. Laitin received his BA from Swarthmore College and his Ph.D. at the University of California, Berkeley. He has conducted field research in Somalia, Yorubaland (Nigeria), Catalonia (Spain), and Narva (Estonia). He is the author of *Politics, Language and Thought: The Somali Experience* (1977), *Hegemony and Culture* (1986), *Language Repertoires and State Construction in Africa* (1992) and *Identity in Formation: The Russian-speaking Populations in the Near Abroad* (1998). He is Professor of Political Science at Stanford University.

Peter Mair is Professor of Comparative Politics in Leiden University in the Netherlands and is co-editor of *West European Politics*. He is author of *Party System Change* (1997), and co-author of *Representative Government in Modern Europe* (3rd edn., 2000). His co-edited books include *How Parties Organize* (1994), and *Parteien auf komplexen Wählermärkten* (1999).

Darina Malová is Associate Professor of Political Science at Comenius University in Bratislava and Academic Director of 'Academia Istropolitana Nova', the first private institute for graduate studies in Slovakia. Her research interests focus primarily on the institutional and behavioural changes in post-communist Slovakia, and since 1993 she has contributed the 'Slovakia' section to the *European Journal of Political Research*'s Political Data Yearbook.

Vladimir Tismaneanu is Professor of Politics at the University of Maryland (College Park), editor of the journal *East European Politics and Societies*, and author of numerous books including *Fantasies of Salvation: Nationalism, Democracy, and Myth in Post-Communist Europe* (1998). He is editor of *The Revolutions of 1989* (1999).

Hans-Jürgen Wagener studied economics in Munich and Berlin, and worked at the Osteuropa-Institut Munich and at the Vienna Institute for International Economic Comparisons. From 1975 to 1993 he was Professor of Economics at the Rijksuniversiteit Groningen, The Netherlands, with which he is still affiliated. Since 1993 he has been Professor of Economics at the European University Viadrina Frankfurt (Oder) and managing director of the Frankfurt Institute for Transformation Studies.

Jan Zielonka is Professor of Political Science at the European University Institute in Florence, on leave from Leiden University in the Netherlands. He is author of *Explaining Euro-paralysis: Why Europe is Unable to Act in International Politics* (1998) and editor of the two-volume work *Democratic Consolidation in Eastern Europe* (2001).

Index